THE ANTI-SEMITE NEXT DOOR

A ZACHARY BLAKE LEGAL THRILLER

WRITTEN BY:

MARK M. BELLO

10 Grand Publications

4301 Orchard Lake Road

Suite 180-124

West Bloomfield, MI 48323

ISBN-: (Paperback) 978-1-956595-17-8

(eBook) 978-1-956595-16-1

TABLE OF CONTENTS

PROLOGUE

Nestled between the Detroit suburbs of Southfield and Birmingham, Beverly Hills is a quaint town of about eleven thousand people. It features mature homes, beautiful parks, nature trails, skating, sledding, and one of Zachary Blake's favorite restaurants, the *Beverly Hills Grill*. One Detroit area magazine acknowledged the 80-seat restaurant for having the area's "Best Brunch," the main reason for the meeting at that place and time.

Rich Cooper was an old college buddy. While he and Zack were still friends, life got in the way. Rich went to Lawrence Tech to pursue a degree in architectural design. In contrast, Zack pursued a bachelor's degree in English at Oakland University and a law degree at Thomas M. Cooley Law School. Both met women, fell in love, married, and had families.

Rich's marriage was still going strong. Zack's ended in divorce. Rich opened his architectural firm. Zack formed a partnership with some law school buddies. Rich's practice was steady, like his life. He was fiscally conservative and socially liberal, like many Michiganders. He loathed the political divide in America and Michigan, preferring to keep his politics and opinions to himself. He despised political discussion. People were set in their way and could not be convinced otherwise. Arguments *always* resulted. Rich Cooper was a man who stayed above the fray and watched positive or negative things happen from a distance.

Zachary Blake was the opposite of his friend, Rich. Zack's law practice and life featured incredible ups and terrible downs. Back in the day, during his initial period of success, Blake was known as Detroit's "King of Justice." He built a fee-churning law practice, scoring several high-profile seven and eight-figure verdicts. He was the envy of his competitors, feared by insurance companies, and the darling of the Detroit area press on legal issues.

But success went to Zack's head—he decided to live the high life, sponge off the labors of his partners, enjoy the social scene, get drunk too often, and ignore his practice and loved ones. At the bitter end of his casual carelessness, his wife divorced him and took his kids and what was left of his money. His partners kicked him to the curb. His historic fall from grace culminated in Zack Blake practicing from a one-room office on Eight Mile Road, handling misdemeanor criminal assignments and traffic tickets.

At his worst moments, a woman named Jennifer Tracey telephoned with the case of Zack's career. A priest sexually abused Jennifer's two sons, and the church was covering up the crime. Blake took the case, cleaned up his act, took on the church and its clandestine cover-up organization, and won the largest verdict in Michigan history.

As most contingency fee lawyers know, large verdicts are only valuable if they are collectible. Zack Blake and Jennifer Tracey collected almost every dime of the nine-figure verdict. Blake was wealthy beyond his dreams in one fell swoop—he reclaimed his title as Detroit's "King of Justice."

While frowned upon in legal circles, Zack began to have feelings for Jennifer *before* the case was resolved. They dated, fell in love, married, and Zack adopted Jennifer's two sons, Kenny and Jake. Granted a glorious do-over, Zack did not take this new-found success in business or love for granted. His practice was booming—he and Jennifer had a storybook marriage.

In recent years, following his historic verdict against the church, Zachary Blake landed high-profile case after high-profile case. He achieved landmark verdicts and donated substantial sums to worthwhile social justice charities, PACs, and progressive causes. He wore his politics on his sleeve. In one case, he even took down a bigoted president of the United States, which led to his appointment as lead prosecutor at POTUS's impeachment trial. Zack enjoyed a happy, stable, and loving home life with his wife and adopted sons when he wasn't taking down corporate or government wrongdoers.

Rich Cooper lived with his family in a modest four-bedroom, ranch-style home in Beverly Hills. Blake lived in Bloomfield Hills mansion off Woodward Avenue, a few miles away. His office was a converted mansion on Woodward Avenue near Square Lake Road, a mile from his home. Through it all, the two men remained friends. Zack and Rich met monthly for brunch at the *Beverly Hills Grill*. Rich had one condition: Zack promised to refrain from discussing politics.

"How's Josh doing?" Zack wondered. "Does he have his shit together? His *Torah* portion nailed?" The boy's bar-mitzvah was in two weeks at Temple Kol Yisrael.

"He's nervous," Rich advised. "He's also excited and trying to keep things in perspective. He's ready, whether he believes it or not. He's worked extremely hard, and I'm proud of him."

"Nose to the grindstone, don't rock the boat, just get the job done," Zack kibitzed. "Sounds like this guy I knew in high school. If I recall correctly, his name was Cooper."

"It's eerie, Zack," Rich observed with a smile. "You're right. The kid is like 'mini-me.'"

Zack laughed. "The apple doesn't fall far from the tree."

"In his case, it doesn't."

"Well, Jennifer and I are looking forward to his special day. Knowing Josh, he'll knock it out of the park. Thanks for inviting us."

"I couldn't have a bar-mitzvah without the King of Justice," Rich remarked. "Justice should be the theme of every bar-mitzvah. If those who peddle hate and injustice had their way, the Jews would be extinct, and this bar-mitzvah would never have been rescheduled."

"Why, Mr. Cooper," Zack observed with a chuckle. "Was that a political observation?"

"No. It's a historical fact. Throughout history, different groups have attempted to enslave, convert, expel, attack, and even massacre us, but we're still here. How about the recent shit that caused us to delay our event? I'm mad as hell! For me, a bar or bat mitzvah is an important and defiant moment for every Jewish boy or girl."

"Sounds like a political statement to me," Zack mocked.

"How is that political? I'm reciting non-political Jewish history."

"Because most of the attacks on Jews are rooted in politics, the pogroms in Russia, the Holocaust, Hamas in Israel, and the neo-Nazis and alt-right here in Michigan peddling their anti-Semitic garbage. 'Jews will not replace us?' Who wants to replace these idiots? When did the Midwest become the old South?"

Rich shook his head. Zack continued. "We're two-point-four percent of the population, plotting to supplant white Christians? What a joke! These jerks even tried to kidnap our governor. I will not cede ground to these bigots, nor will I remain silent. These are the essential causes of my life.

"I've told you my grandfather's escape story," Zack continued. "I'm not sure you know this, but he told me that story the night before my bar-mitzvah. His story and time in captivity helped shape me into the man I am today. Grandpa Max is the biggest reason I'm passionate about this stuff."

"Geez-o-Pete, Zack, how do you really feel? Calm down!"

"I can't, Rich. I don't know how you do it."

"Do what?"

"Stay on the sidelines."

"I don't stay on the sidelines. I am very active at my temple, support Detroit area Jewish causes, and I'm very supportive of Israel. I'm just quieter about it than you are."

"Like a church mouse," Zack laughed.

"Temple mouse," Rich countered.

"Humor? Humor and politics? From Mister Straight Lace? Maybe there is still hope for you! I'll bet you have every dime you've ever made, the original millionaire next door."

"Funny coming from the wealthiest guy I know," Rich observed. "I'm no millionaire, but I do okay."

"Do your neighbors know who lives next door?" Zack continued his assault.

"Does anyone know the real person who lives next door? You'll meet one of my neighbors at the bar-mitzvah. His name is Chip Ellis. He's a very nice guy."

"Is he a quiet millionaire, too?" Zack wondered. "Does he dare discuss politics with 'Mister Disengaged?'"

"That's not fair, Zack." Rich became annoyed. "Just because I'm less vocal does not mean I'm disengaged."

"Fair point. So, what's this Ellis guy like? Is he politically active? Democrat? Republican?"

"I told you, we don't discuss politics. He's a good guy, an art broker; he buys and sells fine art. Travels all over the world. It's quite interesting; he's got a great business going. He also has a wonderful wife, Tricia, and two young sons, Christopher and Bruno. We get together, have backyard barbecues, and stuff. The kids go to school together. They'll be at the bar mitzvah."

"Christopher and Bruno? Not Jewish," Zack kibbitzed.

"No," Rich chuckled, shaking his head. "I think they're Catholic."

"Catholic guilt is quite similar to Jewish guilt," Zack smirked. "Just ask my wife."

"How is your wife?"

Zack smiled. "She's wonderful. Jennifer and the boys are the best things that ever happened to me."

"And Tobey and the girls?" Rich wondered.

"The opposite. The end of my marriage and who I was back then? They were the worst moments of my life. I have only regrets. I must fix those relationships someday. I don't know where to start."

"How about a telephone call to one or all?" Rich suggested.

"What would I say? I'm sorry I was such a disappointing failure as a husband and father?"

"Why not? Sounds like a good premise for a conversation."

Zack sighed. "Let's change the subject."

"I think you should call," Rich encouraged. "No time like the present. Everybody screws up at some point in their lives. You're not the same guy you were back then. What do *you* want to talk about?"

"Politics?"

"Oh, brother!"

CHAPTER ONE

Winger Wright was an active Internet browser. While his past heroes relied on in-person organizing, newsletters, and marches to advocate the cause in the 1950s, the Internet allowed Wright to engage and connect with ideologically like-minded young men and women in much larger numbers nationwide. Wright saw himself as a quiet revolutionary—*these politically correct assholes will never see me coming!*

Like his mentors, Benjamin Blaine and Bart Breitner, Wright was delighted with the stark change in acceptable discourse that began with President Ronald John's shocking rise to power. Suddenly, it was fashionable to "make America pure again." Wright's alt-right views became mainstream, and he became one of America's most accomplished alt-right propagandists.

Winger Wright was a pseudonym. The Internet permitted him to hide in plain sight, mingle with the general population, and pen electronic newsletters that tapped into anxieties and frustrations felt by certain white Christian groups in America. The oppression or perceived loss of status of young white men was one reason why Ronald John was elected president of the United States.

The movement was derailed when President John tried to spew too much hate, too often, too fast, implementing a Muslim ban, building walls on both borders, deporting Hispanics, and criminalizing what he called "Mexican parasitic migration." When he inserted his political might into a couple of "Jew lawyer" Zachary Blake's cases, the mighty Blake brought the president down, had him impeached, removed from office, and prosecuted.

Not to be deterred, Wright, the self-proclaimed leader of a group known as The Patriotic Storm Troopers, announced Phase Two of the group's 'Master Race Master Plan,' which featured marches on the largest synagogues and temples in Michigan. The marches would take place at the same time, on January 27, Yom HaShoah, Holocaust Remembrance Day, and pay homage to 'two men named Adolf,' Hitler and Eichmann.

"My lawyer advises that we have First Amendment rights in this country and are entitled to peaceful assembly on public land," he wrote in a rambling manifesto announcing the event. The plan was to bus alt-right bigots to temples and synagogues all over Michigan.

The national news got wind of the plan, reported on the prospective marches, and scared the hell out of Michigan's Jewish Community. The governor flew to Detroit to meet with the mayor and community, political, and religious leaders of all denominations. Everyone at the meeting publicly denounced anti-Semitism.

Working together, public and private officials assembled the most significant police task force ever, even deputizing private citizens. The task force pledged to place patrols at every synagogue and temple in Michigan on January 27, calling the march a "hateful, life-threatening event that exposes a disturbing and dangerous underbelly in society, putting all Americans at risk." Wright answered back, claiming that European skinheads from all points in Europe were flying into the country to supplement the troops and wreak havoc on America's Jewish "scum population."

"Nothing will deter us," he wrote. "Nothing!"

On January 27, an enormous police presence showed up in defense of every Jewish synagogue, temple, building, funeral home, and cemetery in Michigan. Not a single marcher showed up for the event at any location; no skinhead, white nationalist, neo-Nazi, or alt-right activist in sight.

Governor Whitman, flanked by representatives of the Anti-Defamation League and the World Jewish Congress, gave a speech denouncing hate of all types, especially anti-Semitism. She called the march a "sick hoax orchestrated by a group of cowards."

"We must stand up to bullies and bigots in this country," she announced to a rousing ovation.

Wright's "failure to launch," as the media referred to it, left his readers and supporters wondering whether he was committed to the cause of white men. "Is Wright a gutless coward?" wrote one alt-right rag. Following the January debacle, Wright continued to feed his audience hateful garbage, announcing a less ambitious plan of unannounced, targeted hits when law enforcement and Jewish organizations least expected them. He followed this announcement with almost complete radio silence, taking his message off the Internet, privately meeting with his associates, and planning these events. He would attack the Jews directly, one community at a time, a tribute to the bigots who came before.

Slowly and quietly, Wright began mounting a serious threat to Michigan's Jewish community. His goal was to nationalize the effort. Piece by piece, he assembled his coalition of hate, charting a cautious, circuitous, but alarming course of neo-Nazi activity. He was obsessed with creating a national plan of attack. However, he was also patient, knowing an attack had to begin somewhere. Ultimately, his goal was to become famous for his views. He wanted to be the next Robert Miles or Richard Spencer. Soon, he would return to the Internet.

***

According to his manifesto, this Winger Wright character lived in Oakland County, one of Michigan's more affluent counties. He filed assumed name papers in Pontiac under an alias, using the Internet to raise seed money. He had little trouble raising a war chest of seven hundred fifty thousand dollars held in cryptocurrency. The group's first Internet newsletter publication endorsed Ronald John for president.

Wright was a serial liar who masked his identity and published lies about the group's membership numbers, fundraising dollars, location, and everything else. The lies served a dual purpose: to increase membership and operate in relative secrecy and security. "They can't hurt you if they can't find you," he often said.

The Patriotic Storm Troopers' first activities were a series of phony telephone calls to Southeastern Lower Michigan's Jewish community. On May 4, 2019, Bernard Cohen answered his iPhone and heard machine gun fire. He promptly disconnected the call, but the phone rang a second time. This time, a male voice imitated machine gun fire and predicted a new Holocaust, this one eradicating the entire Jewish population of Michigan.

Cohen immediately called the local police and notified his synagogue and rabbi. The police ignored the intrusion and threat, attributing it to a 'prank call,' probably by mischievous teenagers. They rationalized that law enforcement authorities received numerous 'swatting' calls through the 9-1-1 system.

The rabbi took the call more seriously, advising Cohen that many congregants in the area had received similar calls. He understood there were white nationalists sprinkled throughout the state. The rabbi got the ADL involved, and that initial, early effort eventually resulted in the well-organized defense initiative against the Yom HaShoah rally in January, four years later.

Winger Wright had no problem invading the privacy of Michigan's Jewish citizens. He enjoyed placing harassing phone calls, sending hate mail, and dispatching hateful electronic messages by text or email. At the same time, ever the coward, he resisted all attempts to reveal his identity, preferring to remain hidden in cyberspace. The Patriotic Storm Trooper website rapidly became the number one place to spew hate on the dark web.

Wright was almost single-handedly responsible for digitizing hate, using worn-out Nazi tropes to attract Millennials. He pulled quotes from prominent publications and repeated them out of context, suggesting that they supported his offensive positions on the various issues of the day. Every sourced quote was somehow bastardized to espouse a racist, anti-Semitic viewpoint.

Wright long urged his followers to declare a race and culture war, eliminate wokeness or cancel culture, and prepare for physical urban warfare against Jews, Blacks, Muslims, Hispanics, liberals, and the liberal press, any ethnic constituency that might impede his agenda. He established online culture clubs, created chapters in major U.S. cities, and encouraged his followers to contribute and act. Calls to action included weapons purchases, firearms training, martial arts classes, and paramilitary training. In essence, Winger Wright had declared war on American-style Democracy.

His outreach and rhetoric paid dividends. Notorious mass shooters, after being captured, confessed to reading and adopting the ideology of the Patriotic Storm Troopers' newsletters. Several synagogues and temples were firebombed. Two orthodox Jewish men were seriously injured after being run over by motorcycles on a West Bloomfield sidewalk as they walked to synagogue on a Saturday morning. Several cars parked in a Lansing synagogue had their windows shot out. The cars were empty—no one was hurt—but the event had a chilling effect on future attendance at the synagogue.

In Grand Rapids, police received an anonymous call telling them to visit an address in the city where they would find a hate-filled manifesto, automatic weapons, and explosives. The police obtained an exigent circumstances search warrant, visited the address, retrieved the materials, and arrested six men and women on suspicion of hate crimes and illegal weapons charges. The first person to provide information on Wright was offered immunity from prosecution, but the suspects refused to talk and immediately requested an attorney.

Wright's campaign was wildly successful. While Jewish leaders encouraged their fellow Jews to ignore the threats and cede "not an inch of territory" to these domestic terrorists, the statewide Jewish community was terrified. Rabbis preached near-empty temples and synagogues, special events were canceled, travel was severely limited, and people became prisoners in their own homes.

Suddenly, as quickly as it began and flourished, the newsletters and anti-Semitic activities stopped. Michigan Jews came slowly out of hiding and returned to their active, vibrant lives. Law enforcement officials were puzzled at the sudden end to the threats and violence, wondering if Winger Wright had been killed or otherwise muzzled. They were dubious yet cautiously optimistic.

Canceled events were rescheduled under heavy security protocols. Services were well-attended again. Bar and bat mitzvahs were scheduled and joyously celebrated. Winger's followers were puzzled at his disappearance, afraid to act without his leadership and inspiration. Privately, many wondered if he had been killed in a raid or some such intrusion. Cowards all, none of them had the stomach to lead Winger's revolution, and life began to return to normal.

Rich and Gail Cooper were among the last Temple Kol Yisrael members to climb aboard the Jewish activity train. Rich was a pragmatic, non-confrontational individual who preferred to patiently await safety. He relied on the peacekeepers rather than actively fighting for peace. Finally satisfied that his son could be safely called to the *Torah*, he rescheduled Josh's bar-mitzvah. It was a decision he would soon regret.

CHAPTER TWO

Josh's big day had arrived. The congregation, including several of Josh's friends, trickled in. The kids acted wild, as twelve and thirteen-year-olds are prone to do at bar and bat mitzvahs. Rich and Gail parked themselves at the entrance to the sanctuary, welcoming guests as they entered. When Rich and Gail greeted Zack and Jennifer, Gail and Jennifer strolled away for a moment to engage in private conversation. Zack extended a Mazel Tov to Rich, excused himself, and searched for Josh, hoping to give him a pep talk. He found the boy over by the kids' section, chatting with his friends.

"Hey, Josh boy," Zack called.

"Mr. Blake! Thanks for coming."

"Mazel Tov, young man! Are you ready to kick some ass on the *bimah*?"

The kids, including Josh, guffawed at Zack's language in the sacred temple.

"God is watching, Mr. Blake," Josh joked.

"Forgot where I was for a second." Zack looked up to the sky, expressing regret. "You've got this, kid."

"I hope so, Mr. Blake. I think I'm ready."

"I'm certain of it. And call me Zack. I've told you a thousand times."

"I can't," Josh advised. "My folks won't let me."

"It will be our secret," Zack whispered. "Besides, you'll be a man before the morning is over. Good luck today, Josh."

"Thanks . . . Zack."

Blake turned to the kids. "Behave yourselves today, guys and gals. Have respect for your friend."

"Yeah, sure, old man," cracked one smart-ass kid.

"Old man? Ouch! How about a game of one-on-one?" Zack challenged. The kids cracked up at the suggestion.

At that moment, a family of four approached Josh. The teenage children fist-bumped Josh and ran off to join the kid brigade. The parents stayed behind to wish the Bar Mitzvah boy good luck.

Zack studied the couple. The man was tall, perhaps 6 ft 1 or 2, rugged, quite handsome, well-built, with blond hair and blue eyes. The wife was a stunner, a brunette who resembled Jennifer Connelly.

"Hey, Josh, you ready?" the man inquired.

"Yes, Mr. Ellis, Mrs. Ellis. Thanks for coming. I appreciate it."

"We wouldn't have missed it for the world. After all, you're our favorite neighbor," Mrs. Ellis gushed.

"True that," Mr. Ellis agreed.

"This is my dad's friend and lawyer, Zachary Blake." Josh turned to Zack.

"The King of Justice! Rich talks about you all the time." Chip offered his hand.

Zack took it and thought the man was going to crush his fingers.

"This is my wife, Tricia," Chip added.

"How do you do, Tricia? I'm Zack." *She's gorgeous!*

"We've both heard a lot about the famous lawyer. Your reputation precedes you, Zack," Tricia noted.

"Don't believe everything you read. How do you guys know Rich and Gail?" Zack wondered.

"We live next door."

"Right, right, got it. Rich mentioned you at breakfast the other day. I forgot."

"Good things, I hope," Chip prompted.

"Absolutely. When does Rich ever say anything bad about anyone? The original *nebbish*, that one."

"Nebbish?"

"Oh . . . right . . . you guys are Christian. It's a Yiddish term, kinda-sorta means nerd."

"Interesting. I'll have to remember that word. Lots of Yiddish and Hebrew words have invaded our vocabulary," Chip smirked.

Invaded? Zack paused.

"The service is about to start," Tricia intervened. "Good luck, Josh."

"Thanks again, Mrs. Ellis."

"Nice meeting you guys," Zack offered.

"Likewise." Chip shot Zack a look that caused the lawyer to pause. Attitude? Arrogance? *What's with this guy?*

The rabbi wandered over, retrieved Josh, and brought him to the *bimah* to sit. The service was about to begin. An organ and violin began playing, and the talkative congregation quieted.

"*Shabbat Shalom*," Rabbi Solomon greeted the congregation.

"*Shabbat Shalom*," the congregation replied in unison.

"My dear temple family and honored guests," Rabbi Solomon began. "On behalf of Joshua Cooper and his parents, I am pleased to welcome you here as Joshua is called to the *Torah* to become a Bar Mitzvah.

"Bar Mitzvah means 'son of the commandments.' It is an important time in the life of a Jewish boy, as he assumes the responsibilities of an adult in our Jewish community. Joshua attended Hebrew school and worked for years to achieve this milestone. He is ready to demonstrate his commitment to a Jewish adult's ethical and moral responsibilities. One of those responsibilities is to further his Jewish education and continue to develop his Jewish identity, increasing his knowledge of our precious traditions.

"Our temple has modernized written and oral Jewish law but still adheres to the traditions developed over thousands of years of Jewish history and prayer. The *yarmulke* some of us wear is a sign of reverence to *Hashem*, our lord. During our service, our bar mitzvah will don a *Tallit* for the first time, as will all men past bar mitzvah age. Wearing this prayer shawl reminds us of the commandments *Hashem* gave to Moses on Mount Sinai.

"This beautiful sanctuary contains three essential elements of Judaism, *Hashem*, the *Torah*, and the land and people of *Eretz Yisrael*, Israel as we know it, here in America. Suspended above the Ark is the Eternal Flame, lit continuously to symbolize God's eternal presence. Each of our beautiful stained-glass windows tells a particular bible story. I challenge you to study the artwork contained in each window. Find me after the service and tell me what stories the windows tell.

"Some of you are visiting a temple or synagogue for the first time. *Shabbat* commemorates the seventh day, where God rested after creating the world in six days. Our morning service, which Joshua will lead today, consists of a series of traditional Sabbath prayers, which you may follow in English in the prayer book on the wooden rack before you. You will notice that the book opens right to left because Hebrew portions are read right to left.

"The service highlights are the *Shema*, our sacred declaration of belief in one God, and the *Amidah*, a central prayer recited while standing and chanted during every Jewish service. For some prayers, one of our members or honored guests will be asked to open the Ark. The congregation will rise to show its respect for the *Torah*.

"The *Torah* portion follows the morning service. The *Torah* is removed from the Ark, and the congregation rises in respect. Each *Torah* scroll contains the five books of Moses, known as the Old Testament of the modern bible. Each *Torah* scroll is carefully written by hand by a biblical scholar and takes a year to write.

"The scroll is brought to the congregants in a special procession featuring our bar mitzvah boy, and it is customary to kiss or touch the *Torah* as it passes you. Joshua and I will read this week's portion after the *Torah*'s return to the *bimah*. A different portion is read each week. The entire *Torah* is read over a calendar year.

"The portion Joshua will read is also read on this day in every synagogue and temple worldwide, linking Joshua's special day with the world's Jewish population. Today's portion is Noah from the Book of Revelation. You all know the story where God orders Noah to load all the world's animals, two by two, so they might survive the great flood and repopulate the world.

"During the reading, we will honor family and friends and have them recite special blessings or assist in removing, replacing, or dressing the *Torah*. Following the reading, Joshua will chant his *Haftorah*, a concluding portion connected to this week's *Torah* reading. Finally, we will chant concluding prayers and blessings over the wine and bread.

"At this time, I'd like to call Joshua Cooper and his parents to the *bimah* for the presentation and donning of his beautiful *Tallit*, a gift from Josh's grandparents."

Rich and Gail stood and walked onto the *bimah*, carefully removed the prayer shawl from its ornate bag, and placed it around Josh's shoulders. Gail cried the entire time, which caused most of the congregation to laugh. One of the centerpieces of Judaism is study. A Jewish child is obliged to learn Hebrew and study it throughout his life. The bar mitzvah is a young boy's first public demonstration of his Hebrew prowess, marking his passage from childhood to adolescence. Joshua did his parents proud, reciting all his portions flawlessly. After he read the final portion, Rabbi Solomon and Cantor Finkelstein ducked behind their respective podiums as the temple children chucked soft plastic-wrapped candy at the bar mitzvah boy, symbolic of a long, happy, and sweet life.

Rich and Gail hosted a *Kiddush* following the service. The luncheon for honored guests paid tribute to their son's accomplishment. People approached Joshua, congratulated him, and told him how well he did. Some advised that he was the best in congregation history, praise that every bar mitzvah boy receives from at least one family member or congregation regular.

Following the luncheon, Rich rose and walked to the podium, offering a congratulatory speech, expressing how proud he and Gail were of their young son. As he returned to the table, Joshua thanked him and asked if he might be excused to use the restroom.

"Of course, son," Rich crowed. "This is your day! You can do whatever you want. Have a drink!"

"Really?"

"Absolutely not," warned Gail, shooting the stink eye at her husband.

The boy laughed and wandered off, headed for the bathroom. Chip Ellis headed the same way. A short time later, Gail began to wonder what was keeping Josh.

"Is he sick or something?" she asked Rich. "Please go check on him."

A loud and forceful explosion rocked the temple as Rich Cooper walked toward the bathroom. Rich was thrown backward by the blast and knocked unconscious by shock waves. Congregants and visitors began a mad dash for the exits, pushing each other out of the way, trampling over those who fell to the ground.

When calm was restored, Rich was taken by ambulance, unconscious, along with several other seriously injured guests, to Henry Ford Hospital in West Bloomfield. The West Bloomfield Police were called to the scene. Investigators traced the source of the explosion to an Oklahoma City-style bomb set off in the Temple men's room that Joshua Cooper and Chip Ellis entered immediately before the blast.

The temple was evacuated—the bathroom was roped off until crime tech units arrived and surveyed the lavatory. Gail Cooper was torn between her unconscious husband at Henry Ford and her missing son, presumed to be somewhere in the ruins of the bathroom. She decided to wait at the temple for the crime techs to clear the debris, hoping for a *Shabbat* miracle in which her son and her neighbor were both found alive. When CSI investigators finally emerged from the wreckage, they announced good news and bad. The good news was that no bodies were found in the bathroom debris. The bad news, which caused Gail Cooper to faint, was that Joshua Cooper and Chip Ellis were nowhere to be found.

CHAPTER THREE

Winger Wright's eyes shifted from one television to the next. He had set up three of them side-by-side, each one either tuned to CNN, Fox News, or MSNBC's coverage of the attack at the temple. The TV shots showcased either ground-level or aerial views of the smoke trickling out of the holy place's windows, the feed occasionally cutting to inserts of temple-goers covered in soot, some of them bleeding from lacerations caused by the debris the blast had made.

"Today's attack," one reporter on the middle television said, "demonstrates that anti-Jewish rhetoric and intolerance is increasing here, in the United States and abroad, perhaps at levels not experienced in decades. The events transpiring behind me are the most recent horrible examples of what can only be called terrorism against America's Jewish population—"

Winger's lips pulled back into a tight, self-assured grin. *Good!* He relished in the carnage and mayhem playing out on multiple screens—domestic terrorism he carefully planned and executed. He was far from finished. Part two of his master plan would soon be put into motion. For now, Winger took a moment to scan the scenes displayed by the various networks, stand back, witness the damage and devastation he caused, and bask in righteous glory.

Winger stepped closer to the television sets. He rejoiced in Jewish pain and suffering. The more temple worshippers suffered, the more joy he felt. The Jews in that temple and those scattered throughout the rest of the world would remember this day. Historically, Jews used events like this to seize control of American business and media sectors. 'Oppression and religious bigotry demand no less,' they would say. Winger would work to ensure the failure of that disgusting idea. *That's how the state of Israel came to exist.*

Winger lit a cigarette, took a long drag, and exhaled. He shouted at the screen: "Cry your shifty little eyes out."

The door behind Winger opened—he didn't bother to turn around to see who had joined him. The compound was secluded. There was little chance that anyone could infiltrate his fortified hub of operations.

'The PST,' as it was known, was now Winger's organization, inherited from his patriotic father, God rest his soul. Winger shook his head. Thinking of his father tugged at his heartstrings. He wished his old man was still alive to witness the fruits of his labor and observe how tiny seedlings, planted over 30 years ago, grew and flourished into a movement true to his father's own words:

"Return this nation to the strong, untainted, white-dominated principles upon which it was founded."

Winger closed his eyes. "I hope you're proud, Pop," he whispered. "We'll get this nation back on track."

A hand clapped his shoulder. Winger turned toward whoever was standing behind him and discovered it was his right-hand man and loyal cousin, Carl. Winger's headstrong cousin was an honorable man who demonstrated his loyalty a few years back by spending six years in prison instead of taking the Feds' offer of leniency in exchange for testifying against Winger and PST.

Carl gestured to the television sets and crowed, "That's quite a sight to behold, brother."

"Indeed, it is," Winger nodded, jutting his chin toward the screens. "Just the beginning, though—we have a long way to go to claim victory."

Carl shrugged. "We will. One day, we will."

Winger pulled up a chair, a minor effort for him, thanks to the 200 solid pounds of muscles tacked to his frame. "How is our young guest?" he inquired.

Carl shrugged again. "Kid's a resilient little Jew bastard. Edgar's keeping an eye on him. He'll need some water or grub soon, maybe a toilet. I haven't checked yet, but he may have soiled his cute little bar mitzvah suit. Jews have those dietary restrictions—no this, no that, no pork and shit. What do you want me to do?"

Winger laughed and then dabbed out his cigarette. "Deprive him for a day or two—when he's hungry enough, the kid will eat whatever we give him. Feed him something from our rations. We're stocked up. Parcel it out. Give him no more than he needs."

"When do we make the call, and what do we tell them about Chip Ellis?" Carl snickered.

Winger glanced at the televisions and paused, contemplating his answer. "We'll call soon," he finally replied, continuing to watch coverage of his masterpiece.

"Let the dust settle, create some urgency, then give them a ring—catch them off guard. They'll be grateful to hear from us, delighted to hear the boy is still alive. Considering what I'm seeing on television, the boy and the neighbor might be buried under the rubble. That's what law enforcement now believes. Maybe some Jewish artifacts fell on them and crushed them."

"Poetic, but what about after?"

Winger furrowed his brow. "After what?"

"After they discover no one under the rubble and determine that two people are missing. And take things one step further: What happens after they pay the ransom? What will we do?" Carl inquired.

"What happens to the kid? Will Chip Ellis be released? Does he escape? What's the plan? Are we going to kill a thirteen-year-old kid? Have you thought that far ahead, fleshed those things out?"

Winger shrugged. "No, I haven't. So far, the kid hasn't seen our faces. I'm not worried about Ellis at this point. Maintain the status quo for now. If both escape or get released, no one would be the wiser, barring some major fuck-up on our part."

Carl's eyes narrowed. "On second thought, maybe the kid doesn't survive. Kill the little Jew before he gets married and has children. Several fewer Jews in our future—more room on the planet for our kind. It's in keeping with our mission."

Terminating the kid occurred to Winger on more than one occasion. If he had his way, every single Jewish person on the face of the planet would perish with one swift stroke. Perhaps it was possible in 1940 but nearly impossible in the twenty-first century. These days, surgical precision was required to restore proper Arian supremacy, not mass extermination. One had to be discreet and savvy, think things through, and incrementally chip away at the "Jewish Problem." This is what Winger's father constantly preached, principles Wright still lived by:

"Strategize. Always stay ten steps ahead of your opponents," his father would say.

Winger turned to Carl. "Killing the kid is an obvious option. Doing so, however, may present more serious problems. The eyes of the world are upon us right now. Our mission is front and center in everyone's minds. The Jewish-controlled government will stop at nothing to track us down. If we kill the kid after the ransom is paid, the government and every civil rights organization in the world will want our heads on proverbial platters. Do we want to invite that type of scrutiny? Are we prepared to engage in all-out war? Isn't that a shit-storm we don't need?"

Carl shrugged. "So, we let him live—release him in a blindfold and zip ties on a remote highway somewhere?"

A crooked smile beamed on Winger's face. "I didn't say that either," he replied. "We test the waters. If the kidnapping alone stirs up the same shitstorm, what difference does it make if the kid winds up dead? We kick the hornet's nest, demonstrate that we're serious as a heart attack, and wait for law enforcement's reaction."

Winger shifted his focus to a monitor more diminutive than the televisions they had tuned into news stations. A black-and-white image of Josh Cooper sitting cross-legged on the floor with a canvas bag over his head, his arms zip-tied behind him, filled the small screen.

"I'll decide soon," Winger continued. "In the meantime, let's prepare for stage two of the plan."

Carl flattened his palm over his heart. Winger did the same. They shot their arms toward the ceiling and shouted: "Sieg Heil!"

CHAPTER FOUR

The explosion and evacuation happened quickly. Josh had no time to process the events. He remembered entering the bathroom, hearing a loud boom, and feeling the bathroom shake. He saw walls begin to crumble and then nothing—he must have passed out. His next memory was of a pair of hands pulling his arms behind his back, restraining them with something tight. The blast reverberated in his chest. He heard Chip scream. "Let me go!"

Every moment after that was shrouded in darkness, an occasional voice grunting or barking at another, accompanied by burnt rubber and diesel smells. When Josh regained consciousness, he lay in a small room on a cold stone floor. A canvas bag covering his head prevented him from seeing anything but daylight. His wrists were bound—the struggle to free himself was fruitless. The room smelled like a Home Depot or other large hardware store, with wood smells, fertilizer, and various chemicals like turpentine or paint thinner.

"Hello? Is anyone out there? Where am I?" Josh cried. "Mom? Dad?"

Josh was terrified. His heart beat rapidly as though it might pop out of his chest. His palms were slick with sweat. Panic constricted the muscles in his throat.

"Mom?" Josh shouted through the bag over his head. "Dad!"

On the other side of the door, he heard Mr. Ellis call out: "Josh boy? Are you okay?" The familiar voice filled the young man with an immediate sense of relief.

"Mr. Ellis? Is that you?" Josh cried out in response. "Where are we? What's going on?"

"Easy, Josh," Chip urged. "Try to stay calm. Deep breaths. Okay?"

Josh again strained to unfasten the zip-ties that bound his wrists. The restraints would not budge. "I can't move," Josh cried. "I can't see, Mr. Ellis. I—"

"You must try to relax, son," Chip said. "Listen to me. Just listen to the sound of my voice. One way or the other, we are getting out of here. I promise everything will be okay."

Josh erupted in tears, drew a shaky breath, and nodded. He took a deeper breath, held it, and felt his heartbeat slow. "Thanks, Mr. Ellis. I think I'm okay," he muttered.

"Good," Chip retorted. "Let's slow down, take a moment to think."

"What happened?" Josh wondered. "Where are we?"

"Someone took us, Josh. I don't know if the explosion was meant to disguise our abduction, but it doesn't matter. Here we are."

"Took us?" Josh exclaimed. "Like . . . a kidnapping?"

"I believe so," Chip presumed. "It happened back at the temple bathroom. Remember?"

"Yes. But who took us? What would they want with us?"

"I'm not sure. It was quick. I was stunned by the explosion, but I remember three or four guys bursting in. I'm pretty sure they drugged us and took us away in a truck or maybe a van."

Josh winced. His head was pounding. "Drugged? So that's why my head hurts so bad?"

"I believe so, son," Chip concurred. "Whatever they dosed us with seems to be wearing off."

Josh craned and shrugged, trying to knock off whatever was covering his face. "I can't see," he shrieked. "I can't see anything."

"I know," Chip soothed. "They put canvas bags over our heads."

"Where are we, Mr. Ellis?"

"I'm not sure, Josh. I can't see either. Think about this, though. If these guys wanted to hurt us, they would have done so already, don't you think?" Chip tried to calm the boy.

A single tear streamed down Josh's cheek. "Mom and Dad—are they okay?" he wondered. "What about my bar mitzvah guests and the regulars? What about the rabbi and the cantor?"

"I'm sure they're okay, Josh. We need to be patient. Please do me a favor. Follow my lead and do what I tell you. Okay? Can you do that?"

"I want to go home," Josh wailed, his lips quivering.

"I know," Chip cooed, "I know. Try to stay calm. Not much we can do about any of that right now."

A sharp, metal-on-metal screech cut through the silence. Josh shuddered as he felt a gust of air breezing over his few exposed body parts. He detected scents of mildew and stale cigarettes as booted feet marched slowly and deliberately into the room. The sound sent chills up and down his spine. Then, silence—total terrifying silence—Josh feared the worst. Perhaps another explosion or a gunshot would end his young life. He was terror-stricken once more, awaiting the inevitable.

A door slammed shut. Josh saw hints of light through the canvas bag covering his head.

"Stay calm, you two." A booming and authoritative voice ordered. "As much as we'd like to, we won't hurt you. You're too valuable as bait."

Josh furrowed his brow. The voice was eerily familiar, yet different somehow. *Do I know this person? Does Mr. Ellis?* He wondered where he heard it before, why it was so familiar. *Did I hear it on the news?* Wherever it was, he couldn't quite place it.

The voice bristled. "Listen up, now!" "I'm only going to say this once," it ranted.

What did we do to piss this guy off? Josh wondered.

"You've been taken hostage. You're safe for now, but no one knows about this place. Your friends and family won't find you. If they genuinely love your asses, and we sincerely hope they do, they will pay a fortune for your safe return. If they don't pay, we'll send you back in little pieces, perhaps in those canvas bags that cover your heads. How much time you spend here, whether you go home in one piece or several, depends on whether and how soon they pay the ransom.

"While we wait for that to happen, you will each remain confined to your rooms. You will speak only when permitted to speak. You will not scream. You will not shout. You will not attempt to escape or commit acts of violence against any member of my team. If you attempt to break these rules, you will suffer harsh consequences. If you follow the rules, you will be treated fairly, fed, and cared for during your stay. Any questions?"

Josh deferred to Chip, waiting for him to question his captors. But Chip said nothing. Josh remained silent, afraid to question anyone's authority under these hostile circumstances.

"Last chance," the voice warned. "Speak now or forever hold your peace."

Again, Josh waited on Chip. Silence. Josh cleared his throat and muttered, "Who are you? Why are you doing this? My parents are not rich. They can't pay you much."

"At this moment, who we are doesn't matter. What we want is money. If your folks can't afford to pay, we will kill you. They better find some rich relative to pay the ransom."

"Why us?" Josh queried. "Like I said, we don't—"

"You people," the voice snarled. "You are the reason this is happening. It's because of you that the world is a crap place, and things are in such disarray."

Josh shuddered at his captor's 'you people' comment. His seventh-grade class recently visited the Holocaust Museum in Farmington Hills. Anti-Semites often used this term to express hatred for Jews. Was he being held hostage because he was Jewish? Who would do such a thing? Why?

The abductor continued to spew his mini-manifesto, grumbling that "his people" were oppressed by "you people," promising that he and his men would dismantle the country's current corrupt and oppressive political and social structure.

"Our movement requires capital. You two are fund-raising tools, nothing more," the voice explained.

Josh was surprised at Chip's silence. *Why is he even here? He's not Jewish. Why doesn't he tell them that? "You've got the wrong guys." Say something!*

"Please," Josh pleaded. "May I call my mom and dad? They're probably worried."

Boots clicked slowly across the floor, the sound growing louder as they moved closer to Josh. The boy tensed his body, holding his head high, squinting through the canvas in a vain attempt to identify his captor.

"No!" the voice roared, a few inches from Josh's ear. "I'm in charge. I make the rules. No contact. No free choice. You will do only as I say. No one calls anyone until it suits my purpose. Understood?" he snarled.

The mad man hovered, still a few inches from the boy's ear, awaiting an answer. The kid didn't get it.

"I asked, 'understood?' You will answer me when I ask you a question," the voice rumbled in Josh's ear.

"Understood, sir," the boy peeped.

"That's better," the voice calmed.

Boots clicked back across the floor, lights were switched, and a door slammed. Josh heard a lock engage. He felt glued to the floor, afraid to move. Fear was his primary emotion, with confusion running a close second. The more he considered the voice of the hostage taker, the more he felt he knew the person. *The voice is so familiar. Who is it? Why can't I remember?* He tried to imagine the same voice in a calmer and more peaceful context.

"Mr. Ellis?" Josh spoke. "Are you still here? Do you recognize that guy's voice?" Josh was distracted by a faint, flashing red light. *A camera*, he decided. *They're watching us.*

Josh repeated, "Mr. Ellis? Who was that guy? Did you recognize his voice?"

Chip did not answer. *Have they taken him? Why were we separated? Wouldn't it be easier to keep us together? Where is he?* Josh replayed the sound of the man's voice in his mind. The more he heard it, the more he thought he recognized, no, *knew* who the speaker was. *No, it can't be. It makes no sense.*

CHAPTER FIVE

The living room was deathly quiet. Rich and Gail held each other on the couch. A room that hosted numerous family gatherings and produced happy memories now played host to grief, concern, fear, and pain.

Zachary Blake crouched in front of Rich and Gail, rested his hand on Gail's, looked deep into her eyes, and promised, "We'll find him, Gail. You have my word. No one will sleep until Josh is safe at home."

Gail groaned, nodded, and burst into tears. She fell into Zack's arms and embraced him for quite a while. When they finally terminated the embrace, she thanked him for his support.

"Find him, Zack! Find my baby boy!"

"I will, Gail. I promise."

Zack moved across the room to Chip's wife, Tricia. He repeated his promise, this time, to bring Chip home safely.

"All will be well—Chip will be home before you know it."

Tricia was less responsive. She offered a sleepy head nod. She'd been awake for seventy-two hours.

Zack felt a tap on his shoulder. Rich wanted to talk privately. He asked Zack's wife, Jennifer, if she'd stay with Gail and Tricia while he spoke with Zack in the study. The two men entered the room. Zack closed the door behind him.

"Are you okay?" Zack inquired. "Can I get you anything?"

Rich shook his head, tears misting in his eyes. "I need my son returned to me, Zack—safe and sound. I've never had a quarrel or dispute with anyone. Why would anyone take Josh? What the hell is going on?"

"I'm not sure yet, Rich," Zack cooed with a comforting tone. "We'll get to the bottom of things. We'll make this right, buddy. For now, we hold out hope that he's okay and thank God for the lives that were spared today. What happened was terrible, but your friends and family are resilient people. We'll get through this. Together."

Rich slipped down behind his executive desk, holding his head. He took a deep breath.

"Who would do such a thing?" he wondered aloud. "And . . . why?" His eyes narrowed. Tears formed as he addressed his friend.

"Josh must be found and returned to me, Zack. I can't go on without him. The American melting pot experiment is almost two hundred fifty years old, and we Jews must still endure this level of hatred and violence."

"They'll pay for what they've done, Rich—every one of these terrorists. Mark my words—we'll put them on display for the world and ensure justice is served," Zack pledged.

Rich stood, approached Zack, and wrapped his arms around him.

"I'm going to need your help, buddy," he pleaded. "More than ever before."

Zack nodded. "I'm here for you, Rich. I'm not going anywhere."

The doorbell rang, and several police officers joined the others in the house. A trio of news vans were parked outside. Reporters and camera operators angled to get clear shots of the victims or interviews with whoever walked out the door.

Zack stood in the kitchen with his arm around Jennifer, watching Rich hold Gail in his arms, trying his best to console his wife. Gail was inconsolable, crying almost non-stop, weeping uncontrollably over the past several hours. He was amazed she was still conscious. Her head remained buried in Rich's chest, even as the police stood in front of them, asking question after question. They were trying to do their jobs; Zack understood, but it seemed insensitive.

Zack sighed and closed his eyes. On a positive note, no one was killed in the explosive terrorist attack. He recalled Dearborn, Arya Khan, and the white supremacist terrorist bombing at the Mosque of America a few short years ago. Jack Dylan and his anti-terrorist task force hunted down the perps. All the vengeful bigots, including their aged leader, Benjamin Blaine, currently resided in various prisons around the Midwest. Blaine would, most certainly, die in custody. Innocent people died in that blast, aimed at America's Muslim population.

In this case, there were no deaths, but plenty of injuries ranging from lacerations to mild concussions, and one case where a temple member's pacemaker momentarily stopped functioning. Several hospital rooms were occupied with victims expected to survive the attack. Perhaps he would reach out to Jack and his team for guidance or direct involvement in hunting down these vicious men.

Jennifer rested her palm on Zack's shoulder, startling Zack from his bitter memories. He turned to the love of his life and smiled.

"Are you okay?" Jennifer rubbed circles on Zack's back, massaging muscles knotted from the strain.

Zack nodded. "I feel terrible," he whispered, hoping Rich and Gail wouldn't hear. "You and I have been through some horrible stuff, but what would we do if Kenny or Jake went missing? I can't imagine." He pivoted focus from Rich and Gail to Tricia Ellis, who chatted with a police detective.

Jennifer drew a breath. "I can't believe this is happening. The police are now speculating that the bombing could be a smokescreen to draw attention away from the kidnapping of Josh and Chip."

Zack sensed this was true. *Something bigger is at play. There's a reason these two were taken. This is a smokescreen of sorts. Is the motive terror, money, or both?*

The number of police officers inside the house continued to grow. Uniformed patrol and plain-clothed cops filtered in and out of the house, taking orders from a trio of detectives currently assigned to the developing case. A detective wearing a tweed coat and horn-rim glasses approached and offered his hand.

"I'm Detective Lowery. You're Zachary Blake. The King of Justice?"

Zack shrugged and shook the detective's hand. "The 'King' thing is a marketing tool, Detective. I'm Zack. Nice to meet you. Sorry to meet under such horrible circumstances."

"Agreed," Lowery concurred. "Can we talk in the den?"

"Sure," Zack followed Lowry to Rich's cozy, comfortable den office.

"What can I do for you, Detective?" Zack wondered.

"Your reputation precedes you. I need a few minutes of your time. I'm taking statements from everyone in the temple when the explosion was triggered. We're still sifting through the rubble. I want to be as discreet as possible. Our current concern is that the two missing individuals—"

"Josh," Zack cut in. "They have names—Josh and Chip," he grumbled.

Lowery grimaced, uncomfortable. "My apologies. Where was I? Our people are still combing the wreckage, praying for the best but expecting the worst."

Zack shook his head. "I disagree. You're suggesting that Josh and Chip are dead, but I assure you, they are not. Had this bomb been powerful enough to level the building and claim multiple victims, I might have been on board. But two random victims disappear without a trace? Next-door neighbors plucked from a few hundred survivors? No, sir, this is not random. Josh and Chip are alive. You'll see."

"Again," Lowery assured. "We are combing through the rubble. If they're there, we'll find them."

"You're wasting valuable time and manpower," Zack opined. "Josh and Chip have been kidnapped."

"What makes you so sure?" Lowery inquired.

"It makes sense," Zack shrugged. "The blast was destructive but not powerful enough to kill. Death wasn't their intent. The terrorists are trying to send a message, but they were not trying to kill."

"Message? What message?" Lowery crossed his arms and cocked his head.

Zack had been tossing theories around in his head since the explosion occurred. He'd been waiting for a cop to question him. This was an act of terror, an attempt to grab attention or headlines and raise awareness or money for the cause.

"I've been involved in one of these explosions. Remember the Mosque of America in Dearborn? *That* explosion intended to kill. It was considerably more incendiary and potent. This wasn't as messy—it was more intentionally logistical, meant to attract attention. I wouldn't be surprised if it detonated in an *empty* bathroom."

"If that's true, the terrorists accomplished their mission. They have our attention. I remember that Dearborn case. That was Jack Dylan's case. He and his anti-terrorist task force are first-rate," Lowery commented.

Zack huffed. "Dylan is the best. There is no finer law enforcement officer. You might consider calling him for advice and counsel on this case. His anti-terrorist team ranks among the country's finest.

"As to the temple bombing, I was there. I witnessed the destruction. The bomb caused a huge crater, but it was positioned and detonated in the men's room, a reasonable distance away from the *bimah* and the sanctuary where the congregants were seated. The blast radius shook the building but had nowhere near the force needed to bring it down on the attendees.

"I'll bet you a hundred bucks, right now, that the bomb techs back my theory. Whoever planted these explosives knew how to set the bomb to minimize casualties. The explosion was a diversion."

Shrugging, Lowery replied, "Diversion? Diversion to cover up what?"

"Like I said," Zack repeated. "This was done to divert attention from the terrorist's true intent. This was a hostage-taking, an abduction. Josh and Chip were kidnapped."

Lowery held up a finger. "Perhaps. Let's call it a *possible* abduction," he clarified. "We don't know at this point. All possibilities are on the table."

"But we *do* know," Zack persisted. "Where are the remains? Where is the residual evidence? Has CSI found DNA? It's been five hours—your team is still sifting through the rubble. Wouldn't they have found something by now?"

"Perhaps," Lowry conceded. "Let's run with your theory for the moment. Where do things progress from here?"

"I suspect we'll get a ransom demand sooner than later. The perps are waiting us out, building tension, fear, frustration, causing the Cooper and Ellis families to become desperate," Zack predicted.

"Any idea who might be responsible?"

Zack looked surprised at the question. "Seriously? This is a *Jewish* house of worship. Like the attack in Dearborn on the Muslim community, Detective Lowry, this is a *hate* crime, an act of terror directed at the Jewish people.

"I don't need to tell you there's been a rash of these recently. There are numerous organizations or individuals inclined to carry out anti-Semitic attacks. Fifty-eight percent of all hate crimes are attributed to people of the Jewish faith."

Lowery nodded. "I'm acutely aware," he admitted. "Let's talk about your theory that the bombers have explosives expertise and were able to limit and project the blast to minimize casualties. If they acted with that type of precision, that fact alone drastically narrows the suspect pool.

"Assuming I'm on board, we aren't dealing with a group of backwoods idiots playing dress-up in hand-me-down army fatigues. The expertise, precision, and planning you're speaking about could only be done by a few terrorist groups. Add the anti-Semitic component, and the suspect pool narrows even further. There are only a few groups who have both the technical skills and anti-Semitic organizational roots to pull this off."

"What groups? Get in touch with Dylan and get him involved. It's all he does these days. Better yet, hand the case off to the feds. There's a Detroit FBI agent; her name is Clare Gibson. She's the best at these types of cases," Zack assured.

"I may do that. I know Jack and Gibson. Both are solid. With what's going on in Israel, I would not rule out Muslim extremist groups. The Nation of Islam comes to mind. As to Neo-Nazis and White Supremacist groups, my best guess would be a group that calls itself the Patriotic Storm Troopers or PST. Their leader is a horrible but elusive bigot who calls himself 'Winger Wright.' His group's brand recognition is at an all-time high. The PST's signature is on a host of recent terrorist and anti-Semitic attacks," Lowry advised.

Zack pondered Lowry's theory. He was familiar with neo-Nazi anti-Semite groups like the PST. As a prominent donor to Jewish causes, Zack sat on numerous Jewish advocacy and charitable boards.

Is it feasible that the PST did this? If so, it's a bold attempt at expanding their reach, broadening their brand, increasing membership and dollars raised, and advancing their neo-Nazi agenda.

"Mr. Blake?" Detective Lowery interrupted his thoughts.

Zack snapped out of his trance. "Yes, Detective?"

"This will take some time," Lowery continued. "I'll consider contacting Dylan or Gibson. Please stay close to the families and offer them your support. I know you're a resourceful man, but do not try to interfere with our ongoing investigation."

"Where does *that* come from? What makes you think I'd interfere with an active police investigation?"

"I indicated previously, Mr. Blake. Your reputation, good and bad, precede you," Lowry cautioned. "And, as you've already indicated, you have preferred law enforcement contacts, lots of power and money, and a reputation for acting, sometimes without regard to the consequences. Please try to constrain yourself."

"What a nice thing to say, Lowry! We're going to be good friends. I'll be satisfied if you promise to consider contacting Dylan or Gibson. Don't be shy—ask for help. These are good people."

Lowry stayed silent. Like most local cops, he was not keen on involving other cops, especially the feds.

"We'll cross that bridge when we come to it," he remarked. "Besides, it's not my call to make. Requests for federal assistance must go through the mayor and the governor and a ton of people higher up on the WBPD's payroll to make that happen."

The muscles in Zack's jaw tensed. "You just witnessed the most heinous crime ever committed against the Detroit area's Jewish community. The FBI ought to be sitting here asking questions as we speak. With all due respect, Detective Lowery, how do we leave the case to a small-town police force like West Bloomfield?"

"Insult acknowledged, thank you very much. Blake, I know you're frustrated, but this attack is just seventy-two hours young. Give us a break, would you? You're a grown man. I can't stop you from doing anything you're inclined to do, including calling in Gibson and the feds. However, if you do anything to obstruct my investigation, I will charge you, sir. Fair warning," Lowery threatened.

"Duly noted, Detective. Will there be anything else?"

"No, I think that covers things for now. Nice chatting with you."

"Likewise."

After they terminated the meeting, Zack sat alone in the Cooper's den. He rehashed the conversation and the detective's thinly veiled threat. The lawyer pulled out his iPhone, scanned his contacts, settled on a familiar and trusted name, and pushed 'send.'

CHAPTER SIX

Micah Love was once a smoker. He kicked the habit over twenty years ago with a yeoman-like effort. These days, he followed strangers' smoke trails or automobile tailpipes but proudly refrained from smoking. According to his most recent therapist, Micah had an addictive personality. His ascent to the top of the private investigator world did little to change him. The riches he achieved by hitching his wagon to Zachary Blake, the legal juggernaut known as the King of Justice, probably made things worse. Micah could easily afford to do anything and engage in any vice whenever he wanted.

Under these difficult circumstances—enormous wealth—Micah's therapist advised that kicking bad habits would be difficult. His current effort centered on his voracious porn habit. The shrink opined that kicking porn would be even more difficult than quitting cigarettes. But the love of his life, the beautiful and talented Jessica Klein, challenged him to do something about his porn addiction.

"Why do you need porn when you have the most insatiable girlfriend on the planet?" she pondered aloud. "Is there anything I wouldn't do to satisfy your sexual desires?"

"Not that I can think of," he had to admit. He was, indeed, a lucky man.

As he completed the session and left the therapist's office, Micah smiled at the memory, amused by the absurdity of seeing an expensive shrink to kick a 'habit' he considered completely normal. Smoking was dangerous and addictive. It caused heart and lung disease and was linked to other serious physical ailments.

Who does porn or masturbation hurt? If the cops ever decided to declare pornography a crime, it was a victimless crime. He wasn't a child, although he often acted like one. He was a grown man with an overactive libido.

"No big thing," he muttered, loud enough to turn heads on the street. He got into his latest and fanciest Lincoln—Micah only purchased American cars. He started it up and drove away. Flushing nicotine out of his system would likely prolong his life. *Who did porn ever kill?*

To Micah, experiencing Internet porn was a God-given right—he didn't need or want a flush. While plenty of men tried to kick the habit, the shrink indicated that doing so required a patient willing to admit he had a psychological or physiological problem. Micah recounted the exchange as he headed to his downtown office.

"You have an addiction," the therapist opined. "Like any addiction, you must confront it, head on, then wean yourself off, like a drug."

Micah shrugged and shifted his short, stout frame on the doctor's couch. The sudden shift caused his combover to fall over his shoulder, exposing whisps of leftover hair and a bald dome.

"I don't have an addiction," he retorted. He licked his hands and tried to replace his combover with hands sticky from the saliva.

"I'm just your average alpha male. I love women. I adore women. I adore women's bodies. Women are beautiful, all shapes and sizes."

The therapist scribbled a note and inquired, "What about the . . . uh . . . frequency? You have admitted that you spend an excessive amount of time on Internet pornography sites."

Micah shrugged. "So? What's the big deal?" he wondered, perplexed by the inquiry.

"By your admission, you watch for more than the average male."

"Oh? How would you know? What's average? Have you researched the subject? Hey Doc, do *you* watch porn?" Micah kibbitzed.

"Heavens, no!" the therapist exclaimed. "I'm only reacting to what you have told me. You indicated that you watch multiple types of porn for several hours a day, Micah."

"Why isn't that a good thing, Doc?" Micah queried. "It keeps my libido in check and helps me focus."

"What about your girlfriend? What was her name?"

"Jessica. What about her? I don't understand." Micah cocked his head like a confused dog.

"How does she feel about your pornography obsession?"

"She doesn't like it. She's the reason I'm here. I no longer talk to her about porn," Micah confessed. "Why poke the bear? Know what I mean?"

"But you've told me she's the love of your life, Micah," the therapist reasoned.

"You indicated that you were in a committed relationship with this woman. Things were quite serious between the two of you. Perhaps this is an unwarranted assumption, but aren't you jeopardizing your relationship by carrying on this way? I don't want to see either of you get hurt. Do you want a good relationship destroyed over . . . shall we say . . . your *supplemental* sexual cravings? Healthy relationships function well when both parties have an open line of communication with each other's needs, wants, and desires."

"I know she doesn't care for porn or my interest in porn. But what she doesn't know won't hurt her. There's a *shit ton* she doesn't know. *That's* good for the relationship," Micah concluded.

The therapist and patient were worlds apart on what was important or relevant to a meaningful relationship. The therapist shook his head in disbelief.

"But she should know, Micah!" he bristled. "You should be open and honest with her. This obsession of yours is not healthy. Nothing wrong with taking yourself in hand, so to speak, but there are acceptable limits."

"Who sets those limits, Doc? You? Some psychiatry board? Who? These guys probably sit in a dark room somewhere, by themselves, holding a Penthouse Magazine in one hand and their dicks in the other."

"For the sake of your relationship with this woman, you should try to find healthier outlets, perhaps slowly disengage from this constant and incessant objectification of woman," he warned.

"I fear that if you can't do that, your current relationship, or any other future relationship with the opposite sex, will end badly. You are not on a good path, Micah. Think about Adam, Eve, and the forbidden fruit. Nothing good will come of this porn obsession."

Micah knew the therapist spoke the truth—he couldn't decide whether he cared. He never considered porn detrimental to his mental health. Quite the contrary, porn got him through many years of abstinence. He did not wish to be free of porn.

For the sake of his relationship with Jessica Klein, he only wanted to taper his desire a tad. He once objectified women as beings put on this earth to please men sexually, get pregnant, have babies, and perpetuate the species.

Jessica Klein changed his perspective. She was more intelligent than him, better than a mere equal. Her stunning beauty was a lucky strike extra. He didn't desire an alternative relationship—he and Jessica were the real deal. She didn't care if he dabbled in porn, but she considered it unhealthy to engage whenever he was alone. And what Jessica wanted, Micah wanted—but three weeks into 'operation porn-less,' he was frustrated.

He sat at his computer, fighting the urge to visit a site.

"Control . . ." he whispered to himself, "baby steps . . ." *You can do this!*

According to the therapist, in a few short months, he'd have his obsession under control. *Does it have to be cold turkey? Like an alcoholic?*

A chill shot through his body. He shivered. He felt a sudden buzz in his pants. Initially shocked at what seemed to be a physical reaction, Micah realized it was his cell phone, in silent, vibrator mode.

He composed himself, appreciating the sudden distraction, and accepted the call without checking the screen.

"Love Investigations, Micah Love speaking. How may I help you?"

"How's the best sleuth in America?" Zachary Blake chirped.

"The King of Justice," he chuckled. "How the hell are you?" He adjusted his pants and straightened his shirt like Zack could see him.

"I'm so honored that the King has taken time out of his busy schedule. To what do I owe the pleasure?"

"Is this a good time?"

Micah glanced down to his lap, up his computer screen, and finally shuffled some paperwork on his desk.

"Just wrapping up a case for another client. I *do* have other clients, you know—a police brutality situation. Long story short, I've got a slew of bad cops caught in my crosshairs. However, I *always* have time for the King."

"Can you take a new case? It's a big deal and a big ask," Zack advised.

"I'm listening," Micah leaned forward in anticipation. Working with Blake was usually an exciting adventure and a huge payday. The two friends handled lots of tough cases together. Micah was a multi-millionaire, thanks to Zack.

"Have you heard about the recent terrorist attack in West Bloomfield?"

"Saw it on the news. At the temple, right?"

"Right. It happened during my friend's son's bar mitzvah. You remember Rich Cooper. Lives in Beverly Hills?"

Sure. Nice guy, as I recall. When did he move to California?"

"Not *that* Beverly Hills," Zack advised. "The one in Michigan, you know, near Birmingham."

Micah smirked. "Nothing happens to anyone in *that* Beverly Hills."

"I guess that's true here. The actual incident occurred in West Bloomfield, with an explosion and two missing people at Temple Kol Yisrael. I was there, Micah. It was a terrorist attack act with a small glitch. I witnessed the whole thing."

The muscles in Micah's chest knotted. "Shit, Zack, are you okay? My God!"

"I'm fine," Zack assured him. "Luckily, there were only minor injuries. You may recall from the Hayley Shultz case that West Bloomfield has a small police force—they'll have difficulty getting organized. I need your help."

Micah grunted, "Why me? Won't the state or the feds get involved?"

"Probably, at some point, local police will reach out, but I want to grease the skids. And it can't come from me. Point blank, the lead detective told me to stay out of his way and not interfere with the investigation. Perhaps he doesn't like attorneys, especially somewhat famous attorneys who occasionally make cops look bad. Can you help me out, buddy? West Bloomfield isn't equipped to handle this. I need someone I trust to get the investigation rolling with the state or the feds. Two people, last seen in the building before the explosion, have gone missing."

"Who?" Micah wondered.

"Rich Cooper's son, Josh, the bar-mitzvah boy. Again, he's the reason I was there," Zack replied.

"Whoa! Nothing like a terrorist attack to ruin a kid's big day. Who's the other guy, the dad?"

"No, Rich's next-door neighbor, Chip Ellis. Neither has been accounted for. Police don't believe the blast was powerful enough to kill anyone. Get my drift?"

"They were kidnapped. Is that what you're saying?"

"Yes, I believe they were," Zack declared. "No one has claimed responsibility, but they will. It's a given, only a matter of time. Will you contact Clare Gibson? You remember Clare."

"How could I forget Clare? She the best."

"I'm glad you feel that way," Zack remarked. "Will you get in touch with her right away?"

Micah shrugged. "Sure, but why? The FBI will stick their nose into a kidnapping sooner than later."

"I agree," Zack replied. "But there have been local shake-ups at the Detroit Bureau, and I want to make sure Clare gets the case."

"Understood. And I also understand why you want to keep your name out of this thing."

Micah was quite aware of the local FBI's current state of disarray. Multiple terminations, resignations, and politically motivated reassignments placed several people in positions they weren't qualified to handle. Rumors surfaced from highly placed news sources and unnamed Bureau insiders that local directors and assistant directors were borderline incompetent.

The inmates were now running the asylum with little or no training for the top jobs. Clare Gibson was either passed up or voluntarily passed on a director's assignment, preferring to stay in the field. Zack was buoyed to hear she was still an agent and not a supervisor.

"An antisemitic terrorist event at the largest temple in the area should light a fire under the FBI's ass. They'll throw everything they have at this until they figure out who's responsible," Micah speculated.

"Perhaps," Zack agreed, "but I want the investigation managed by people I trust, you and Clare. I won't leave anything to chance, and some rookie supervisor will not cut his teeth at the expense of my friend."

Micah pulled up a Google Maps display of West Bloomfield Township, a short distance from Zack's Bloomfield Hills home and office. Micah was quite familiar with the community. There was a large Jewish population. Micah had attended services at Temple Kol Yisrael in the past. While Zack filled him in on details of the attack, Micah searched the Internet for the names of the township supervisor and the chief of police. He would eventually need their cooperation if he wanted to investigate in their town. He wondered why the perps chose Detroit rather than New York, Los Angeles, or another larger city. Detroit wasn't as large as it used to be. *Wouldn't NYC have attracted more attention?*

"I'll call Clare," Micah promised. "Get the ball rolling. Consider me on board."

"Thank you, Micah." Zack sighed appreciatively. "Usual fee structure?"

Micah pulled up a Free Press article about the temple attack. A large, color photograph of a young mother and her child, soot on their faces, tears streaming down inflamed cheeks, graced the paper's front page.

"*Bupkis*, Zack—you're paying me *bupkis*," he declared. "I want these *mamzers* brought to justice. My fee is your promise to get me front-row seats at the trial of these anti-Semites, especially at their sentencing."

"The Coopers will appreciate it, Micah, as do I," Zack replied. "I'll get you everything you need to get started. Please let me know when you reach Clare. The three of us will need to meet and coordinate."

"What will you be doing?" Micah wondered.

"I've got a few calls to make," Zack advised. "I'm pulling out all the stops on this one. Anything else we need to discuss?"

Micah sifted through a few more articles. The online reporting was virtually identical—no suspects in custody, two people missing, and no official bomb techs or squad in West Bloomfield. The locals had not developed any clues or leads, at least none they made public.

"Does the temple have security cameras? And, if so, where do they keep the footage?"

"It's a Jewish place of worship—the largest congregation of Jewish people in Metro Detroit. I noticed at least a pair on the outside of the building, one in front, one in back, and several more inside. I'm sure there are some hidden ones, too."

"And the footage? How do we get our hands on the footage for the day of the bombing?"

"I'm not sure . . ." Zack hesitated, looking for something. "I've got the name of the company here somewhere. Here it is, a company called 'Secure Systems.' Schmucks! Real secure!" he grumbled. "Wouldn't the local police have grabbed those already?"

"Who knows? I'll check with the cops and the company. It will allow me to introduce myself. Do you know the clergy, executive director, or board members of the temple? I need to speak to anyone involved in the day-to-day. I'll need a list of everyone with keys and, you know . . . access. Temple Kol Yisrael is a big fish in a small town. The terrorists seem to have known the lay of the land at the temple. How could that be? At least one of these guys must have been there before."

"Are you suggesting that a member or officer might be involved? That is almost impossible to believe, Micah." Zack almost choked on his own words.

Micah sighed. "I don't think we can rule out anyone or anything at this point in the investigation. Let's take things one step at a time."

"You're the high-paid private dick—I defer to your sleuthing greatness."

"You love calling me a dick, don't you? And 'free' is not high paid."

"A testament to past investigations and compensation paid, free or not, I defer."

"Until you can't resist and decide to stick your nose where it doesn't belong," Micah chided him.

"What can I say? Sometimes I want what I want. I'm willing to do whatever it takes to get it."

CHAPTER SEVEN

Clare Gibson sat back from her computer. Her eyes burned from staring at the screen. She rubbed them, then reached back and massaged the muscles in her neck. Eye doctors failed to understand that FBI agents couldn't take breaks from backlit computer screens. Tired or burning eyes were hazards of the occupation.

Clare persevered, doing the math inside her head, trying to guesstimate how many hours she'd been sitting in front of the computer. She still had more reports to type and files to collate. Clare often worked unpaid overtime for the Feds, investing at least a third of her life to the job.

Eleven months earlier, Clare had been a victim of a Bureau shake-up and was suddenly transferred from her home in Detroit to the Las Vegas field office. She didn't request the transfer. She hated Nevada and its one-hundred-plus-degree heat. She considered protesting, but Clare Gibson was a team player. Besides, she was promised the posting would be temporary, a short-term assignment.

Clare's job was to crack down on a money-laundering operation orchestrated by the owner of a string of casinos on the Vegas strip. "Real, old-school mobster kind of stuff," a supervisor told her on her first day in the office. "We haven't seen anything like this since maybe the mid-to-late 60s."

After multiple tax audits, select casino tax returns were flagged by the Internal Revenue Service and forwarded to the bureau. Some Ivy-league whiz kid at the IRS noticed Ponzi Scheme-type irregularities in the casinos' business returns.

When the auditors turned up nothing, at least nothing criminal, the whiz kid contacted the FBI, which launched a cursory investigation into the matter. Clare was recruited at that point, did some heavy lifting, and three months later discovered that the whiz kid's hunches were right on the money.

Dozens of late-night interviews, sting operations, and an in-depth forensic examination of the casino's tax returns led Clare to discover a name that popped up on casino payrolls under investigation. On paper, this person didn't exist. He had no driver's license—his Social Security Number was bogus. After another round of intense digging, Clare uncovered a massive illicit money-laundering operation orchestrated by the Sinaloa Cartel. The scandal made the local and national news, piquing the interest of the Central Intelligence Agency, which promptly took over the investigation.

Clare feared she would be tossed aside, but the bigwigs were so impressed with her work on the case that they offered her various options to achieve her career goals. The FBI was in turmoil at that moment. Field office positions were being filled, vacated, and filled again. Supervisors came and went, suddenly transferred. Clare wanted out of Nevada. The notion that the summer heat was tolerable because "it was only a dry heat" was absurd.

Clare longed for a return to Michigan, with four seasons and a director's position open in the Detroit office. Her request had to go through the proper channels, but her work on the money-laundering case, she was told, would help grease the skids. It was a waiting game, and her public desire to leave Nevada did not sit well with the local brass. She now occupied a desk and sat in front of a computer, performing what she viewed as remedial tasks in anticipation of a transfer. Clare Gibson was an agent in limbo. A file suddenly slapped before her, startling her from her thoughts. She again rubbed her eyes and gazed up at her colleague, Jules Paulson, a lanky FBI agent leaning against her desk.

Clare grimaced. "What the hell, Paulson? You scared the shit out of me!"

"Sorry to interrupt your afternoon daydream, Gibson, but Kavanaugh needs a favor."

Clare rolled her eyes. If there was one reason to leave the Nevada office, it was Bryce Kavanaugh. She couldn't go so far as to call the man an idiot, but it took great restraint from her and every other field agent not to call him inept. Who died and made him a special agent in charge?

Clare sighed. "My old buddy Bryce," she muttered with a simpering tone. "How is it he's not on cold case duty in Upper Mongolia or someplace similar?"

"Did you hear?" Paulson teased.

"Hear what?" Clare wondered.

"The thing in Michigan," he floated. "A terrorist attack on a place of worship."

"What are you talking about?" Clare was intrigued.

Paulson glanced over his shoulder, scanned the area for busybodies, and lowered his voice to just above a whisper.

"Someone set off a bomb at a Jewish temple in the Detroit area. The Detroit field office is short-staffed—they have no SAC. They're scrambling to work with the local cops to figure things out. Kavanaugh just ended a conference call with the SACs, asking for files on all violent extremist groups."

Clare leaned back in her chair. "That's terrible," she uttered. *Aren't I the obvious choice? I've been down this road in Detroit.* Her thoughts pivoted to the previous case, a religious attack on a Muslim mosque. A young woman was accused of murdering the White Nationalist who detonated the bomb. Clare worked the case with a local private eye, Micah Love, and a prominent attorney, Zachary Blake. *Doesn't Zack live in West Bloomfield or nearby? Is this his temple?*

Paulson turned to a file sitting on the opposite desk. He repeatedly nodded at the file, attempting to re-direct her attention.

"What's your problem, Paulson? Something wrong with your neck?"

"No, my neck is fine. Check this out." He picked up the file and handed it to Clare.

"Kavanaugh's supervising a check fraud case—this guy in Iowa is cashing Covid relief checks belonging to other people and absconding with the dough. He's ripped off CARES Act money to the tune of five hundred big ones. We're having a tough time tracking the guy and the funds."

Clare peeled open the file. She began to peruse the contents, overstuffed into a thick manila folder. She quickly sifted through the contents.

"Brian Alpert," she read the man's name from the file jacket. "File says he works for a tractor dealership."

Paulson held up a finger. "Only on paper," he advised. "Kavanaugh made a few calls and had someone from the Iowa field office investigate. No one at the company ever heard of a Brian Alpert."

"When Kavanaugh looked up Alpert on the usual databases," Clare inquired, "what did he find?"

"The guy's dead," Paulson advised. "He's been dead for six years. Alpert was an elementary school teacher, killed in a car crash."

Clare nodded. "Someone stole his identity," she surmised.

"That's where Kavanaugh left things," Paulson advised. "Once Alpert turned out to be dead, our fearless leader punted the football. In other words, the case was too complicated."

Clare scanned the file again, quickly learning about Brian Alpert. His bio now engrained in her memory, Clare began to reassemble the facts like puzzle pieces, shuffling them here and there. After a short while, an important piece fit into place. Clare smiled—her 'ah-hah' moment.

"It's the tractor company!" She exclaimed.

Paulson was impressed but curious at the same time. "How do you figure?"

Clare pressed her finger on a page in the file.

"The owner of the tractor company is Alpert's former brother-in-law. It says so right here." She pulled the document from the file and shoved it in Paulson's face.

"The case isn't difficult at all. Kavanaugh did not need to punt. Tell that moron to pull up the guy's record. Something will smack him right in the kisser—I guarantee it."

"The brother-in-law stole his identity?"

"Who knows? Probably, it's a lead, at the very least. I'll bet the tractor man stole his dead brother-in-law's identity or did something else of a criminal nature. I'm *positive* it's something like that."

Paulson retrieved the file, smirked, and nodded to Clare. "You're the best, Gibson. I'll let the boss know," he assured her.

"Keep me in the loop," Clare requested. "Tell Kavanaugh that if I'm right about this and he gets credit for a solve, he owes me a beer and a transfer."

"I'll do that, Gibson. Thanks for your help," Paulson replied, ducking out of the cubicle.

A few minutes later, Gibson's desk phone rang.

"FBI, Clare Gibson speaking," she answered.

"Remember me?" a familiar voice chirped.

Clare sat back in her chair, grinned, and shook her head. "Well, I'll be damned. I was just thinking about you, Micah. How the hell are you?"

Micah chuckled. "Doing well, Clare, doing well."

Clare smiled at her memories of the man at the other end of the line. She was all business; he was all nonsense. Yet, he found time to be an extremely talented private investigator. They worked a northern Michigan case together, a cop wrongly accused of murdering a White Supremacist. Two completely different approaches to crime investigation with excellent results. She was glad fate threw them together; they would otherwise never have crossed paths. Micah's casual approach to investigation, coupled with his obnoxious objectification of women, would have been abhorrent to someone like her, an agent who took her job seriously. But fate threw them together, and Clare learned a valuable lesson. There was more than one way to close a case, more than one way to look at the facts and the evidence. Micah was not only a master private investigator, the best she'd ever encountered, but he was also a lot of fun to hang with.

"What's new with you?" she chirped.

"Surviving," Micah replied. "You?"

"Same," Clare said, momentarily reflecting on her time at the Detroit field office and the case they solved together. She blinked away her thoughts and sat up in her chair.

"I heard what happened in West Bloomfield. This isn't a social call, is it?"

"I'm afraid not. Have you followed the case on the news? It's déjà vu all over again, but it's *my* people this time."

Clare shook her head as if Micah could see her. "I've been stuck in the office for almost thirty hours straight. I hardly have time to breathe, let alone follow the status of cases I'm not handling."

"This attack hits way too close to home, Clare. The temple is in Zack's backyard."

Clare sighed. "I heard. Is he okay?"

"He's fine. He's mad as hell, but he's fine. He asked me to reach out to you."

Clare opened her web browser. She typed "temple bombing West Bloomfield" into the search engine. In a few seconds, multiple local and national headlines filled her screen. There was a major terrorist event, a hate crime, in her old stomping grounds. A temple bombing, with multiple injuries and two people missing, including a thirteen-year-old boy. Her eyes began to burn for reasons other than eye strain.

"I realize this happened near his home and office, but why is he taking this so personally? And what does he want from me?" Clare wondered.

"The bar mitzvah boy was his friend's kid. He was invited to the celebration. He attended services that day. He was *there* when the bomb exploded, Clare! Plus, the kid and the family's next-door neighbor are still missing," Micah seethed.

"Why are you involved?" She knew the answer.

"Zack called me," Micah sighed. "Like I said, he was *inside* the temple when the bomb detonated. I've never seen him so angry or determined. He doesn't trust the locals; they're still scrambling to assemble things."

"I understand why he's frustrated, Micah, but the wise thing to do is let the police do their jobs. There isn't much I can do from Las Vegas."

"I get that, Clare. But you know Zack. He's quite worked up over the situation. And when the King gets worked up—"

"I get the picture. I pity the locals. Hang on a second; I'm reading some of the stories."

Clare continued to scan news reports about the bombing. The headlines became more dire as she sifted through them:

'JEWISH TEMPLE EXPLOSION RATTLES WEST BLOOMFIELD'

'MICHIGAN TEMPLE THE TARGET OF EXTREMIST ATTACK'

'POLICE INVESTIGATE POSSIBLE TERRORIST ATTACK'

'ANTI-SEMITIC ATTACK IN MICHIGAN SUBURB'

"They don't report fatalities," she noted as she continued to read. "No one was killed?"

"We were lucky this time," Micah advised, "No one was seriously hurt. A few people spent the night at Henry Ford, West Bloomfield, the local ER. Everyone appears to be fine. Unless you count Zack's buddy's son and neighbor. The kid is Josh Cooper; the neighbor is Chip Ellis. They're both missing. The cops believe they may be under the rubble. Zack is convinced the explosion was a diversion, a literal smokescreen to disguise a kidnapping."

Clare's mouth dropped open. "They've been abducted? Is there any evidence?"

"Depends on how you look at it. They haven't found their bodies, and no one wants to presume they're dead. As I said, Zack strongly believes this is a well-conceived kidnapping," Micah sighed. "Considering the time that's passed and the lack of serious injuries to other attendees, I agree with Zack. And, as you know, he's got a sixth sense, good radar for shit like this."

"What is the police saying?"

"It's a small-town force in a big-city atmosphere. You know how Detroit and its suburbs work. There's not too much coordination or cooperation unless we're talking sports. They're scrambling. It's only been a few days. The township supervisor is going live in a few minutes, giving a press conference. Hang on, I'll pull it up."

"You've got to love the Internet. I can do it here, too." Clare pecked on her keyboard and pulled up a live CNN feed of the West Bloomfield Township Supervisor standing beside a podium with several cameras focused on his sullen face. He was flanked on one side by the Oakland County Sheriff and on the other by Chiefs of Police in West Bloomfield and Beverly Hills. The Oakland County Prosecutor was also on hand but off camera. The room was silent but for a couple of coughs and the clatter of camera equipment. The township supervisor stepped up to the podium. Clare and Micah settled back to watch.

"Good afternoon," the supervisor began, with reading glasses perched on his nose and his brow furrowed from the strain.

"Last Saturday morning, members of West Bloomfield's Jewish community fell victim to a vicious terrorist attack at one of our many houses of worship.

"There are no fatalities to report, some minor injuries, cuts, bruises, and the like, but nothing serious. Victims were treated and released by the professional staff at nearby Henry Ford Hospital."

The supervisor glanced at the cameras, smoothed his tie, and braced himself against the podium.

"The West Bloomfield Police Department is working tirelessly to identify the person or group responsible for this heinous attack. We cannot provide details; this is an active and ongoing investigation."

The supervisor gestured to a man dressed in police blues, standing to his left. "I have been assured by Chief Strozier, here, that every available member of the department is probing every detail in the case with the utmost scrutiny—"

Micah spoke into the receiver. "Run-of-the-mill bullshit rhetoric," he lamented. "This guy must be up for re-election. They don't know anything."

"But they'll pull out all the stops to catch these guys," Clare opined. "That's for sure."

"As well they should," Micah growled.

"What are your plans now that Zack asked for your help, Micah?"

"I'm not sure yet, Clare. I told him I'd work the case for free. He asked me to contact you. He probably thinks you're still in Detroit. I believe he wants the Detroit Field Office to assign you the case. The local police department is ill-equipped to handle an investigation of this magnitude."

"I've been in Nevada almost a year now. I've been trying to transfer back. The Detroit office is not in good shape, and there's no SAC. I've requested the assignment, but the federal bureaucracy is molasses, not motor oil."

"Zack is well-connected. You know that. A call to the governor here or the president there . . . if anyone can grease the skids for your transfer, it's our pal, the king, Zachary Blake."

"Yada, yada, the self-proclaimed King of Justice. What an ego!"

"It's more than ego; it's well-deserved. Would you handle the case if Zack makes a well-placed call and arranges for you to come to Detroit?"

"Absolutely. Do you believe that Blake has that kind of clout?"

"Let's put the theory to the test. Up for a three-way?"

"You're disgusting as always," Clare scoffed.

"Whose mind is in the gutter? Not *that* kind of three-way!"

"Oh, you meant a conference call. Go for it! In my defense, I am speaking with Micah Love, right? The porn king of Detroit?"

"You know me well. Should I make the call?"

"I thought he didn't want his hands on this thing."

"*I'm* adding him to the call. You aren't calling him. His number won't show up on your call list."

"Knock yourself out." Clare was happy to speak with Zack. She waited patiently while Micah pressed the numbers on his cell phone.

"Micah?" Zack answered

"Zack? Say hi to Clare Gibson."

"Dammit, Micah, I asked you to keep this on the down low . . . Hi Clare, how the hell are you?"

"You sure know how to make a woman feel welcome, Zack," Clare chuckled.

"It's not you—"

"I know. Micah briefed me on your situation. He says that the call will register from him to me and from him to you. You're safe, on the 'down low,' as you called it."

"He's the master. I'm sorry I jumped down your throat, bud."

"That's okay, Zack," Micah replied. "I know you're going through some bad stuff right now. We've got a problem that requires your skill and power."

"I'm sure about the power thing, but I'm happy to be of service. What can I do for you?" Zack asked.

"As you may or may not know, Clare was recently transferred to Nevada. She is not currently stationed at the Michigan field office."

"Shit! I want her here. I don't trust these guys! What do you need to make this happen?"

"There is a SAC opening in Detroit. Clare put in for it, but the FBI is in disarray, and politics are involved. Might you contact the governor or the president and grease the skids?"

"Is *that* all? If I can get it done, how soon can you get to Detroit, Clare?"

"Tomorrow? I just solved my biggest case. I'll probably have to return to testify, but nothing else will keep me in Vegas if they consent to the transfer. Besides, I hate it here! It's too hot! A dry heat, my ass! I much prefer Michigan's four seasons. Get me back there, please?"

"If I'm reading the tea leaves correctly, Zack, West Bloomfield will soon implement the usual playbook. The cops will roust the usual suspects and try to pin this on the first person or group who makes sense. As we all know from personal experience, there is no shortage of racists with extremist ties—we've put a few of them in prison. West Bloomfield will haul a few in for questioning, investigate, parade the suspects in front of the cameras, and hope that the public begins to relax, especially the Jewish public. West Bloomfield lacks the resources and is not equipped for this level of terrorism. Having said that, though, I doubt they'll seek assistance."

"You think they'll give the public a scapegoat, or scapegoats, to be more accurate?" Clare floated.

"Exactly," Micah concurred.

"I have to disagree, Micah. These guys are pros. They must get this right; a lot is riding on the investigation, and the election is not far away. I doubt the supervisor will risk pinning the tail on the wrong donkey. If something bad happens, he loses one or both missing people, and the city's Jewish community will crucify the guy. I don't see him taking a risk that might come back to bite him in the ass."

"I agree. I'm not suggesting he'd arrest the wrong guy and quit looking for the right one. I'm suggesting he needs a face for primetime news to buy time to track down the real bad guys," Micah suggested.

"That would be a terrible mistake," Clare countered. "If he does that and later arrests the real terrorists, there is reasonable doubt all over the place. Were you right then, or are you right now? He'll look like an idiot and give the prosecutor a bum case to try."

"She right. If I'm representing the real perps, I'm arguing that the first set of patsies committed the crime. Who does the jury believe? Were the cops right the first time or the second?" Zack opined.

"That's why we need you to spearhead this investigation, Clare. We need to arrest and convict the real perps the first time, not some prop-ups to appease the public," Zack concluded.

"Get me to Michigan and get me into the Detroit Field Office Director's chair. I'll do you guys proud," Clare promised.

"I know you will, Clare. Micah and I trust and respect you without hesitation. This is a scary situation—it needs to be handled by an experienced pro," Zack reasoned. "There's more to this case than meets the eye. Things don't add up for me."

"It's a bombing," Clare replied. "Of course, it doesn't feel right."

"That's not what I mean. These guys are smarter than the average white nationalist group. I believe the explosion was exactly what they intended.

"They intended no fatalities. They sought people's attention. They rallied the troops, dominated a news cycle, raised awareness, and probably, a lot of cash. As far as I can see, the strategy worked. The Detroit area is talking about nothing else," Zack observed.

"What's their objective, Zack? Why set off a bomb if you don't intend to hurt or kill someone? There are other ways to get attention," Clare winced.

"I am quite certain that this will turn out to be an abduction. We can expect a ransom demand. The reason may be as simple as a fundraising event for their racist and anti-Semitic agenda. Perhaps they're content with scaring the hell out of the Jewish community but I believe it's a money grab," Zack opined.

"Or all of the above," Micah added.

"I agree that both make sense, gentlemen," Clare agreed. She leaned back in her chair and switched the phone to her other ear.

"I'll see if I can get a few federal CSIs to process the scene. I need to figure out how to get there as quickly as possible. Can you finagle a plane, Zack?"

"Pack your things. I'll commission a private jet. I'll need an hour or two. Text me the address of the nearest private airstrip to where you are right now."

"You're that confident you can get this done?" Clare marveled.

"These guys owe me a ton of political favors. I'm calling one in. No big deal," Zack advised, unimpressed with the level of his political power.

Clare glanced at her watch and did the math quickly in her head. "About five hours by jet," she calculated. "I should be there this afternoon if all goes according to plan."

"What about your Nevada boss? Will he give you the green light?"

Clare turned to the window of the Nevada SAC's office. Blaire Hawthorne, her immediate supervisor, the SAC, had a stack of papers clutched in his hand.

"I'll call you back," Clare promised. "Give me two minutes."

Gibson knocked on Hawthorne's office door. Eyes glued to his paperwork, Hawthorne called out, "Come in." He was a scrawny beanpole of a man. He stood about six feet tall and weighed less than one hundred forty pounds.

"Sir," Clare entered, stood at attention, and held her head high. She respected Hawthorne's rank but did not like the man. He was promoted over her, primarily because Clare was a woman. Women weren't receiving ASAC assignments in those days.

Hawthorne was six years younger than Clare. He once worked in the Hoover building in Washington, D.C., but ended up in the Nevada field office. He was a politician's son, which might explain his rapid ascent into the hierarchy of the FBI. Clare was itching to get to the bottom of his meteoric rise. Perhaps he was just another rich kid whose political connections got him shoehorned into an FBI power position. He was competent, clever even, but was no supervisor. His eagerness to accept credit for Clare's work on the casino case was a graphic illustration. He lacked talent, undercut his agents, and pissed off everyone who worked under him. His was not the glowing resume of a leader.

"What's up, Gibson?" Hawthorne mumbled from his office chair, still fixated on the paperwork he was reviewing. "What can I do for you?"

Clare hesitated and took a small step forward. "Sir, are you aware of the bombing that just took place just outside Detroit?"

Hawthorne put down the papers, studied Gibson for a second or two, and nodded. "I just got off the phone with an agent in the Detroit Field office."

"What did he say?" Clare inquired.

Hawthorne pushed the files away on his desk and eyeballed Clare. "He wanted detailed information about neo-Nazi and White extremist groups."

"Forgive me, sir, but why from you?" Clare observed. "The information is in the central database, accessible to agents in all fifty states. He doesn't need you to provide him with the information. He can access the same files you access, depending on his clearance level."

Hawthorne's jaw muscles tensed. He was angry about something.

"He's asking for other information, Agent Gibson," Hawthorne snarled.

Clare was now curious. There were multiple ongoing investigations, some of them shrouded in secrecy. "What kind of information? Might it compromise—"

"What are you driving at, Agent Gibson?" The SAC glared at Gibson.

"I'd like to go to Detroit, sir. I want to handle the case."

Hawthorne cleared his throat. He stared at Clare. "Why would I let a Nevada agent under my command go to Detroit to handle a local suburban investigation? Besides, you're needed here."

Clare was not easily intimidated. She'd encountered numerous bullies during her tenure with the FBI. "You have only six months left in your posting, sir," she replied. "We both know the reason."

Hawthorne's face slackened. Clare continued. "The casino investigation put you back in D. C.'s good graces. You didn't even have to break a sweat. My work, my investigation, I put you in good standing. I'm the reason that this field office now enjoys a certain reputation—you didn't lift a finger. I never once complained, nor did I throw shade your way. Your elevated status was achieved on the blood, sweat, and tears of every agent who worked that case, especially me. You owe me, Hawthorne," she demanded. Hawthorne again cleared his throat. He could not hold eye contact, deliberately averting his eyes.

"I'm going to Michigan," Clare insisted. "You're going to arrange for me to ride to Detroit in the G5 the field office has on standby, so I forego the hassle and time of flying commercial. On top of that, I will apply for the open SAC position in Detroit, and you will recommend me for the job. In the meantime, you'll run interference and make all necessary excuses so I don't have to explain myself. And if things don't work out in Detroit, you will welcome me back to Nevada with open arms and recommend me as your replacement here when you decide to leave. Is that understood, sir?"

A moment passed. Hawthorne continued to stare at a wall. The only sound heard was the static of a pair of failing overhead fluorescent lights. Hawthorne blinked, turned to his desk phone, and scooped up the receiver. A receptionist for the government's private airstrip answered the phone. Hawthorne identified himself and authorized her to have a G5 ready for travel to Detroit in one hour.

Five minutes later, as she drove to the airstrip, Clare called Micah.

"Hello?"

"On my way."

"Great!"

"Please tell Zack I won't be needing his plane. I commandeered a government jet."

"I'll bet that's a good story."

"I'll tell you when I see you in about five hours from now."

"Safe travels."

"Thanks."

CHAPTER EIGHT

Seventy-two hours after the bombing, Zack Blake was functioning on very little sleep. He was either on the phone, ping-ponging between Rich and Gail's house, or coordinating with Micah and Clare.

Gail had become so emotionally exhausted she fell asleep for several hours. Rich constantly checked on her, knowing she'd be angry at him for letting her sleep so long. He reasoned that sleep deprivation relief triumphed over marital harmony. She'd eventually come to realize he made the right decision.

Tricia Ellis was equally exhausted but unable to sleep. She appeared relaxed and calm, but Rich Cooper was convinced that the stress of worrying about young Josh and her husband weighed heavily on her shoulders.

"I'm worried," Rich whispered to Zack. "She acts like this is a walk in the park."

Zack nodded, glancing at Tricia in the dining room, setting the table for dinner. "She's in shock," he decided. "Different people process trauma in different ways. Jennifer and I handled the boys' trauma with the church quite differently. Recently, I handled a wrongful death case where the client, a widow, insisted that her husband was still alive. I had to get Doc Rothenberg involved. I've represented thousands of clients over the years. While there are common denominators, no one handles trauma the same."

Rich massaged the muscles in the back of his neck—the tension was causing a headache. "I'm running on fumes, Zack," he admitted. "Between my back and forth with the police, agonizing over the fate of my son, where he might be, and whether he's okay, I'm going to have a serious meltdown. I may be on the verge of collapse."

It was easy for Zack to put himself in Rich's shoes. He was estranged from his natural children but had a special bond with his adopted sons. They shared the trauma caused by the abusive priest. When Kenny, Jennifer's eldest, was shot in the leg during a mass school shooting, the family pulled together to help heal the community. They experienced their fair share of trauma. He assured Rich everything would work out but wasn't sure he believed his words. *Josh will turn up safe and sound, won't he?*

"The not knowing is the worst. This eerie silence. If they want money, why don't they make contact? Make a ransom demand? Why can't the cops come up with a lead? Anything will do . . . some sign . . . any sign that my son is alive."

"If they wanted to kill him, why not do it at the temple? They took him for a reason, Rich. I don't know why. Probably ransom, but that's no more than an educated guess. That he's missing gives me hope he's alive. Hang in there, buddy."

"I'm trying, Zack, but the cops don't seem very swift."

"Help is on the way, my friend. I'm putting a team together."

"Who?"

"Some old friends. People I trust with my life. They'll get to the bottom of this."

Early the next day, Zack cruised down Maple Road toward the temple. On the way, he called Jennifer, who was checking on the status of victims at Henry Ford.

"They're discharging everyone this morning, Zack," Jennifer cheered. "A couple of concussions, a cracked rib or two, the worst injury was a fractured kneecap. She'll be assigned a home health care nurse, but we seem to have dodged a bullet. This could have been a lot worse."

Zack hadn't shared his suspicion that the explosion was intended to cause chaos, not serious injury. He still believed the bombing was a smokescreen to cover up an abduction. If everyone was going home, he now had a new worry to consider.

"I'm worried about the media," Zack confessed. "If the names and addresses of victims are leaked to the press, we'll have a horde of reporters and news vans camped on people's lawns. I've seen this time and again with the press. God bless the First Amendment, but these vultures have little compassion for victims if they get in the way of a good story. They don't know when to stop. The last thing these people need is a reporter sticking a microphone in their face when they arrive home."

"So far, Henry Ford has been keeping a tight lid on things," Jennifer advised. "Ambulance companies and EMS have volunteered to pick up the released victims and take them home. No names have been released. Reporters are lurking, but they're not getting any information. The doctors and nurses are under strict orders from the hospital administrator and the West Bloomfield police to maintain HIPPA guidelines. Things will be fine over here. What are you going to be doing this morning?"

"Meeting Clare Gibson and Micah at the temple. We need to get Clare up to snuff."

"I'm good here, Zack. Meet with Agent Gibson. Don't worry about the other victims or me—between the hospital staff, the ambulances and EMS, and the West Bloomfield police, we've got it covered."

Zack was relieved. "How are the boys?"

"They're okay," Jennifer sighed. "A bit shook up from the other day, but they're fine. God knows they're strong boys. I'll stop by and check on them before I head back to Rich and Gail's. They asked me if *you're* okay—I told them you were fine, but I guess I'm asking too."

Zack pondered the question. He was exhausted and desperately needed a break, but he could not stop now. He needed answers. He needed to meet with Clare and get the federal ball rolling. Most importantly, he needed any lead about Josh, his condition, or whereabouts. If he could identify those responsible for the attack, everything else would likely fall into place.

Members of his faith were maliciously attacked. Before and after the Israel-Hamas conflict, Anti-Semitic activities were on the rise—could this be a hate crime? If so, he would do everything in his power to bring the bigots to their knees and hold them accountable for their crimes. One day, they would answer to him. But today was not that day. Today, they had *bupkes*.

"I'll be fine," Zack finally assured his wife. "I'm mad as hell, worried about what's coming, concerned about the unknown, but buoyed that Clare is joining us. She's a top-notch agent, and this is right in her wheelhouse."

"I love you, Zachary Blake," Jennifer gushed. "The things you do for people . . . I'm so fortunate that you're my husband."

"I'm the lucky one, my sweet. I'd be lost without you. I love you, too." They said their goodbyes, and Zack ended the call. He arrived at the temple, parked, and texted Micah for an update.

CHAPTER NINE

Micah stepped out of the Lincoln and took in the grim scene. His heart lodged in his throat. Yellow tape cordoned off the entirety of the temple. Uniformed patrol officers walked the scene, sifted through damaged parts, and searched for clues. Micah sensed frustration and confusion—most of these officers were local kids. Their most significant cases were reckless driving or DUI investigations, burglaries, or family disputes.

Micah appraised the building. Once beautiful stained-glass windows were charred. Chunks of brick were dislodged, bits of debris scattered along the sidewalk. Micah's throat constricted. He waited behind the yellow tape, sighed, and closed his eyes. He recounted what had been learned, frequently checking the time on his iPhone. After twenty minutes, he received a text from Zack Blake, who had just arrived at the temple.

As Micah scanned the parking lot looking for Zack's car, a dark Ford Crown Vic pulled into the temple entrance and drove up to the yellow tape. A patrolman with a lousy attitude trotted over to the car to redirect whoever was behind the wheel. When the patrolmen bent over the driver's side window to chastise the driver, he stepped back, eyes wide, hands raised in the air, apologetically. He lifted the tape and waved the vehicle inside.

Micah leaned forward, still behind the tape, and squinted his eyes, trying to see who was inside the Crown Vic. The passenger door opened, and Agent Clare Gibson slipped out of the vehicle, a grim look on her face. Her expression changed when she eyeballed Micah standing at the tape.

"Micah!" Clare exclaimed. "How nice to see you! Wish it were under different circumstances."

"Claaaaarrrrre!" Micah shouted, a standard greeting during their old case encounters. "It's great to see you, too."

Clare turned to the still-embarrassed officer and nodded toward Micah. "He's good. Let him in."

The officer lifted the crime scene tape. Micah ducked under it and jogged toward Clare, who smiled and stuck out her hand.

"Handshake, schmandshake," Micah guffawed. "Give me a hug!" He hugged her, planting a wet kiss on her cheek. Clare first stood there awkwardly, like a rag doll, finally smiling and returning the embrace.

"You sure know how to make a woman feel welcome, Micah. How the hell are you?"

"Much better, now that you're here. It's hard to investigate when denied access to the crime scene."

Clare again turned to the officer. "This guy is good," she repeated. "Full access. Get him credentials, please."

"Thanks, Clare," Micah gushed. They stood side-by-side, assessing the damage, their silence interrupted only by the steady hum of traffic or an occasional horn sounding on Maple Road. Traffic was slow, as gawkers had to take in the scene as they drove past the temple. A West Bloomfield Police vehicle was stationed at the entrance, and an officer stood on the shoulder of Maple, waving at, ordering drivers forward to continue their journey.

To Micah Love, the temple felt like a family member or a good friend, the victim of an anti-Semitic attack, scarred, lacerated, but still standing. Micah often joked about the holidays that celebrated the heritage and history of his people:

"They tried to kill us; we beat them; let's eat!"

The temple was a shining example of this theme, damaged but still welcoming Jewish worshipers and others in fellowship, a beacon of peace and love for Judaism.

"Micah?" Clare interrupted his thoughts. "Let's take a look, shall we?"

"Zack is around here somewhere," Micah looked around, doing a three-sixty.

"Claaaaarrrrre!" Zack shouted from the parking lot. He trotted up to the crime scene tape.

"He's good, too," Clare laughed, addressing the bewildered officer.

"How the hell are you?" Zack crawled under the tape to embrace her, like Micah had done moments before.

The three entered the building. Clare flashed her credentials at the uniformed officers who stood guard. They moved aside and allowed the group to enter. Micah and Zack gasped at the sight. The damage inside was far worse than the damage outside. Like the two men at this moment, the building was shaken to its core, pockmarked, but still standing, beautiful and proud.

Zack was speechless, a rare occurrence for the vocal advocate. Micah, the trained investigator, reminded himself to be analytical, to take in the scene like a crime tech expert, and to be devoid of emotion. They toured the entire building, first, the lobby and bathrooms, which suffered the brunt of the damage. They moved to the mammoth sanctuary and social hall where congregants pray and celebrate. Zack proudly showed Clare the *bimah* and the ark, where the precious *Torah* scrolls were housed. An eternal light burned in a candelabra before the ark.

Zack closed his eyes, recalling the sanctuary on that infamous *Shabbat*, filled with congregants, Josh on the *bimah*, chanting his

Haftorah, finishing the blessings, a broad smile on his face. He walks away. Shortly afterward, the bomb explodes, destroys Josh's *simcha*, and terrorizes his guests and the congregation's regulars. Josh disappears in a cloud of dust.

Focus, Zack reminded himself. *Keep your head on straight*. He gestured to Micah.

"There," he pointed. "The damage is more severe. You can see the scorch marks from where the blast went off."

Clare nodded. "Good catch, Zack. Do you see that crater? That's the epicenter of the blast, where they planted the explosives."

Micah led the way to the back of the temple. The three gazed at a large hole in the lot behind the temple.

"I notice there are security cameras. Have either of you seen the footage?" Clare wondered.

"West Bloomfield has been tight-lipped. Understandably, we are not in the loop. Hopefully, that changes with you around," Micah smiled. "I know there is footage, but we have not seen it. The temple installed cameras and a whole new security system after a spike in anti-Semitic attacks in 2018 and 2019. Temple security keeps tabs on suspicious behavior and people."

"That's good to know. I'll want to talk to their security people."

"There's another snag, as well," Micah advised.

"Oh? What's that?" Clare inquired.

Micah pointed at two spots near the crater. "The security company, Secure Systems, established surveillance outside the temple. The primary units and the hard drive were positioned here and here." Micah pointed to the two spots.

"Unfortunately, the main drive was severely damaged in the blast. The restoration of data does not look promising. With your permission, I'd like to get Reed Spencer involved." Reed was Micah's tech guy. A former criminal, Reed was now Micah's go-to person for all things cyber.

"That is unfortunate," Clare agreed. "I'll alert our tech people and greenlight Reed's clearance. He's an asset."

"These guys knew what they were doing. It's no coincidence that the drives were targeted," Micah suggested.

"What about backups?"

"That's the only good news. The backups are stored at Secure Systems' home office. I've spoken to them to ensure the preservation of the footage. West Bloomfield, however, has stonewalled my access. The Deputy Chief says I'm "sticking my nose up the ass of their investigation." He even kicked me off the scene. I'm hoping there are shots of a vehicle or person who looks out of place or appears up to no good. If we get fortunate, perhaps there's footage of someone back here, messing with the equipment, concealing a bomb," Micah advised.

Clare grimaced. "You will have full FBI clearance from now on. I'll get personnel from the Detroit field office to grease the skids to get that footage. Do you have the address for Secure Systems' home office?"

"Yes. It's in my phone, somewhere." Micah turned and began to scroll through the names and addresses contained in his phone. "Here it is." He turned and handed the phone to Clare. She pulled out her phone and snapped a photo of Micah's screen.

"Ain't twenty-first-century technology grand?" Micah snickered.

"Livonia, huh? Not too far. I'll contact the field office," Clare promised.

Micah shook his head. "Remember, the temple must permit Secure Systems to release the drive's contents. Board members, clergy, and professional staff have been in the hospital."

"I just got off the phone with my wife, Jennifer," Zack advised. "She says that everyone is being released this morning."

"Then a release shouldn't be a problem. Besides, we're the FBI— we can be very persuasive," Clare mused. She shifted her attention back to the crater. The surface looked like a small asteroid had struck Earth.

"No sign of vehicle damages or a gas or oil leak. If the bomb was delivered in some vehicle, the blast was too small to obliterate or shatter it. Someone must have dropped off a crate or box."

Micah needed more convincing. "Someone would have seen it. Whoever was monitoring the security cameras should have been able to spot something out-of-place at or near the time of the attack."

"The device itself wouldn't have been too large," Clare speculated. "Perhaps it was a single, barrel-like object containing the explosives. And don't forget, the blast might have been remotely detonated—whoever planted it could have set it off from a mile or two away."

Micah looked around the neighborhood. Was it possible that the person who detonated the bomb lived close by? Perhaps they rented a nearby apartment, found a loophole in the system, or camped out nearby. How could the bomb have been delivered without anyone noticing? *Was this an inside job?*

"Micah," Clare hesitated. "I have a rather difficult question to ask you."

"Go ahead," Micah prompted her. "I can't be shamed or embarrassed. I won't take it personally, either . . . well . . . depending on what you're asking."

Clare drew a breath. "You don't think someone with prior access might have been responsible?"

Congregants? Day-to-day administrative or professional staff? Clergy? Micah's head was spinning.

"A regular? A Jewish person? Someone who attends frequently? It's not impossible, I guess, but it's highly improbable. Maybe a clerical worker, delivery guy, or someone on the maintenance staff?"

Clare shrugged. "We have to examine all possibilities."

Micah's skin crawled. "Hopefully, that will not be the case."

Shuffled footsteps caught everyone's attention. Micah, Zack, and Clare turned and observed a young patrolman, barely out of his teens, coming their way.

"Excuse me," he inquired. "Are you the FBI agents?"

"She is," Micah chuckled, pointing at Clare. "I'm just a lowly private eye, and this guy's an attorney." Micah pointed to Zack.

Clare rolled her eyes and stuck out her hand. "Special Agent Clare Gibson, Detroit field office," she introduced herself. "And you are?"

The patrolman took Clare's hand. "Mills," he replied. "Mills Miller."

Micah wrinkled his brow. "Mills Miller?" he chuckled. "Do you curse your folks for that one?"

The young officer laughed. "It doesn't bother me. I rather like it. Rolls off the tongue. My chief advised me you were coming, Agent Gibson. He said you might be bringing a bomb specialist. He wanted you to know that we don't have one, and yours would be greatly appreciated."

Micah interrupted. "West Bloomfield is a small town. Are your guns even loaded? Is yours a volunteer force?" he kibbitzed.

Miller paused. *Is he serious?* Clare shot Micah a glance, hand motioning him to cut the crap. He'd reached his joke quota for the day.

"Let your chief know that we have a team of experts en route, courtesy of the Detroit Police Department's bomb tech unit. They should be here any minute," Clare assured him.

Ten minutes later, only one expert arrived, a diminutive woman with strawberry blond hair and glasses perched at the end of a button-like nose. She looked more like a librarian than a bomb technician. "Dana

Shaw," she introduced herself, shaking Clare's hand, "Detroit Police Bomb Tech Unit. You rang?"

"I did. Good to meet you. Let me show you around."

"I like that, all business, no small talk. Lead the way," Shaw extended her arm for Clare to take the lead. Clare led Shaw through the building, taking a second look and renewing her search for clues. Shaw studied every nook and cranny.

As Shaw carefully padded her way through the crime scene, she never looked at Micah, Zack, or Clare. She might as well have been alone, strolling the route, taking photographs, jotting notes, and collecting samples with gloved hands. She kneeled at the crater, measuring it, testing the scorched marks, holding her hands up like a film director envisioning a shot, and, finally, coming up with a baseline theory.

"The bomb was placed here," she pointed to a spot near the men's room. "The crater is where it detonated. I've found traces of Tovex Blastrite Gel, ammonium nitrate, and nitromethane. There were no blasting caps or a fuse, which tells us the device was remotely detonated. These are preliminary conclusions—don't hold me to them—I've got to do more in-depth testing."

"Where have I heard these ingredients before?" Micah searched his memory. "Sounds so familiar."

"Oklahoma City," Clare refreshed his memory. "Timothy McVeigh. These ingredients were part of the bomb that took down the Murrah Building."

"Do you think there's a connection?" Same group as McVeigh?" Zack wondered.

"It's too early to tell. What I can tell you is that McVeigh was linked to a militia group here in Michigan, the same group that recently plotted to kidnap Michigan's governor. The group is called the Wolverine Watchmen. They advocated for civil war after the recent elections. They're in Michigan, and these are McVeigh-type components. It might be too coincidental to ignore. The main point here is that it's not the first time someone with Michigan connections constructed a bomb using those same components."

"Our working theory is that the bomb was a tool used to create a distraction. The terrorists had an alternative mission planned," Clare advised Shaw.

"Care to elaborate?" Shaw was intrigued.

"They weren't trying to kill anyone. That's what Clare is suggesting," Micah blurted.

"I suppose that's possible. As you can see, it produced quite a blast and caused lots of damage," Shaw responded. "I don't necessarily disagree with the theory, but I would amend it to say they didn't care if people died. Your hypothesis may prove to be correct. I need to do more comprehensive testing."

Micah turned his back and drafted a text to Zack:

What's it like always being right? She's going to conclude that the bomb wasn't meant to kill. She's cute.

Micah hit 'send' and Zack's phone pinged. He looked down at the message, rolled his eyes, and shot Micah the stink-eye. He composed a response.

Grow up, juvenile!

"Shut this damn thing down, now!" A voice shouted from behind Micah, Zack, Shaw, and Clare. They turned around as a burly man with a thick mustache and a permanent scowl approached, escorted by two frazzled-looking patrolmen. "Shut this down," he repeated, almost on top of them now. "And get the hell out of here."

Clare stepped forward. "Special Agent Gibson, FBI," she crooned, syrupy sweet, "and who might you be?"

The burly man shook his head in anger. "I don't give a rat's ass who you are, lady," he boomed. "I want all of you out of here, now!"

"And again, sir," Clare purred. "Who are you?"

The burly man stepped closer, so close that Micah could smell his foul breath. The name "Garber" was engraved on a badge pinned to his shirt.

"I'm the Oakland County Sheriff," Garber advised. "This is my county, my investigation, and I want—"

"Yeah, yeah," Clare interrupted. "You want all of us out of here. We heard you all three times you barked at us. There is one problem, though."

"Yeah? What's that?" Garber demanded.

Clare showed Garber her badge and her orders. "As you can see, I'm an FBI special agent. I am here at the request of Michigan's governor and . . . wait for it . . . the president of the United States. You might want to tone down that attitude."

Garber huffed. "I haven't heard anything of the sort."

"Go ahead, hot shot." Clare remained soft-spoken, almost polite, but she was tired of being bullied by inferior male cops. "Call the governor. You can use *my* phone. I have her on speed dial. Or we can call POTUS. Which do you prefer?"

Garber walked up to Clare, close, almost nose-to-nose. Micah stood beside Clare and opened his mouth to protest Garber's chauvinist behavior. Clare put a hand on his arm and shook her head. "Make the call, Garber. We'll wait by the car."

"Chauvinist pig, asshole," Micah whispered under his breath as they headed toward the car. "Doesn't he realize the governor is a woman? Can't we all get along? What's his damage?"

"Who knows, Micah?" Clare replied. "If I had to guess, I'd say he doesn't like his authority questioned or higher-ups usurping that authority. On the other hand, he probably did the same thing to the West Bloomfield police. The governor will not be as nice as I am."

Micah forked a thumb over his shoulder. "We need to be in there. We need to green-light this investigation. This political nonsense slows down the investigation. The more they pull this crap, the more time we waste without finding the people who did this."

At that moment, Zack walked up to the duo, holding his phone.

"Where have you been?" Micah asked. "We didn't notice you walk away."

"We're all set."

"What do you mean, 'all set?'" Micah demanded.

"I just got off a conference call with the president and the governor. We're all set."

"Stop saying that! Make him stop saying that!" Micah recited lines from an old Barbra Streisand comedy.

"Take a look. Garber should be getting his marching orders right about . . . now!" Zack pointed at the offensive sheriff.

They all turned toward Garber. He was on the telephone, his body language transforming from defiant to graciously compliant. "Yes, sir. Right away, sir. It's been an honor to speak with you. Yes ma'am. I'll say hello. Nice to hear from you again. I'll do that, ma'am. Thank you."

Garber terminated the call and stuck his phone in his pocket. He summoned his deputies and ordered them to return to their cars. Then he walked over to Clare, Shaw, Zack, and Micah.

"I just talked to the governor and the president. Change of plans— the crime scene is all yours. I was not advised. I wish the different branches of government would communicate better, red tape and all. We could avoid all this unpleasantness. No hard feelings?" He stuck out a hand in friendship.

"I was nothing but pleasant and respectful to you, Sheriff Garber. You treated me worse than you might treat a boot patrolman in her first week of service. I displayed my credentials and my orders. Still, you persisted. I believe you have a problem with female authority figures. I'm surprised that you were so respectful to the governor. Of course, she is your female superior. I would suggest, in the future, that you curb the attitude. Take some anger management courses. No hard feelings? You must be joking. Let's just part law enforcement colleagues, shall we? Oh, and by the way—"

"Yes?" Garber sighed.

"Get the hell away from *my* crime scene, and don't come back."

Micah cheered and applauded as Garber walked away with his tail between his legs. Clare watched him go, shaking her head, tired of the disrespect the law enforcement community continued to show for women in authority. Zack walked away to take a telephone call. Micah and Clare turned as he approached, grim-faced, his voice strained.

"Clare? He called," Zack grimaced.

"What are you talking about, Zack? What's wrong? Who called?"

"The guy who took Josh and the neighbor. He just telephoned Rich and Gail Cooper."

CHAPTER TEN

Four of Winger's men, dressed in combat gear, stood at attention inside the Patriotic Storm Trooper's compound bunker. Tensions were high in the cold and windowless room as Winger paced in front of the PST pennant, a swastika intertwined with elements of the American flag, a symbol created by Winger's father. The senior Wright hoped to convey mixed messages of patriotism, authoritarianism, and fear, common alt-right themes. Wright was on the phone, speaking in his disguised, alternate voice, distorted even further by a voice distorter app on his cell phone. He glanced at Carl, who provided a thumbs-up to confirm that the call was not being traced.

"Rich Cooper?" Winger smirked.

"Yes," Rich whispered. "This is Rich Cooper. Who is this?"

Winger expelled a deep, sinister laugh. "I'm your white knight, Mr. Cooper, the one man who can assure the safe return of your son."

"You have Josh? Are you the person who attacked the temple? Is my boy alright? May I speak to him? Why are you doing this, sir? What have we done to deserve this?"

"I thought Jews were supposed to be smart, Cooper. Your questions are rather stupid, don't you agree? Besides, I'm calling you. Of course, I have your son. Of course, I'm the person who bombed the Jew haven. Why am I doing this? Simple. Two reasons: One, I hate Jews. Two, I want money—lots and lots of money. Why you? Wrong place, wrong time, sucks to be you. It sucks worse to be Josh and his neighbor; what's his name, the older guy. Can you talk to your son? That depends on your behavior over the next several hours and days. For now, he's okay. That may be a very temporary condition. Totally up to you."

"I understand, but what do you *want*?"

"Still playing stupid. I told you! What do you think I want?"

"If you harm a single hair—"

The call suddenly disconnected. Rich glanced at Gail and shrugged. A shocked expression crossed his face; tears welled up in his eyes. He felt helpless, terrified he had just killed his son. The phone rang a second time.

"Hello?"

"If you want to see your son, never threaten me again."

"I'm so sorry, sir. I'm just frustrated. Put yourself in my shoes."

"I could never place myself in Jewish shoes. Such small feet. Small heads, small hands, small . . . ha-ha-ha-ha-ha-ha-ha-ha!" The caller laughed a haunting laugh. Rich was terrified but stayed silent.

"Yes, Cooper, I have your son. You don't threaten me. The last thing you want to do is agitate the man who, at a moment's notice, might decide to put a bullet in your son's head. Make sense? You might end up attending your only son's funeral . . . without a body. Understood?" Wright heard a woman sobbing in the background.

"Are the authorities with you? Tell me the truth. I know the answer. I have people watching you. I only ask to test whether your responses are truthful."

"Yes, they are here, listening."

"That's fine. I appreciate your honesty. I know there's a trace on the call. Tell them they're wasting their time. The call will originate from Juarez, Mexico, not where we are calling from or holding your son and neighbor." Wright glanced at his men. The group exchanged childish giggles and sinister smiles, quite proud of the mental torture they were inflicting on a helpless father.

"Sir, whoever you are, may I please speak to my son? His mother and I need to know he's alright. Please?"

Winger motioned to the men holding Josh, still bound, gagged, and blinded by a hood. They carried him over to Winger and placed the boy on his knees close to the terrorist. Winger held the phone to Josh's ear and instructed him to speak.

"Go ahead, Jew boy," Winger ordered. "Say hello to your father."

Josh pressed his ear to the phone. "Dad? I-is th-that you?" he stuttered.

The man promptly hoisted Josh up and whisked him back to his cell.

"Josh!" Rich hollered. "Son, are you okay?"

"He's no longer here, Cooper. You got what you asked for—proof of life," Winger replied.

"Please!" Rich insisted. "Let me talk to my—"

"Was that a challenge to my authority, Cooper?" Winger cut in. "I told you what would happen."

"I'm sorry. Please tell me. What do you want? What are your demands?"

"In due time, Jewper," Winger laughed. "Clever, huh? A portmanteau, hilarious, right?"

Cooper stayed silent.

"Well, my guys thought it was funny," Winger chuckled. "This call was a simple courtesy to inform you that your son is alive and well. The call also serves the purpose of informing you, the police, the press, and anyone with a social media account that the man responsible for the temple bombing and Josh's kidnapping is Winger Wright, supreme leader of the Patriotic Storm Troopers. Look us up."

"Please listen to me, Mr. Wright," Rich pleaded. "I'll give you whatever you want. Just don't hurt my boy."

Winger smiled. This was music to his ears. "I know you'll do everything possible to save your boy. This is simple. I am in charge—you do everything I ask you to do. Understood Jewper?

"The first thing I want you to do is tell the world that the Patriotic Storm Troopers are here to stay. We will not rest until our people prevail. This is merely the first strike of many to come. Tell them, Jewper. Give the world this message. Afterward, say your prayers, wait for Jehovah to help you, and wait by the phone for further instructions."

***

Rich Cooper's hand trembled as he tried to place down the receiver. His skin was ashen white, and anxiety and fear overwhelmed him. He looked around for the nearest seat. Gail gasped and took his hand, eyes wide, brimming with concern.

"What's going on?" she cried. "Is Josh okay? What's happening? Who was that? What did he want?" she rambled, near hysterical, when Rich could not reply. All he could think about was Josh, bound up in a cold room somewhere, terrified, in mortal fear, his parents virtually helpless to save him.

Gail cupped her hands around his face. "Rich!" she barked. "Rich!" She slapped his face. He turned to her, confused, panic-stricken. "Snap out of it! What's going on?" Gail demanded.

Rich squeezed his wife's hand and muttered, "Where's Zack? We must talk with Zack. Can someone please get ahold of Zack Blake?"

CHAPTER ELEVEN

Barrett's parents drummed Jew hatred into the boy at an early age. Jews were terrible people, a stain on society, a threat to white Christians, and subpar humans who sought to dominate multiple industries. The fate of society depended on preventing the Jews from their planned takeover of the American way of life. Jews were greedy, selfish, and driven to replace every man, woman, and child on God's white Christian earth.

Barrett was orphaned at eleven years old. The police killed his parents during a Klan uprising that turned violent. A ward of the state with no relatives, Winger stepped in and assumed guardianship of Barrett, recruited him to the cause, furthered his 'education,' and cemented his destiny as a White Supremacist. Years later, Barrett's indoctrination was so complete that he was trusted to guard Josh Cooper during his internment at the PST facility.

Barrett was a little man, no more than five feet, five inches tall. While he was twenty-five years of age, he was very young-looking. To the casual observer, he looked like a teenager. He wore his brown hair shaggy, usually kept under a hooded sweatshirt. Winger relished the man's boyish, unassuming looks because they enabled him to mingle with or cross paths with the enemy without detection. Barrett could travel anywhere, scout venues for planned terrorist activity, and raise almost no suspicion.

"You will go places in this organization," Winger praised. "You're not ready for combat or rifle duty. Be patient—we'll get you on the front lines sooner rather than later. You'll see. Keep your head down. Follow orders. Prove yourself and demonstrate your devotion to the cause; good things will happen for you. You're a grunt now; you probably think your assigned tasks are minor and inconsequential, but they are not. They are important to the cause and stepping-stones in your development."

Barrett bristled at the notion that he was anything but ready to contribute but was careful to display no emotion. 'Inconsequential' was, indeed, how he felt. He now carried a TV dinner to Josh's cell.

I'm a glorified waiter to a Jew! Winger's a great leader. He knows a thing or two. I'll take his guff, slow but sure, and, one day, I'll be in charge. Instead of feeding this kid, I'll lead the charge to free our kind from those who seek to take us down.

He reached into his pocket and produced the key to Josh's cell. He twisted open the locks, swung the door open, stood on his toes, puffed his chest to appear taller, and sauntered inside.

"Rise and shine, little piglet," Barrett cackled, growling to sound more menacing. "Time to eat."

Josh Cooper looked only a few years younger than Barrett, but the teenager shuddered as the older boy entered his cell. He backed up against the wall, cowering in fear.

"Take it easy, squirt," Barrett snickered, placing the dinner on the floor. "My orders are to feed you, not hurt you, but give me a reason. I'll smack you around."

As the boy calmed and reached for his dinner, Barrett stepped forward and growled louder, like a wild animal, once again sending Josh cowering to the corner.

"Just kidding," Barrett laughed. "Eat your food, Jew boy. I won't hurt you."

Josh was starving. He, once again, crawled toward the container. Barrett towered over him and lit a cigarette, leaning his back against the front wall. "Eat the whole thing," Barrett ordered. "I have to stay to make sure you finish. Winger needs you alive. Can't have you getting sick or dying on us . . . yet," he guffawed.

This guy is nuts. Josh grabbed at the container, afraid to make eye contact. "W-where's Mr. Ellis?" Josh gibbered.

"Who?" *Idiot!* Barrett rumbled. He kicked the container away. "He's in another cell being questioned. He'll be back soon enough."

Barrett kicked the TV dinner again, sliding it across the cement floor at Josh. Josh stopped it with both hands and secured the container. "Eat it, you little prick! Don't make me cram it down your throat."

Josh pulled the plastic off the TV dinner and palmed a piece of bread. He nibbled at it gingerly, tasting a sample, before devouring the whole thing. Usually, they served him mush or water-downed stew. This was a treat.

"It's not kosher," Barrett snarled. "Does the Jewper family keep Kosher?"

Josh furrowed his brow. "Jewper?"

"Your new nickname, dumb-ass! Your family name. Be honored. Winger bestowed it upon you," Barrett explained. "A Jew named Cooper? Jewper! Get it? Hilarious!"

Shrugging, Josh rationalized, "I've heard worse. Kids call me names sometimes. There are lots of hate words for Jews, Blacks, and Arabs. It doesn't bother me. My dad tells me to ignore them. They're just words. Words can't hurt you."

Barrett took a long drag on his cigarette and blew the smoke in Josh's face. "Bullshit, kid! I saw the way you reacted when I walked in. You were terrified."

"I thought you were going to hurt me."

"Eat! Keep up the smart mouth, and I *will* hurt you, punk. I'm in charge here. I'll lay a beating on you if you don't behave. Got it?"

Josh hung his head and averted Barrett's gaze. The boy ate silently, chowing through the cornbread, spinach, and what he assumed was dried-out meat or steak. When he finished eating, he nudged the container toward Barrett and returned to his corner, hugging his knees. He watched Barrett collect the refuse.

"Thank you," Josh whispered.

Barrett looked confused. "What the hell are you thanking me for?"

"You brought me food. Thank you."

"Who thanks the person who holds him captive, dumb-shit? What's wrong with you?"

Josh bit his lip. "I'm sorry. I was grateful for the food. You said you were in charge. I wanted to be polite. Thought you might . . . I don't know . . . hit me or something if I wasn't polite or grateful."

Barrett puffed his chest again. "Good thinking, little Jewper," he snickered. "Glad you know who's in charge."

"You're in charge, sir," Josh nodded.

Barrett grinned, "And don't you forget it." He walked to the door, grabbed the handle, twisted it, and pulled it open. He looked back and thrust his nose in the air before turning to leave.

"How old are you?" Josh asked.

Barrett spun around, angry and paranoid. "Come again?" he demanded.

Josh shrugged. "I was curious how old you were."

"What do you care?"

"Because you look young," Josh retorted. "I just turned thirteen. Are you much older?"

"I'm twenty-five," Barrett responded, forgetting he was conversing with a hostage. He was surprised the kid took an interest and even more surprised he answered the little Jew.

Barrett was used to his role as an uninteresting lackey, the gopher for everyone in the PST. If someone wanted coffee, Barrett fetched it with no expression of gratitude from any recipient. If a member needed gas, groceries, or whatever, Barrett was expected to accommodate that member. He had no brothers or sisters—only his fellow PST members, who treated him like dirt. He was not used to anyone being polite, asking nicely, thanking him, or treating him like a superior. Barrett enjoyed the experience.

"I'm just about half your age," Josh retorted.

"A little more than half."

"Do you like Xbox?"

Barrett's eyes narrowed. "What?"

"Xbox," Josh smirked, happy to engage in a fleeting moment of cordial conversation. "You know, video games."

Barrett had seen a few gaming consoles. He usually watched while some other kid played a game. These were products for wealthy people who had little serious to do. Hate was serious business, so Barrett had little time for such nonsense. That's why he was such an easy mark for Winger Wright and his gang. The young man never played video games—but, secretly, he wanted to.

"No," Barrett muttered. "Never touched one."

"Really?" Josh sounded surprised. "They're fun. My dad says they're addicting, though. How about sports? Do you play sports?"

Barrett became annoyed with all the questions and back and forth. They were making him feel inferior. He did not like feeling that way, especially to a Jew. His head began to hurt, pain creeping up the back of his neck. The kid sounded like a cop questioning a suspect. *Why is any of this his business? What does he care?*

"What's with all the questions? What the fuck do you care, anyway?"

"I was just curious. I'm sorry. I shouldn't have said anything."

Barrett glared at Josh, thinking about himself before Winger took control of his life. Bigger kids in the trailer park used to punch, kick, and bully him. They treated him like an abandoned dog.

He's just a kid, Barrett considered. Josh continued to cower in the corner. *He's a **Jew** kid, but he seems no different from other kids his age.* Barrett paused and collected himself. *Stay focused. You're in charge. This kid is your prisoner, not your buddy.*

"Shut the hell up! You talk too much," Barrett growled. "Keep your mouth shut. You'll be fine if you don't give the older guys any guff."

"You think so?"

"Yeah, I do."

"Thanks."

Barrett grimaced. "Whatever," he grumbled. He grabbed the food container and left the room. As he locked the door behind him, he reminded himself: *He's just a kid.* He padded down the hallway, rehashing the conversation. *The kid didn't do anything. He was born Jewish. How is that his fault?* He tried to shake away the thoughts. *Do your job—no sympathy for the Jew boy.*

Barrett glanced back and over his shoulder at the locked door. *Maybe I can find a book or a magazine—the kid would probably like that.* Barrett turned, eager to report to Winger and get his next assignment.

CHAPTER TWELVE

Clare Gibson and Micah Love arrived at a complex of warehouse office buildings. Like any other run-of-the-mill warehouse complex, this was a place where companies might store wholesale furniture, industrial supplies, or confections. A chain-link fence gated off the site. An overweight guard stood at a shack at the main entrance, eating fast food.

Clare approached the shack, flashed her badge at the guard, and informed him that she had an appointment with Robert Harbor, the owner or manager of Secure Systems. The guard gave them location instructions, opened the gate, and waved them through. Following the guard's directions, they arrived at an industrial white building with a striking electric blue flashing company sign. Clare drove to the front of the business and parked.

A good-looking kid in a logoed white and blue polo shirt greeted them at the door, smiling. His clothing resembled the building sign. He waved, turned, and opened the door, gesturing for them to enter like a valet or hostess at the door of a restaurant.

"Thank you for coming," he greeted them. "My dad is in his office."

"Your dad?" Micah inquired.

"Yeah . . ." the kid was confused for a second. "Oh, you think I'm Robert . . . no, that's my dad. I'm Anthony, Anthony Harbor." He offered

Micah his hand. The kid had a firm grip and a laborer's rough hands. "Nice to meet you."

"Why so jittery, young man?" Clare wondered.

Anthony appraised Clare's FBI badge clipped to her hip. "I've never met an FBI agent before," he shrugged. "Makes me nervous. Not sure why. I feel like I must defend myself. I've done nothing wrong."

Clare chuckled. "No? Are you sure?"

Anthony shrugged. "Weed's no longer illegal, right? So, no, I have not done anything wrong," he giggled. Clare and Micah didn't react. The kid cleared his throat and steered them down an aisle, changing the subject. "This way," he pointed and motioned for them to follow him.

They passed towering shelves stacked with servers, security cameras, and other surveillance equipment. Micah stopped at a rack and eyeballed some of the inventory.

"Holy shit!" he marveled. "You guys are rocking some state-of-the-art gear here."

Anthony proudly jutted his chin and nose at the cameras Micah was appraising.

"Top-of-the-line," he beamed. "We supply almost half the state. We just locked down a contract with some State Department people who want to test our gear in a few embassies. That's my old man's department. I install the stuff." He pounded his chest a couple of times. "Yes, sir, I'm a whiz at installation."

"Answer a question for me, Anthony," Clare asked. "With state-of-the-art equipment like this and a top-notch staff, how could your father's security company have a backup footage failure at a religious institution? I'm in charge of the investigation into the Kol Yisrael temple bombing in West Bloomfield."

Anthony surrendered his hands. "Way above my pay grade. You'll have to talk to my dad about that one," he waffled—the response sounding rehearsed. "Besides, I'm not permitted to answer questions like that."

He pointed to an office cordoned off by walls and plexiglass. A robust man sat inside, behind an ornate executive desk, talking on the phone. The guy was balding, with blatant hair plugs where a bald dome used to be. He was built like someone who might have once played defensive end for the Lions, perhaps in the late eighties or early nineties.

Clare and Micah knocked on the office door.

"Enter," the man covered the receiver and shouted from the other side of the door.

As they entered the office, the man behind the desk held up a finger, gesturing 'one moment,' and continued the conversation. "Right," he said. "Okay, yeah," he nodded. "I'll get right on it, bye." He hung up the phone, rose from his chair, and smiled at Micah and Clare. He immediately changed his expression to grim.

Clare offered her name, rank, and serial number. Micah identified himself.

"Rob Harbor," the man behind the desk introduced himself. "I'm sorry you guys had to trek over here. No one gave me a heads-up. I'm a bit angry about that. I'm rather upset about this whole fiasco."

Micah sought clarification. "You mean the temple bombing or the failures in your security technology?"

Rob's nostrils flared, but he quickly calmed. "Honestly?"

"No, *lie* to me. I hate that expression," Clare bristled.

"Sorry, bad habit. Frankly, I'm angry about both. Everyone has system failures from time to time. However, cloud storage and automatic backup technology should easily prevent such failures. We're still investigating security footage storage errors on primary servers and backups. There's no excuse. I feel terrible." Micah sensed genuine remorse. He glanced over at Clare but could not read her thoughts.

Clare wanted clarity. "Can you elaborate, please?"

Rob stuffed his hands into his pockets. "The backup drives for the temple," he stated again.

"What about them?" Micah asked.

"They were wiped clean late last night by one of my guys. I've demanded his attendance here at the office. He should be down in a moment."

Micah's mouth dropped open. "Someone wiped the backups? What the hell are you talking about?"

Rob held up his palm. "I don't know what happened. It has never happened before—"

"Continue, please," Clare encouraged.

"We were about to dump the footage onto a hard drive for you guys to review. When we accessed the server, something happened."

"Something happened?" Clare exclaimed. "Mr. Harbor, I need specifics. What are you going on about here?"

"That's just it. At this moment, we don't have specifics. We don't have a clue!" Rob bristled. "We're scrambling to figure this out. It is unprecedented. As I stated earlier, it's never happened before. The only thing I'm sure of is that we are victims here. We had nothing to do with it."

At that moment, a young, nerdy-looking guy entered the office. He held onto a laptop for dear life. His eyes remained glued to the floor. He nodded at Rob, then lingered in the back corner of the room, looking ready to bolt at any moment. He clutched the laptop like it was the nuclear football.

"That's Pete," Rob pointed with his head and nose. The introduction was venomous—Rob was unhappy with the guy. "He was the tech on duty last night."

Rob sat down in a huff. "These people are law enforcement, Pete. Tell them what happened last night. If what you tell them helps with the investigation, maybe, just maybe, I won't fire your sorry ass."

Pete fidgeted, began to talk, stuttered, stopped, and started again. His eyes remained fixated on the floor, talking to no one in particular.

"It-it was bizarre," he stammered. "I-I don't know what the hell happened. I went to Cal Tech—nothing like this happened before. No red flags, nothing out of the ordinary. I never saw it coming!"

"Let's calm down a bit. Take a deep breath and walk me through it," Clare soothed. She and Pete took a few deep breaths in unison. "Start from the beginning."

Pete nodded over his shoulder. "It would be better if I showed you."

The group left the office, made a right, then a left, then another right, down to a section of servers. Pete approached a terminal, pulled out, and then connected his laptop.

"This should have been a routine dump," he spoke as he clacked away on the keyboard. "I planned to download the footage from the temple directly from our Cloud server. It wasn't there. That caused some alarm. Protocol dictates that we notify management, so I contacted Rob. It must be on the Cloud . . . *somewhere*. I'm also working to access it directly from the drive. That's all I can tell you. It's still there! It has to be!"

Rob huffed. "Incompetent Pete is trying to say that he and I are the only ones with access to the cloud. I didn't do this. If he didn't do this—" Rob left things hanging.

Pete ignored his insult and continued. "I jacked in right here." Pete looked around the terminal area. "I pulled up the footage and dumped it onto the drive. Then I went to confirm that the footage was on the drive." He pulled up a screen on his computer. "See? The drive is empty—it's not possible!"

"Define empty," Micah demanded.

"In layman's terms, someone planted a bug into the hard drive. As the footage downloaded to the drive, the dump triggered the bug and wiped it clean the second it was accessed. Unfortunately, that someone, the guinea pig, if you will, was me. But I promise you, I had *nothing* to do with this." He was equal parts terrified and impressed.

His eyes widened. "This was all done remotely. Whoever did this has serious tech skills—this is some next-level talent!"

Micah snapped his fingers and posed an idea. "What about—" He searched the ceiling for the words, "an IP address or something?"

Pete rolled his eyes. "It's not that simple."

"Make it simple," Clare suggested. "Losing this footage makes your company look complicit in a bombing and kidnapping, which does not bode well for its future."

Pete gulped, a terrified expression on his face. "I'm telling you guys, someone tapped into our servers off-site and remotely caused the footage to self-destruct the second someone tried to access it. This is Tom Cruise, Mission Impossible-type tech! They are so good they made it look like it happened here so that it couldn't be traced back to them. And they left no digital fingerprint, at least none I've uncovered."

"Despite going to Cal Tech, asshole, what am I paying you all this money for?" Rob chastised him. Pete bowed his head in shame.

"Is it even possible to leave no digital footprint?" Clare wondered.

"Not in my world. It's there, somewhere. It *has* to be," Pete replied.

"How about we go through this, line by line?" Clare suggested, perhaps more of an order.

They spent the next two hours scanning every line of code. The search and scan yielded no trace. When they completed their interrogation and exercise with an exhausted and terrified Pete, they interrogated Rob ad nauseam, getting nowhere. These guys were either innocent victims or the best liars Micah and Clare had ever encountered.

The day wasn't a total waste. Clare and Micah discovered that the perps had next-level computer tech skills. Micah promised to get Reed Spencer together with Pete and any techie Clare decided to employ at the FBI. Micah hoped Reed's lengthy record of computer crimes before going straight and hooking up with Love Investigations would be helpful in *this* criminal enterprise.

Clare and Micah left Secure Systems and headed to Little Daddy's on Woodward, Zack Blake's favorite diner. On the way, Micah called Zack and asked him to meet at the restaurant to commiserate over the day's failures.

Clare had Rob Harbor create two complete paper copies of the temple file, detailing what Rob and Peter claimed occurred when Pete attempted to access the files on the drive.

"I'll get my tech people on this. You do the same with Reed. Our cybercrimes division might have to fly someone in, but between Reed and our tech guys, if there's a breadcrumb of a trail, they'll find it." Clare tried to put a positive spin on things.

Zack was dumbfounded when Clare and Micah tried to explain the problem. "These are right-wing, redneck, Jew-hating lowlifes. How do such lowlifes have the technical skills to pull this off? It sure as hell isn't this Winger Wright character!"

Clare sipped on her coffee mug and placed it back on the counter. "Wright's telephone call to Cooper," she wondered. "What exactly did he say?"

"A whole lot of nothing, bluster more than anything. He wanted to make his presence known and scare the hell out of Gail and Rich," Zack snarled. "He's having a good old boy time, toying with us. There's more to come, in my opinion. This is about more than a ransom. He wants to *torture* these people, make a statement, and enhance his brand to supremacist degenerates everywhere."

"So, no ransom yet? No demands? Nothing?"

Zack shook his head in frustration. "He hinted at a ransom and told Coop to stay by the phone. He said he'd be back in touch. 'Don't be stupid. I'm in charge,' blah, blah, blah, stuff like that."

"Not to be morbid, but did they provide proof of life?" Clare inquired.

"Yes. Rich demanded he speak with Josh. Winger brought him to the phone for no more than a second. Rich heard his voice. They've got the boy. He's alive and sounds okay, at least, according to Rich."

"Were the police involved? Able to trace the call?"

"They're monitoring the phones in Rich and Gail's house. As you guys probably know, it takes about sixty seconds to pinpoint the exact place where the call originated. Winger stayed on the line for precisely fifty-eight seconds. And, as we now know, with advanced technology in his arsenal, he can probably make those calls look like they originate from *anywhere*.

"For a Jew-hating alt-right bigot, he's rather clever. He's smarter than Ben Blaine's or Bart Breitner's crew from back in the day." These were alt-right supremacists, some now dead, others residing in federal prison. Zack, Micah, and Clare had previous case experience with *those* guys in their two Dearborn cases.

"Where did this call purport to originate from?" Clare wondered.

"Mexico," Zack sighed, rolling his eyes. "Like I said, smart. Winger's screwing with us."

Silence settled over the table as the three sat, thinking things through, contemplating the next moves on both sides, concerned for Josh's safety. Clare broke the silence.

"Something's off about all of this. The level of sophistication is far beyond what one would expect from an organization like Winger's. A few years ago, back when Ronald John was POTUS, his open bigotry opened a Pandora's Box, and the alt-right White Supremacists came crawling out with protests and violence all over the country. "Jews will not replace us—one, two, three, four, let's start a race war— preserve the white race—" The worst president in American history gave these guys broad license. These threats continue today."

"We were there, Clare. We watch the news, too. Tell us something we don't know," Micah grumbled.

Clare laughed. "I know, Micah, but that's not my point," she continued. "While these cretins talked a big game and strutted out and about in neo-Nazi protests and the like, they were idiots—easy to track, monitor, and pinpoint. Within twenty-four to forty-eight hours after they mugged for the cameras out on the street or posted online hate, the FBI was at their doors. Most of these bigots were shaking in their boots, singing for supper. These are not Rhoades Scholars—they're chumps. Maybe this goes beyond Winger's organization."

Zack nodded. "Maybe so, but Winger's got his act together. He's sophisticated. He planned this out far in advance, and from what I gather from your visit to Secure Systems, he's either working for black hat-level hackers or has them working for him."

"Hackers?" Micah chirped. "Great movie. Do they still use that term? Isn't it nineties?"

Zack ignored him. "What's your next move with Secure Systems, Clare?"

Clare pondered the question and decided. "I'll pull a few field agents from the Detroit office to assist and probe every square inch of

Secure Systems, their data, and every employee, including the cleaning staff. While I sense that Harbor and Pete are telling the truth, I'm not ruling out an inside job. It makes the most sense. If I even *mention* the words 'domestic terrorism,' I'll have a solid number of agents at my disposal."

"I'll get Reed Spencer on this immediately," Micah promised. "He thinks like the bad guys do. And while he's doing his thing, I'll do a deep dive on the employees from top to bottom. If anyone has a rotten past, I'll find it. If anyone has the tech knowledge to download porn, Reed will flesh them out. Hey, porn—flesh—get it? Am I clever, or what?"

"Definitely 'what,' Zack rolled his eyes. "I've got to hand it to you, Micah. You have a radar for identifying anything perverted."

Clare laughed out loud. Micah winked, clicked his tongue, and shot a finger gun.

"Where do you start looking for Wright?" Zack asked Clare.

"Known associates," Clare replied. "Anyone with whom he's come into contact, everywhere he's slept, shacked up, stayed, or bought groceries. We'll turn it upside-down, shake it, and see what falls out. I'll have to speak with the Detroit SAC. And I've got to brief the Director—get his people involved.

"Now that the terrorists have made contact, this will become the most-watched news story in the country. The eyes of the nation will be upon us, and the pressure will intensify. Winger will love it and bask in the glory."

"Fuck him! So far, no one inside has leaked anything to the press. Winger's call to Rich has not been reported anywhere. At least, not yet. We still have time to maneuver," Zack speculated.

"Good," Clare replied. "Let's keep it that way for as long as possible."

***

The sewer system is a revolutionary tool that has modernized and benefitted humankind. Its main claim to fame is that it processes and disseminates human waste. The Internet has also revolutionized information and communication, but, like the sewer system, it can often be used to process and convey garbage and waste. The World Wide Web is humankind's most significant technological sewer or cesspool.

Online, Carl had gotten into multiple altercations with numerous people of different races, stirring the pot, hoping to inspire inferior races to turn on each other or themselves. Perhaps some angry moron turns on the next white guy he sees and spends the rest of his days in prison. But this mission was different. He sat at his desk and clacked away on his keyboard. His station was in a dark room deep in the recesses of the PST compound. Carl wasn't rabble-rousing; he was checking in, keeping tabs on the online sect of the movement, conversing one-on-one with a man he and Winger knew only as "Darth Synister."

Winger's tech guy, Stebbins, had created a private server chat box. This allowed various supremacist groups to converse and conspire with each other with relative anonymity.

Carl cracked his fingers and neck and focused on the screen as he opened Stebbins' chat box. Carl typed in a username and password, verified both, and then typed in a message. He hit the return key, sat back, and waited for 'Synister' to reply.

The computer chimed two minutes later.

"Greetings," the message read. "A glorious day for the movement."

Carl smirked. "A glorious day, indeed," he responded with a voice command. "How are things on your end?"

"Progressing nicely," Synister retorted. "We're almost there. The final members are rallying. They'll soon organize at Location Two."

"Excellent," Carl replied. "As soon as you have confirmation, please forward coordinates."

"Will do," Synister promised. The screen went blank for a moment, then came to life. "I look forward to shaking hands with Mr. Winger. I do not relish breaking character, but I have been awaiting this day for some time. I love the playbook. Can't wait to use it."

"Amen," Carl replied.

"Would it be possible to communicate with Winger directly?" Synister wondered.

Carl shook his head, forgetting that Synister couldn't see him. "I can inquire—probably not likely now."

"I've got considerable equity on the table. Relay my request. Remind your esteemed leader that I have a secure channel—a dedicated VPN network to speak through. For increased safety, I will also limit the time window to under sixty seconds."

Carl nodded to himself. "Wait a moment," he entered. He rose, headed to Winger's quarters, and knocked on the leader's door. Winger was hunched over his journal, recounting the day's events, entering handwritten notes into a black leather-bound notebook, a tradition that started with his father. He was immediately annoyed at the intrusion and placed the journal on a shelf with fifty others, including his late father's journals.

"Do you have a good reason for this interruption?" Winger fumed.

"We have a request, boss."

"From the Jew kid?" Winger furrowed his brow.

"No," Carl shook his head. "Darth Synister wishes to speak with you."

"Not wise. I'll connect with him in the next forty-eight hours. Until then, he'll have to wait."

Carl started toward the door. "Figured as much," he replied. "The man is eager. Considering what he's done for the cause, I felt it my duty to pass along his request."

Winger huffed. "What is this, Carl, a guilt trip?"

"No, sir! Not at all," Carl repented. "He knows the decision is yours."

Winger sighed, placed down his pen, and rubbed his stubble. He retrieved the pen, twirled it through his fingers, and contemplated his next move. "Can we talk securely with him?"

Carl nodded. "We can."

"You're sure?

Carl nodded again. "I'm positive."

Winger mulled things over, stood, and gestured Carl to the door. "I've changed my mind. Lead the way."

He followed Carl through a maze to the room where the computers and other tech were housed.

Carl returned his chair to the front of the monitor and resumed his prior position. He typed, "Still there?"

"Yes," came the immediate response.

"Wonderful. Permission granted," Carl responded.

"Outstanding," Synister wrote back. "Be right back."

A few seconds went by as Carl traded chairs with Winger. Properly situated, Winger glared at the screen, awaiting a prompt from Synister. Carl stayed in the room and stood toward the back. The computer suddenly chimed, scaring the hell out of both men.

Synister had shared a link with text below it that read, "Click here. This chat will last for no more than sixty seconds. The network is secure. All call traces are scrubbed seconds after the call terminates."

Winger clicked on the link, crossed his arms, and sat back. A moment later, he heard a voice disguised with an equalizer that sounded like a robot with throat cancer. "Winger?"

"Yes, Synister," Winger responded. "A pleasure to speak with you again."

"The pleasure," Synister noted, "is all mine. Thanks for taking the time to chat, especially considering your established protocols about direct communication."

Winger shrugged. "You've earned sixty seconds. You've done some amazing things for our movement. I'm extremely grateful."

"I will use my time wisely. Thanks for everything you're doing for the movement. It means everything. You and your followers give me hope, purpose, and direction. The future looks brighter and whiter, largely because of protocols you have established."

Winger smiled at the compliment. "I'm glad to have you by my side, soldier."

"And I'm pleased to follow your lead," Synister brown-nosed.

"Winger sat back in his chair and clasped his hands behind his head. "How is the next operation shaping up?"

"Nicely. Without a hitch, so far. As I was explaining to —" Synister caught himself. No names.

"As I said before you came on the line, the troops are mobilized and heading for the rendezvous. I'll be joining them soon. After the initial rendezvous, we'll head to the second location and initiate Stage Two."

"Your gear is being prepped as we speak," Winger advised. "My men will transport it to the drop point at your request. Will you be set to receive?"

"We will be set on my end," Synister assured. "Every element of the op has been discussed, briefed, re-discussed, and re-briefed with all participants. We've left no room for error. We have practiced and rehearsed to the point where we could almost do this with our eyes closed."

Winger was pleased. "Outstanding, soldier. Don't get over-confident," he cautioned. "I will rendezvous with you at the appropriate time. Until then, keep your eyes open and ears peeled. Relish this moment. It is one more step toward a glorious, white Christian world."

"Amen to that," Synister agreed. "Will do."

Winger terminated the call and turned to Carl. "Phase two of our mission will begin as soon as we complete this one."

CHAPTER THIRTEEN

Clare stepped out of the shower in her hotel room. She walked to the counter and wiped the steam off the mirror. Her phone suddenly buzzed, causing her to jump. Her towel fell to the floor. She retrieved the towel, re-wrapped herself, and looked at the screen. She fielded fifty to one hundred daily calls from other agents, superiors, witnesses, lab techs, and local or federal governmental officials.

She sensed that *this* call came from the upper echelon of the FBI. Was she imagining things? Or did the ring seem louder, slower, like it rang in slow motion?

Clare cleared her throat, took a deep breath, and answered the phone. "Clare Gibson."

"Gibson?" An authoritative voice bellowed the inquiry on the other side of the line. "Director Beeman, here."

I knew it, Clare mused. "Deputy Director Beeman," she uttered, inserting false pleasantness in her tone. She checked her watch. "Good afternoon, sir."

"I assume that you're in Michigan, Agent Gibson?"

"Yes, sir," Clare's eyes narrowed.

"And you're running point on this unsanctioned investigation into the temple bombing in the Detroit suburbs?"

Clare cringed at his choice of words to describe her involvement in the case. She paused and finally replied, "Yes, I'm in Detroit. However, this—"

"Agent Gibson," Beeman cut her off.

"Yes, sir?"

"I just got off the horn with SAC Hawthorne at the Nevada field office. While Michigan's Governor formally requested the bureau's involvement in this Detroit thing, how is it that you were in Detroit, and we had boots on the ground twenty-four hours *before* the governor requested our assistance?"

Clare stayed silent.

Beeman continued. "Did I lose you, Agent Gibson?"

"No, sir."

"Why is it that when I call Detroit to coordinate the op, the acting SAC tells me that Detroit, West Bloomfield, Beverly Hills, and the Michigan State Police are already coordinating and trouble-shooting this case with an agent from the Nevada field office? Who authorized *that*?"

Clare paused a second time. *No answer will appease him. He'll be livid either way.*

"Detroit is short-handed, sir. I spent a lot of years in this jurisdiction. The SAC in Nevada authorized my return to assist after I received a call from an old colleague, asking me to investigate the matter."

"Old colleague, Gibson?" Beeman roared. "I don't care if POTUS asked you to go to Detroit. I *talked* to Hawthorne, Gibson. I wanted clarification before I spoke with you. Can you guess what he told me, Agent?"

"No, sir."

"Not only did you fly to Detroit without authorization, but you also had the temerity to commandeer a bureau-owned G5 to do so."

Clare grumbled under her breath. *Squirrelly little prick Hawthorne threw me under the bus to save his ass.* "That's not accurate, sir—" she began her mini-protest. Beeman cut her off.

"You are aware," he continued, "that this agency functions on a strict chain of command. We *fire* rogue agents who engage in unsanctioned ops while wasting Bureau assets."

"I am aware, sir, but—"

Beeman cut her off a second time. "Then why pull a stunt like this? Who do you think you are? Elliot Ness? The rules don't apply to you? What do you have to say for yourself?"

Clare closed her eyes. *I'll be at a desk, chasing bad checks for the rest of my life.*

"An old friend requested my involvement—I thought I might lend my assistance. In retrospect, perhaps my decision was misguided. But Hawthorne authorized my intervention and the use of the G-5."

"What friend requested your assistance?"

"His name is Zachary Blake, sir. He's a prominent lawyer here in the Detroit area."

"Ah," Beeman sighed. "I know the man, the so-called king of some such shit. I'm surprised you didn't drop his name earlier. He's got friends in high places and more pull and nerve than any attorney I've ever met."

"I didn't drop his name because I am responsible for my conduct, positive or negative. Zack made the request. I believed I could help. They're short-handed here, as you well know. Detroit is my old stomping ground. I hit the ground running and offered a fresh perspective. I didn't drop Zack's name because I didn't see the need. SAC Hawthorne authorized the assignment and the transportation."

"The bureau doesn't function in a post 9/11 capacity anymore, Gibson. This cowboy stuff may have flown back then, but now it is an egregious disregard for the chain of command and a gross dereliction of duty. Do you read me, agent?"

Clare was becoming unnerved. *Is he listening to me?* She pushed back.

"I confess that the initial request came from a private citizen, but I followed protocol and obtained permission from my immediate supervisor, SAC Hawthorne. *He* made the assignment. I've done nothing wrong. I'm sorry if the Bureau sees things differently. I intend to hunt down and capture those responsible for this heinous terrorist attack on Detroit's Jewish community. I will not apologize for doing my job, going where I was most needed."

"I should haul your ass back to Nevada, order you to pack your things, and post you in a basement in rural Mississippi. However, your stellar performance on the casino case and your previous fine work in Detroit has earned you some leniency."

"Thank you, sir. I appreciate that."

"Not so fast, Gibson. This is no free pass. You have no SAC experience. I'll leave you in place in Detroit and keep you on the temple bombing, but I'm assigning a new lead agent. You will take orders from this person. Understood?"

"Understood. Who is it, sir?"

"Who is what?"

"Who's the agent in charge? When will this person arrive?"

"Harrelson," Beeman declared. "I believe you've crossed paths with him once or twice."

Clare expelled an exasperated sigh. Harrelson was perhaps the bureau's most calculated, emotionless, and cruel agent. He was universally disliked but had an unparalleled record of success. His case closure rate was the highest in bureau history.

On the other hand, his callous treatment of crime victims and agents assigned to work under his command was equally legendary. He had a reputation for burning those agents to get ahead. His antics earned him a nickname in the bureau—everyone who knew him referred to him as 'Dirty Harry' Harrelson.

Beeman continued giving Clare her new orders. "You will march to Harrelson's drum. Do not so much as wipe your nose without his permission. I will have your shield if I hear you've been anything but conciliatory and respectful of his authority. I've drafted and executed your termination papers in anticipation of your failure. It will save me time later. Do you read me, Agent Gibson?"

"Loud and clear, sir."

"Do not make me regret this decision." She heard an abrupt click, terminating the call as she prepared to respond. She stood stunned, holding the phone to her ear. She looked at herself in the bathroom mirror—the steam had long evaporated during the one-sided conversation.

I held my own, she decided. *I did the right thing for the citizens of Detroit.* She continued to study herself in the mirror, wondering whether her decision would have some long-term effect on her career. She composed herself, walked out of the bathroom, dressed, gathered her belongings, and left the hotel.

The hotel valet brought her bureau-owned Ford Explorer. She hit I-75 and drove to Zachary Blake's office. When Clare arrived, the office receptionist ushered her to Zack's office. Zack was holding court with Micah Love and finishing a telephone call. Zack hand-directed her to a chair next to Micah. He gave Clare the "one-second" gesture with his finger.

"How many?" Zack asked into the receiver. "I see . . . Of course. And he and his team will coordinate with the local police departments? Got it. Progress? Snail's pace, so far. These guys do a marvelous job of covering their tracks. We're looking into a few things. The FBI has the surveillance footage. Micah Love also has talented tech people. Hopefully, we can obtain additional clarity."

Zack rolled his eyes and gestured to Clare. "One of their best agents just arrived in my office. Yes, I will. Thank you, Governor." Zack stood and hung up the phone.

Clare furrowed her brow. "Whitman?" she presumed.

Zack nodded. "Just providing her an update." He grimaced, bowed his head, and rubbed the back of his neck, feeling the effects of two days without sleep. "Any movement on the security footage?"

Clare sighed. "If you call being this close to getting terminated," she held up her index and middle finger a half inch apart from each other. "I guess you could say there's been movement."

"Terminated? You're kidding me." He sat back down in a huff.

"I may have ruffled a few feathers when I arranged to visit Detroit. They're not pleased that I came at your request, even though I had approval from my immediate supervisor. While the DD coordinated with the SAC at the Detroit field office, he discovered I arrived in Detroit before the bureau officially became involved.

"My SAC in Las Vegas threw me under the bus, so I got chewed out for breaking the chain of command," Clare explained with an exasperated sigh.

"Ruffled a few feathers," Micah repeated. "I like that expression."

He gestured to his phone. "I'm hearing kids talk on these things and social media, and the phrases they use make me feel like I'm listening to a foreign language. Have you ever gone on TikTok or tried to read a text between two teenagers? How are we going to communicate with each other in the future?"

"TikTok? Do yourself a favor, Micah," Clare advised. "Delete the app. Half of China is listening to your conversations, including this one."

Micah waved at her in disagreement. "Fuck'em. I don't care. Neither do they." He held up the phone. "Besides, I'm following this one bikini model. She wears this tight two-piece and reviews gourmet meals that you can order directly to your door. The delivery people arrive in bikinis, too—"

"We get the picture, Micah," Zack growled.

Micah ignored him and rambled on. "If the Chinese want to follow my bikini model—"

"Damn it, Clare!" Zack erupted. "I wish you'd told me about your situation before I talked to the governor.

"She could have greased the skids for you, run interference with the Detroit field office, told the brass you were here at her request, something like that."

"It's Bureau politics, Zack. It's been going on for a long time. Everyone worries only about their own ass. In this case, Hawthorne tried to screw me. I pushed back. I can take care of myself. This isn't on you. Hawthorne didn't want to take responsibility for sending me to Detroit, especially in a G-5, so he tried to throw me under the bus. He wants to stay in charge in Vegas—the spoiled little rich boy was making sure he didn't piss off the wrong people. My penance is that I'm not running point anymore. Beeman assigned his fair-haired boy."

"Who?" Zack inquired.

Clare rolled her eyes. "A horrible asshole by the name of Dan Harrelson."

Micah snorted. "Sounds like an alias. Who is this guy? Woody's brother? No one has an original-sounding name anymore," he joked. "Except for me, that is."

"Harrelson is a real piece of work. He made his name in Boston, chasing down a gang knocking off armored trucks. You might remember the case. A father/son/brother team pulled off a string of heists?"

Zack nodded his recollection. "The Boston Dynasty Robbers—they made a movie about those guys. Didn't Jon Hamm play Harrelson?"

Micah recalled the movie, snapping his fingers. "Great movie."

"Harrelson looks nothing like Jon Hamm. And he's a sleazebag of the highest caliber, which is putting it mildly. On the other hand, he's an excellent agent, perhaps one of the best. He's committed and has an unblemished record."

"On the other hand," Zack prompted her to continue.

"He'll throw anyone under the bus and rat out any agent, cop, or attorney who gets in his way," she sighed, glancing at Zack.

"He's unstoppable, a great asset. He'll help us solve the case and find Josh, fill some gaps in the evidence, but—"

"But he's an ass. He'll take over and cut the rest of us out of the investigation. If we solve it, he'll take all the credit," Zack surmised.

Clare nodded. "Exactly."

"So, what? If we get Josh back safely, who cares?" Micah reasoned. "Besides, this guy doesn't know Detroit or Michigan. He doesn't have the juice or the pull we have," he uttered, pointing to Zack. "We've got Michigan's fucking lawyer king, the best attorney in the state, with a direct line to the Governor."

Clare was dubious. "It doesn't matter," she sighed. "Harrelson is well-connected. In many ways, his connections exceed yours."

Slowly closing his eyes, Zack remarked, "He's related to Senator Matt Harrelson, isn't he?"

Clare nodded. "Yes."

Micah stood up from his chair. "Who?"

"Republican Senator from Ohio," Zack explained. "Chummy with your old buddy Ron John."

"He's not my buddy. Worst president in history. Glad he's in prison. How's FBI Harrelson related to *Senator* Harrelson?" Micah wondered.

"They're brothers. Politically, let's hope Harrelson is nothing like his brother," Clare warned.

"If he is, we'll have a Grade-A, America Pure, right-wing sympathizer taking over our case. Hell, gentlemen, he might be on the side of the bombers!" Zack bristled.

Before any of them could further react to that piece of news, Clare's phone rang. She excused herself and walked away. Micah and Zack commiserated while she was tied up with the call. She hung up and glanced over at the investigator and the mouthpiece.

"Interesting news, gentlemen. We've made some progress on the security tapes," she announced, pointing to Micah. "Hand me your laptop."

Moments later, Zack and Micah were leaning over Clare, glaring at the investigator's laptop screen, watching security footage outside the temple. The footage showcased multiple angles of the building from four different vantage points. The sun was shining, the wind was blowing, but nothing looked out of whack. The precious place of worship was intact and untainted, a stark contrast to the charred rubble caused by the explosion.

"We know this footage pre-dates the explosion," Zack observed. "What's the timeline? How did they get a hold of this?"

Clare smirked. "We've got tech people. The best of the best—people being paid a handsome penny to work for the good guys. Some of them, like Reed Spencer, used to play for the other team. These days, with cybercrime on the rise, our people make salaries on par with Silicon Valley, almost what they might make as criminals, but without the risk of incarceration. Mothers all over the country are saying, "My son, the code cracker," rather than "My son, the doctor." These people are the best and the brightest."

"Please don't tell Reed what these guys are making," Micah cracked.

"I don't doubt their talent," Zack agreed, "but that wasn't where I was going with my question. How did they obtain this footage? What's the timeframe of these images?"

"That's classified," Clare smiled and winked at Zack.

"Come on, Clare. Give me a break!" Zack grumbled.

"Okay, not exactly classified," Clare continued. "More like complicated. When they forwarded the footage, they tried to explain how they procured it. Two sentences in, I stopped them. "Hold the phone. Sounds like brain surgery," I told them."

Micah was irritated. "Fine, Clare. Who cares? Stop with the worthless explanations. Where are we with the bombing? What's the time sequence?"

Clare sifted through her notes, looking for the exact moment the bomb exploded. She finally pinpointed it and gave the sequence to Micah. He hit a few keys, fast-forwarded the footage, and stopped it. A play arrow highlighted the screen. Micah hovered the mouse over the arrow and hit return.

"Here we go," he noted.

They watched the screen, with Micah seated, while Clare and Zack flanked and leaned over him on both sides. The image displayed the outside walls of the temple, peaceful and tranquil. Despite knowing what was coming, they all jumped when the footage shook, and a fireball burst out of a stained-glass window. Billows of smoke poured out of the window shortly after that.

Zack was nauseated. He fought the urge to look away, glued to the computer screen. Reigning in his fear and anger, he watched the entire portion.

"How does this help us? I'm not seeing anything that leads us to any conclusions about who and why," Zack concluded.

"Who knows, Zack?" Clare cautioned. "To the tech people or the ATF, something might stand out that a layperson doesn't see. That's why they get the big bucks. You know this."

"I'll concede the point," Zack replied, shaking his head, reeling from the footage, reliving the horror he saw firsthand.

"We're looking for suspects here. Your tech people need to revisit the boring segments. Nothing may be something. Is anything out of place? Someone stands out as doing something they shouldn't do. Perhaps he's in a restricted area. Look for out-of-the-ordinary things or people. Scour through the footage at least a week leading up to the attack. Even further than that—did something get delivered? Were the delivery people expected? How long were they there? Were they seen anywhere they shouldn't have been seen? Did they take a leak and stay too long in the bathroom?" Zack glanced at Clare. "You're the pro here. Are they looking for things like that?"

"They are the best of the best. If there is a needle in this haystack, they will find it," Clare promised.

Micah continued to forward and rewind the footage, studying it at various points. I'm going to clone this stuff and give it to Reed Spencer. I'm guessing that when Agent Hotshot gets here . . . what's his name again, Clare?"

"Harrelson."

"Right. When Woody arrives, he's going to shut us down, commandeer this stuff, and keep us out of the loop. Clare will be relegated to fetching coffee and unfurling yellow crime scene tape for the foreseeable future."

Clare cringed at the imaginary image. "Thanks for that graphic description of my future role in this investigation, Micah. I appreciate it," she lamented.

Her cell phone buzzed, and Clare turned her attention to a text message. "Uh-oh! I believe the time has come sooner than anticipated."

"What do you mean?" Zack wondered.

"He's here," Clare advised. "Harrelson is about to touch down in Michigan."

CHAPTER FOURTEEN

Over Clare's protests, Zack accompanied Clare to greet Agent Harrelson. "Bad idea, Zack—this guy does not like lawyers."

Zack remained cocky and confident. "Trust me. I'll behave. I will also ensure that this Harrelson character doesn't kick us out of *our* investigation."

"Our investigation? The minute you called me in, this became FBI Washington's investigation. I presumed you knew and appreciated that," Clare moaned. "We aren't talking about some small-town Michigan police force where you can dial up your connections and charm the brass into your desired result. Harrelson's a pro. He's a prick but still a pro."

"Noted," Zack ignored her. "So am I," he laughed. "Well, the second part, not the first."

Clare's SAC provided navigation instructions. The team arrived at a private airfield in Waterford and waited for the plane to touch down. Thirty minutes later, an official-looking plane landed on the runway. The aircraft taxied up to the terminal building. The side door opened, a stairway lowered, and a lanky man appeared at the top of the stairs. Harrelson had thinning hair, beady eyes, and a sharp Roman-era nose. He started down the stairway, sauntering like he owned the world, the tails of his crème-colored raincoat flapping in the breeze.

The small terminal building was close to the runway, and he quickly closed the gap between himself and the building. He greeted Clare with a jut of his chin while simultaneously snubbing Blake.

"Agent Gibson," he acknowledged, saying her name as if it placed a sour taste in his mouth.

"Good to see you again, sir." She stuck out her hand and forced a thin smile.

Harrelson turned away, ignored her handshake offer, and turned toward the plane. Terminal staff members were unloading his luggage.

"Grab those bags, Gibson. I've booked a room at the Westin in Southfield. I'll check in after I've visited the crime scene." He pulled up his coat sleeve and checked the time on his Rolex.

Most people check their cellphones, Zack noted silently.

"I'll need a rundown of investigators, city, state, and feds currently looking into the explosion."

Zack wasn't intimidated or amused by Harrelson's attitude, especially how he treated his local colleague. Clare was a skilled agent, not a baggage attendant. This was hardly the first time she had crossed paths with a nasty law enforcement official. Most likely, it wouldn't be the last. Unfortunately, there were too many assholes in law enforcement.

"It wasn't an explosion, Agent Harrelson. It was a bombing. I'm Zachary Blake. I'm an attorney. Rich Cooper is a client and a good friend of mine."

"Who the hell is Rich Cooper? What's an attorney doing here, Gibson?" Harrelson was annoyed. He said 'attorney' like it was a dirty word.

"He's the victim, sir. Cooper's son was having his bar mitzvah at the temple when the bomb went off. The Cooper boy, Josh, is one of the two people who were abducted. The working theory is that the act of terrorism was a distraction to pull off a kidnapping," Clare explained.

"I represent the Cooper family. I'm financing whatever ransom demands are made. I will be an active part of this investigation," Zack insisted. His comment was intentional. He wanted to get a rise out of Harrelson and establish his essential role in the investigation. This crisis was personal. No one would stand in his way, not a cop, not the FBI's best and brightest, not even the President.

Harrelson turned to and sized up Zack from head to toe. "Excuse me?" he scoffed. "Who died and left an ordinary citizen in charge?"

Zack shook his head. "I never said I was in charge, Agent Harrelson. I'm here to work with law enforcement. I'm also a witness to the attack, close friends with, and a representative of several victims. So, in this case, for lack of a better way of phrasing it, I guess you could say I'm a polygonal person of interest in this investigation."

Harrelson curled his lip. "Well, Counselor," he huffed. "As much as I appreciate your take on this situation, this is an FBI matter. You're a witness, nothing more. I'll keep you as informed as I would the attorney for any other victim of a kidnapping."

Clare finished stuffing Harrelson's bags in her trunk. Harrelson demanded to be taken to the temple, a short distance from the private airfield. Upon arriving, they surveyed the scene, getting Harrelson up to snuff.

"Surveillance tapes?" Harrelson inquired. "Security footage? Where do we stand on getting tapes?"

"We've got the tapes," Clare advised. "Took some doing, but we've procured the footage."

"What was the problem?"

Clare explained that Secure Systems had been hacked and had only recently authorized the bureau tech gurus to work the case. "Now that the techies have the footage, sir, hopefully, they can work their magic."

"I'd like to review the footage," Harrelson advised, more of a demand than a request. "Where are the tapes?"

"Sent to tech, as I indicated, sir."

"Do you have a copy?"

"That's against protocol, sir, but—" Clare bit her tongue, immediately sorry.

"But what, Gibson?" Harrelson grumbled.

"A . . . uh . . . a colleague of ours is reviewing them as we speak," Clare conceded.

"Colleague? What kind of colleague?" Harrelson demanded.

"I've retained my private investigator to assist in sifting through the footage. His reputation is—" Zack began to explain.

Harrelson held his hand out like a traffic cop stopping a car. "Whoever this individual is, thank him for his efforts and relieve him of his duties. See that he is paid for his time," he glared at Blake. "He works for you? You hired the guy?"

"That's right," Zack nodded.

"You've overstepped, Counselor," Harrelson growled, shifting his attention to Gibson. "You know better to involve lay people in an active investigation, Agent Gibson." He clasped his hands behind his back and paced the scene like a wartime general.

"From this moment forward, Mr. Blake, you will steer clear of this investigation. I've done my homework on you, sir. I was forewarned about your relationship with Agent Gibson in past cases. I understand you were instrumental in helping to resolve a previous case involving a white nationalist. But you are a layperson and a material witness in this case. Stay out of our way, and don't even think of impeding my investigation," he commanded.

"I'll keep you in the loop, but only if necessary. Someone will be in touch to take your statement," he ordered, turning to Gibson.

"As for you, Agent Gibson, I'm unhappy with your work on this case. Pack your bags and catch the first plane to Las Vegas. Rejoin your cronies back at the Vegas field office. Draft a full report and debrief of your time in Detroit. You are relieved of any further duty on this case."

"Agent Harrelson—" Clare started to protest, eyes narrowing.

"Done deal," Harrelson insisted. "Head back to your hotel, draft your report, turn it in, and I'll arrange to fly you back to Vegas on a bureau-commissioned aircraft."

"May I speak with you privately, Agent Harrelson?" Zack interrupted. Harrelson scowled at him. "Just for a moment?" Zack cooed.

Clare was ready to strangle the guy but maintained her composure. Her face paled. Her lips curved into a slight grimace.

"Mr. Blake," Harrelson muttered. He was about to enter the car and turned back. "I've made myself clear. Now time is of the essence—"

Blake interrupted him mid-sentence. "I'm Zack," he chirped. "The president is a friend. I've tried my best to avoid a confrontation with you, but I must insist on a moment of your time," Zack demanded, folding his arms over his chest and glaring at Harrelson.

Harrelson cleared his throat and started to say something. Instead, he nodded and followed Zack. Clare was left standing alone with a smirk on her face. *This should be interesting.*

The two men walked to a bench outside the crime scene tape. Zack crossed his arms behind his back, like a television lawyer about to grill a key witness on the stand. He waited for Harrelson to catch up before smiling and addressing the agent.

"I've learned much about you, too, Agent Harrelson. You've got a stellar reputation."

Harrelson's expression changed to smug and proud. "Great. Then you understand that I've got no time, nor am I interested in whatever this little sidebar is attempting to accomplish. I'm only indulging you because you also have quite a reputation. However, I will only grant so much leeway. Understood?"

"I get the picture."

"Good," Harrelson advised. "It is quite unusual for a lawyer to be as, shall we say, *involved* as you have been," his eyes narrowed as he continued.

"As time passes, I'm certain your exploits will, one day, procure a true crime development deal at one of the major networks or on some streaming service. 'My Take on the Law with Zachary Blake,' or some such nonsense," Harrelson blustered, pleased with his sarcastic, manufactured television role for Blake, the pain in his ass.

"Clever, Harrelson. Come up with that all by yourself?" Zack inched closer, almost face-to-face with the agent. "Let's cut to the chase. Our investigation and the safe return of the hostages will surely benefit from your insight and professional acumen. Nonetheless, I find aspects of your modus operandi disconcerting."

"Tough shit for you and your fancy ten-dollar words," Harrelson snarled. "This is an FBI investigation. I'm in charge. I have full authority. Not you, not Gibson," He roared, glaring at Gibson.

"I've been briefed, brought up to snuff, gotten a complete rundown of the investigation to the present moment. I know all about it, the whole enchilada. Agent Gibson overstepped her bounds—she's lucky she's only being transferred and not terminated. I've been ordered to clean up her mess, Blake, to ensure this investigation is resolved promptly without loss of life. I will catch the men who did this and bring home these hostages."

"I do not doubt your intentions are honorable," Zack agreed. "I welcome your involvement if you become a team player. I'm no schmuck. You're a despicable person. I wouldn't want to be your friend or colleague, but I will again acknowledge that you might be an asset."

"Kind of you to say," Harrelson snarled, waiting to pounce. "Enlighten me, please," he continued, "why are we wasting time with this trivial back-and-forth? I have authority— you don't."

"Your main purpose here is to relieve Agent Gibson of her command, correct?"

"Quite true," Harrelson responded. "I owe you no explanation, but she has played an insignificant role in this investigation, made serious mistakes and errors in judgment, and the brass decided to replace her with someone with a higher solve rate. Shit happens. I will contact her if I require her services. Same for you. As George W once said, I am the decider. Understood?"

"Absolutely, and that is where we are at an impasse."

Harrelson paused, salivating for a confrontation, sizing up Zack like a boxing opponent. "What the hell does that mean?"

Zack nodded toward Clare. "I have personal experience working with Agent Gibson. She is an exceptional agent—one of the bureau's best. The issues raised are related to her attempts to accommodate me. And these complaints are *politically* motivated," Zack charged.

"How do you figure?"

"I know who you are, Harrelson," Zack continued. "I'm aware of your family lineage. This isn't the first time I've dealt with the brother or son of some senator or member of Congress—you name it. As you probably know, I once took on the president. You *know* how that turned out.

"I'm on to you, sir. You're here only because you tugged on the right strings and got put in charge. The stakes are high. Rescuing the hostages, securing arrests and convictions without bloodshed, all of this will pave the way for advancement."

Harrelson bristled at Blake's hubris. "You've crossed the line. I suggest you exercise your right to remain silent, counselor. One phone call from me and you'll be facing disbarment. Your career will be in the toilet—I understand that's already happened to you once."

"You don't intimidate me, Harrelson," Zack retorted. "You don't scare me in the slightest."

"I should."

"Sorry. I'm not easily intimidated," Zack snarled. "You think you can go toe-to-toe with me? Call your brother. I'll call my close friend, the governor of Michigan. Better yet, I'll text the president to thank him for his recent kindness before I tell him how you've treated a decorated agent. Think I'm a headache now? You haven't seen anything yet."

"You can't get rid of me, Blake."

"I told you, Harrelson. I'm a team player. I don't want to get rid of you. I'm counting on your assistance and expertise. Whether we like each other or not is beside the point. I want to get Josh and the other guy home without a scratch. I'll work with anyone to accomplish that."

"What is it you want from me, Blake?"

"Clare stays. She and Micah Love, my investigator, work a shadow investigation. Each investigation has access to all information and evidence that the other acquires. You guys share everything with a common goal—to bring Josh Cooper home safely. What do you say?"

"I say that I need access to the building surveillance footage. I say that your failure to produce the footage is grounds for obstruction."

"I've not withheld the footage. You just landed. Is this a DNA problem of some sort? Are you incapable of being a *mensch*?"

"What did you call me?" Harrelson seethed.

"I didn't call you anything. I asked if you were incapable of being a *mensch*. It's a Yiddish word. It means 'nice guy.'

"Look, Harrelson. If you want a pissing contest, you got one. Let's assume that we both have considerable political clout. Do we both want what we want? Yes. At the end of the day, though, we want to resolve this case with a safe return of the hostages. Not working together would be counter-productive and might endanger them."

Moments passed with little sound but a breeze rustling through nearby trees. The two men were locked in a stare-down. Harrelson broke the stalemate.

"Okay, Counselor. Where do we go from here?"

"Easy. We get you the footage. You leave Clare and Micah alone except to share information. Hopefully, the relationship and investigation will blossom into a shared endeavor. Otherwise, may the best team win," Zack suggested protocol.

"One caveat, Blake. If Clare's team loses, or this so-called shadow investigation somehow obstructs or delays a successful outcome, you and Gibson will face significant repercussions. I secure the safe return of the hostages—you've been a thorn in my side, sucks to be you. I get to tell my superiors you tried to blackmail me into keeping Clare on the team. Deal?"

"If that's the game you wish to play, I'm in. In my scenario, there are no winners or losers, only the safe return of the hostages and swift and severe justice for the perpetrators."

"I can't say it was nice meeting you, Blake."

"Likewise, Harrelson—the displeasure was mine," Zack grumbled. He turned his back to Harrelson and walked away.

CHAPTER FIFTEEN

Days merged into sleepless nights for the Cooper family. Time slowed to a snail's pace. What little food Rich Cooper could eat was tasteless. His mind and body had become numb, ready to crash at a moment's notice. He sat at the edge of his couch, thinking only of Josh. He held a water bottle and forced himself to take an occasional sip. Someone he couldn't remember advised him to stay hydrated. Zack Blake walked into the room.

"How are you doing, bud? Are you okay?"

Rich was lost in thought. He didn't hear Zack.

"Rich? Are you okay?" Zack repeated.

Rich grimaced and rolled his eyes. "Kind of a silly question."

"I had to ask. I'm concerned about you. You look like you've shed a few since we last saw each other. You must stay strong."

"I suppose," Rich conceded. He looked down at his abdomen. "Not much of an appetite these days."

Zack took a seat on the couch next to his friend. "How's Gail doing?"

Rich pointed over his shoulder to the bedroom.

"She's asleep. This has been too much. She's zonked—can't blame her. Crying too much—eating too little. It's all catching up with her."

"You want me to send a doctor?"

"I'm not sure how receptive she'd be to a doctor, especially a stranger."

"It doesn't need to be a stranger. Just tell me who to call. It might be good for you both to get a quick exam. Maybe they can prescribe you something—"

"I'm not cramming pills to cope with Josh being gone. He's suffering. I'm not going to numb my pain when he can't numb his own. That's not happening."

"That's not what I meant," Zack tried to explain. "You know that."

Closing his eyes, Rich sat back, ran his fingers through his hair, and turned to his friend with tears in his eyes.

"Sorry, Zack. I didn't mean to snap at you. That's the stress talking. Will this ever end? I don't know how much longer we can cope."

"I know," Zack acknowledged. "We're doing everything humanly possible to track down these thugs and bring Josh home, safe and sound."

Rich took another swig from the water bottle, set it down on a nearby table, and leaned forward.

"Any progress to report? Any kind of headway at all?" he pleaded.

"We've got the security footage. Micah's team and the FBI are combing through it, hoping to see anything or anyone out of place in the month or weeks before the attack. Hopefully, we'll catch a break."

"That sounds promising. There should be some serious planning for a terrorist event like this, right? Some form of prior reconnaissance?"

"Makes sense to me, Rich. That's why we're reviewing the footage, frame by frame," Zack agreed, trying to provide a glimmer of hope.

Rich nestled into the couch. "Find my son, Zack. Bring him back to me, safe and sound. I need to see him, hold him, hug him. Then, I need to wrap my fingers around the throats of the guys who took him. Where the hell is he? How do people learn such hate?"

"I just had a thought, Rich. You and your family must have been frequent visitors to the temple in the days leading up to the bar mitzvah, right?"

"True," Rich responded. "Lots of planning to get ready for Josh's big day."

"Think for a moment. Does anyone or anything seem out of sorts on any of those visits? Did you see anything strange or unusual?"

"I'm not sure what you mean."

"You know the place. You know its members. It's a large congregation, but most of us know each other. Were there any visitors who weren't regulars? Workers? Delivery people, perhaps? Guests? Does anyone come to mind? The perp could even be someone you've encountered in the past."

Rich searched his memory. "No. We were focused on planning a joyful event, not scouring the place for hostile forces, anything or anyone out of the ordinary."

"Understood, but try to think, man. The clue that cracks the case often hides under everyone's nose."

"Lawyers and investigators take a pragmatic approach to these things. Perry Mason, Matlock, Benson and Stabler, Will Trent, Columbo, and even Sherlock Holmes are wonderful entertainment, but are they realistic? Are clues uncovered like that in real life? I'm dubious."

"Perhaps the approach is counter-intuitive, Rich, but this is personal. Turn off your pragmatic button and focus on anyone you saw or met that you hadn't seen or met before. Were there any square pegs in *shul* on that Saturday? Any other day before the Bar Mitzvah? Who fits that profile?"

"I appreciate what you're getting at, Zack. I've been racking my brain. Caterers, flower arrangers, decorators, delivery people—I can't place anyone. Can you?"

"No, but when we finally solve this thing or identify these perps, we'll be shocked we missed the obvious. Whoever it is, we'll say: "Yes, that guy makes perfect sense. Can't believe I missed it." And, when we find him, I'll make it my life's mission to see that he's prosecuted to the full extent of the law."

"I know you will, Zack," Rich replied, acknowledging his friend's commitment. "I'm going to lay down, close my eyes, and retrace my steps during the weeks leading to the bar mitzvah. It's worth a try."

"That's the spirit," Zack encouraged.

Rich closed his eyes. Images of friends in the area, temple members and visitors, brief glimpses and bits and pieces of conversations and faces he recalled before the bar mitzvah, clergy, administrators, event planners, and delivery people danced in his brain. This is a tight-knit community—most people were members, staff, friends, or family. Was anyone out of place? Try as he might, no one stood out. The same people, day in, day out. Nothing changed. Nothing or no one out-of-the-ordinary. The same people—

Rich opened his eyes. Zack's were closed. He had decided to engage in the same exercise. "I can see the wheels spinning, Zack," Rich noted. "What's on your mind?"

"I can't shake the feeling this is an inside job."

"What do you mean? A temple regular? Not possible. No way, no how," Rich responded, shaking his head.

"I understand how you feel, Rich. But an insider makes sense. I don't know how or why. Here's an idea. Can you determine if any member has severe financial problems?"

"That's worth a look. There's a candlelight vigil at the temple tomorrow night," Rich advised.

"News to me. When was this organized?"

"Word went out via group text a few days ago. It caught fire. Everyone will be there—Temple members, the media, prominent religious and community leaders, and ordinary citizens. I'm having a hard time getting Gail on board."

"I'll be there," Zack assured. "And so will Special Agent Clare Gibson of the FBI and a strong contingent of local, state, and federal law enforcement officials. I'll see to it. Better safe than sorry."

CHAPTER SIXTEEN

"**R**eturn this nation to the strong, untainted, white-dominated principles upon which it was founded." Winger closed his eyes. "I hope you're proud, Pop," he whispered. "We'll get this nation back on track."

Winger Wright was preparing for his second ransom call. This one would contain more detail, a heavily encrypted video call to the Cooper family demanding three million dollars for the safe return of Josh and Chip. He would also require the release of several prominent brothers and sisters of the movement, currently in prisons across the United States. Wright's technology experts assured him that the call could be processed to avoid the usual open and unencrypted transmissions that would make the hostage-takers easy prey for law enforcement tracking efforts.

GPS signals are relatively easy targets for anyone wishing to record, track, or alter them. Stebbins, Winger's tech guy, devised a workaround. At the time of the call, the tech guy planned to use a radio transmitter to send a counterfeit GPS signal to the Cooper's area antennas. This tracking detection avoidance technique, also known as spoofing, overrides the original signal from the satellite. A fake signal is broadcast from the ground, and all satellite navigators in the locality will show the wrong location. This is consistent with technology used to hijack drones or interfere with transportation navigation systems. Tech-smart *kids* can spoof to avoid being tracked by their parents or to use apps or sites prohibited by over-protective parents. The bottom line is that the technology prevents precise movement tracking.

To avoid the possibility of tracking, after the ransom call, Wright planned to destroy the burner phone immediately following the call. The tech was also rigging the call for broadcast. One of Winger's operatives would leak the 'signal' to Fox 2 Detroit, and eventually, every media outlet in America could broadcast the call live. Winger wanted to use the exchange with the Coopers for the ransom demand but also to promote the group's alt-right, anti-Semitic terrorist agenda to like-minded citizens. Ransom was only one method of fund-raising. Wright believed that post-broadcast dark web donations could easily dwarf the ransom amounts. People were angry. Winger wanted to seize the opportunity to tap into their anger.

The following morning, an anonymous and untraceable call was placed to Fox 2 Detroit, the local Fox affiliate. Someone claiming to be a member of the hostage-takers, the Patriotic Storm Troopers, had a proposal. At six that evening, a video telephone call was to be placed to Rich and Gail Cooper.

"The PST cordially invites Fox 2 Detroit's news department to participate in the call and to make the broadcast feed available to local and national stations all over the United States."

The heads-up was to permit the local station time to coordinate a national broadcast. Fox 2 Detroit was chosen because it was a 'Fox affiliate.' The PST incorrectly associated the local station with Fox News, the national right-leaning political news network.

The general manager of Fox 2 News was excited about the opportunity. She immediately contacted her local news competitors, Channel 7 (ABC), Channel 4 (NBC), Channel 62 (CBS), and Channel 56 (the local PBS affiliate) to alert them to the broadcast and arrange the feed. Newswires and press releases were posted nationally to Fox News, CNN, and MSNBC networks. Reuters, the Associated Press, and even international news services were also alerted to what the Fox 2 GM called an "emergency broadcast." By three o'clock that afternoon, every media outlet in America and beyond was prepared to pick up a live feed of the telephone ransom call.

At the Cooper's home in Beverly Hills, the embattled couple's landline began to ring nonstop. Television and print reporters across America wanted statements from or interviews with Rich or Gail Cooper about the upcoming ransom call. Rich and Gail were unaware of the call. They issued a terse "no comment." The couple turned on the television to discover that the PST planned a ransom call at six that evening.

At the same time, local and state police also learned of the call. They implemented a massive call-tracing operation—local law enforcement officers, FBI special agents, and agents of the FBI's National Cyber Investigative Joint Task Force descended upon the Cooper family's Beverly Hills home. Tech experts installed sophisticated audio and video equipment, hoping to trace the call, narrow down the location, or acquire some remote evidence that might cause a break in the case.

Rich Cooper contacted Zack Blake. He wanted Zack present to hear the ransom demands. Zack arranged for Micah Love and Reed Spencer to be present. All the tech experts expected the call would be highly encrypted, perhaps untraceable, but they planned to use every piece of modern technology available to defeat the PST's encryption techniques.

By six that evening, the entire country and most of the world were tuned in to watch the live feed of the ransom call. Winger Wright was ecstatic about the public's reaction. News stations all over the world were broadcasting live. Reporters offered almost universal condemnation of the despicable broadcast. At the same time, they chastised hate groups, anti-Semites, and White Nationalists. Despite their efforts, dark web contributions were pouring into the PST website. Ransom amounts, if paid, would be dwarfed by the amounts of money contributed by White Nationalists and anti-Semites across the globe. Everything was going according to plan. The Patriotic Storm Troopers, virtually unknown before the abduction, were now an international phenomenon.

At precisely six o'clock Eastern Standard Time, Rich Cooper's cell phone rang. Technology experts hooked the video feed to several large-screen televisions, computer monitors, and laptops throughout the house. An FBI tech expert silently directed Rich to answer the phone. A hooded, face-covered man appeared on the screen.

"Hello?" Rich answered. He held his iPhone close to his face. The caller could not appreciate the chaos that was once the Cooper's private home.

"Richard Cooper? Father of Joshua Cooper and neighbor of Chip Ellis?"

"Yes."

"Are you alone?"

"I am not."

"Who is there with you? Be specific, please."

"My wife, some friends, several local and state police, and some FBI agents."

"I appreciate your honesty, Cooper. Efforts to trace or otherwise monitor or source this call are futile. We have your son, Josh. He is safe, for now. We abducted the boy for two simple reasons."

"Yes?" Rich's voice cracked, near tears.

"First and foremost, we hate Jews. Everyone listening to this broadcast must know that the Jews are an all-present, parasitic evil. Jews control our country, the television and entertainment industry, the media, banking, our political system, and education in America. They have manipulated social order and unleashed colored people, blacks, browns, and other undesirables into the center of white America, creating an impure society.

"At the turn of the last century, one of our heroes, Henry Ford, warned of this Jewish conspiracy to control the world. He was right. We did not heed his warning. As a result, Jews are now the driving force behind the turmoil at the southern border, immigration of other non-white minorities, the Black Lives Matter movement, and equal rights for women. All of this is designed to erode the rights of white men in our society. The Jew is the true enemy of humanity—all racial and impure issues in this country and across the globe lay at the doorstep of the Jews. They are left-wing terrorists. We do not negotiate with and shall never cede ground to terrorists. Jews will not replace us—Seig Heil!"

The speaker paused, awaiting a reaction from Cooper or someone else in the room. Rich looked around at the law enforcement officials spread out across the room. Some shrugged, others put their fingers to their lips, suggesting silence. The pregnant pause did not last long. The terrorist continued.

"We would be pleased to end your son's suffering. One less Jew in this country is what some might call a good start. However, we believe that a better alternative is to have Jews finance our current effort to eradicate Jewish scum from our planet. Our fund-raising campaign, launched with your son's abduction, has already resulted in millions in online contributions. In addition, the ransom you will pay for the safe return of your son will also contribute to the cause of eliminating Jews. Everyone knows Jews control the money in this country. It is high time we redistribute that wealth. Our ransom demand is three million dollars for Josh Cooper and Chip Ellis. That's one point five each. While Ellis is not Jewish, he consorts with Jews, is friendly to them, and lives in Jewish neighborhoods. He is non-Jewish scum. We also require the release of all brothers and sisters of the movement, currently in prisons across the United States.

"We will provide more details and a potential drop site in the coming days. Stay by the phone."

"I want proof of life," Rich demanded, prompted by Clare Gibson.

The caller paused. He moved off camera, pointing the phone away for a moment. The view temporarily moved to a window. Voices could be heard, but listeners could not make out the words. Finally, a voice said, "Bring the boy."

"I want to speak to Chip Ellis, too," Rich announced, again prompted by Clare Gibson.

"Why?" The caller was intrigued.

"Because you asked for one point five million for his safe return. We need proof of life," Rich advised.

"Bring Ellis, too," the caller requested to an unknown companion.

Everyone in the house awaited the appearance of Josh and Chip. The caller paused the call—nothing could be seen or heard while they awaited the hostages' arrival. Suddenly, the audio and video came to life once more. Chip Ellis appeared on the screen, a blindfold over his eyes.

"Hello?"

"Chip? It's Rich. Are you okay?"

"Yes, Rich. Good to hear your voice. I'm okay. I've been keeping tabs on Josh. He's doing as well as can be expected. Screw these bigots! Don't give them a thing!"

The audio and video were suddenly interrupted. The call was paused. The terrorists did not appreciate Chip's attitude. When the caller turned on the video, Chip Ellis was gone.

"If you want to see your son, Cooper, you will ignore those comments. Ellis will receive appropriate punishment," the caller warned.

"I want to see my son," Rich pleaded.

"Hold on." The call went dead again. When the audio and video returned, the hood-covered image of Josh Cooper filled the screen.

"Josh!" Rich cried.

"Dad? Is that you?"

"Yes, son, it's me. Mom is here, too. Gail?" Gail Cooper moved toward the telephone screen so that both faces were visible.

"Josh?" Gail burst into tears.

"Hi, Mom. Please don't cry. I'm okay."

"How are they treating you? Are you eating? What are they feeding you?" Gail sobbed.

"I'm fine, Mom." The terrorist yanked the phone from Josh. The boy disappeared from the screen.

"He's fine. You've seen him. He's in good health—proof of life. Now get us our money and adhere to the rest of our terms." The call terminated. The Coopers, other spectators, and cops from all agencies sat stunned at the intense level of hate, hostility, and depravity of the terrorists. No one doubted that the hostages' lives were in danger.

"What do we do now?" Rich wondered.

"Unfortunately, we can't do anything but wait."

"Were you able to get a trace? Come close to a location?" Zack inquired.

"The call hopped everywhere—Vancouver, Mexico, Amsterdam, Switzerland. We will have to analyze the data," an FBI tech person advised.

"Reed?" Micah turned to his cyber-specialist.

"What she said. It's too early to know whether there are clues. I do want to talk to you and Zack, though, privately," Reed replied.

"Privately? I thought we were sharing everything," Harrelson grumbled.

"I have nothing to share," Reed advised. "I just want to get marching orders from the people who pay me."

"Okay. But don't hold out on me. I'll shut your ass down, and fast!" Harrelson warned.

"Yeah, I heard what a wonderful guy you were," Reed chided.

"Want to be kicked out, smart ass?" Harrelson threatened. Reed remained silent, figuring anything he said would be used against him.

The television networks and stations continued reporting, calling the house, and attempting to obtain interviews with law enforcement or the Coopers. All requests were denied. Talking heads spun the hostage-taking and terrorist playbook, speculating about the next steps that might be taken to resolve the standoff. Speculation centered on whether the call brought law enforcement any closer to identifying the actual terrorists and whether it was wise to pay the ransom and trust that the hostages would be released. Would law enforcement be permitted to release prisoners whose sentences have not been served? The consensus among the so-called experts was that Josh Cooper and Chip Ellis were in grave danger, whether a ransom was paid or not.

CHAPTER SEVENTEEN

"What I love about you is that you think like a criminal!" Zack remarked.

"Thank you?" Reed chuckled.

Following the ransom call. Reed Spencer convened an impromptu meeting with Zack Blake, Clare Gibson, and Micah Love.

"I meant it as a compliment. So, what did you want to discuss that couldn't be discussed in front of Harrelson and the others?" Zack wondered.

"Not much. Micah told me how Harrelson treated Clare. Besides, I don't trust law enforcement types, especially those with whom I've had no experience. Clare is an exception."

"Why, Reed Spencer! Did you pay me a compliment? Am I 'trusted law enforcement' or the 'criminal type' you prefer?" Clare joked, hand-signing quotation marks.

"You're what I call progressive law enforcement. You're not always exclusively by the book, which is good."

"Thanks . . . I think. So, what's up? What's this clandestine get-together about?" Clare wondered, cutting to the chase.

"I have two observations about the video call. Did anyone else notice anything worth talking about?" Reed inquired.

"Not really, nothing stood out. We've recorded the whole thing. I would have to study. Why? What did you notice?" Clare wondered.

"I noticed that the guy is a raving, Jew-hating lunatic. This two-percent minority population caused everything bad in his life. What a stupid, bigoted moron!" Zack ranted.

"Not new information, Zack," Micah observed. "But I agree with you." He turned to Reed. "Let's get back to Clare's question, Kemosabe. What did you notice?"

"I picked up two leads. The first is obvious. Follow the money."

"After the ransom is paid, right? There's no money to follow until Zack pays the ransom." Micah replied, confused.

"Not true. The caller identified himself as a member of the Patriotic Storm Troopers. He claimed they had a presence on the dark web. Right?"

"Right. Go on—I get where you're going with this, I think," Clare advised.

"The guy said something to the effect that the abduction and notice of the ransom call resulted in millions of dollars in dark web donations to the group. He may have been exaggerating or lying, but what if he wasn't? What if we could track online donations to the PST to an account in the States or offshore? Who suddenly received millions? The FBI can track that stuff, can't they?" Reed floated.

"That's a great idea, Reed. I'll get our counterintelligence and cybercrimes teams on this."

"Keep me out of it. Take all the credit. Say it came from you," Reed suggested.

"Why?" Clare asked.

"Because of the way they're treating you, Clare. You don't deserve it. You need the brownie points."

"I can handle myself. I don't need anyone to help make me look good," Clare pushed back.

"I know you don't, Clare. But I get no benefit from disclosing this to them. You will directly benefit from posing the suggestion. Please?"

"Yeah, Clare. Do it," Micah added.

"I agree. Nothing to gain for Reed. Everything to gain for you. No-brainer," Zack added. "Besides, the suggestion has more credibility if it comes from you. Harrelson probably hates the idea of Reed even being present during the call."

"True enough. Okay, you've convinced me. I'll get on it. What was the other thing?" Clare wondered.

"Right, I almost forgot. Did anyone notice that pause when Rich asked to speak to Josh? The caller paused and then said: "Bring the kid," or something like that," Reed recalled.

"I'm positive it was "bring the boy," wasn't it?" Zack corrected.

"It doesn't matter what words he used. I'm asking if anyone remembers the video."

"No, what about it?" Micah asked, motioning for Reed to continue.

"The phone moved and, for a short time, pointed at a window, remember?"

"Yeah, so?" Micah grunted.

"I could have sworn that something outside that window looked familiar. Did anyone else notice? Does the FBI have any landmark identification tools? If we can identify what was outside the window, how far away it was, and at what angle, we may be able to figure out where they're holding the hostages. Grab them back and arrest the bad guys before paying the ransom or releasing dangerous prisoners. That would be easier, no?"

"Reed Spencer!" Clare snapped.

"Yeah?" Reed cowered, frightened by Clare's sudden aggression.

"I've never been more attracted to you! I could kiss you here and now!"

"Please don't. You're not my type," Reed deadpanned.

"Oh? What's your type?" Clare flirted.

"Someone who is not in law enforcement."

"Understood."

"Does anyone have the video?" Zack asked.

"I have it in my laptop," Reed advised.

"Fast forward to the spot you're referring to," Micah demanded.

Reed did as Micah ordered. They all leaned in to see what was outside the window in the video.

"Can anyone tell me what we are looking at? It looks like the sun is behind the image. The call was at six. The sun sets in the west. This time of year, we're about two hours from sunset. The sun would be to the southwest. So, the window exposure was southwest. Now, what is that?" Micah wondered.

"It looks like . . . a lighthouse . . . maybe? But . . . which one? There are a ton of these in Michigan. Does everyone agree that it could be a lighthouse?" Micah asked.

"I don't want to rain on anyone's parade, but I can't tell. And don't forget, even if it is a lighthouse, the location might not be in Michigan," Clare warned.

"Party pooper," Micah sighed.

"Point taken, though. Let's first conclusively identify *what* it is. Then, we can determine *where* it is. We'll call this mission 'Operation Identify.' Sound good?" Clare suggested.

"Sounds good to me," Micah agreed. "What's the next step?"

"Download this piece and get it to my forensics folks in Washington. They do this stuff all the time. The bigger question: Tell Harrelson or don't tell Harrelson?" Clare wondered.

"He's got to know sooner or later. You think he'll take credit for the discovery?" Micah asked.

"I don't know. He's hard to read. Sometimes, I think he's all about the case. Other times, he's crapping all over some excellent agents," Clare concluded. "I vote we tell him."

"Your vote is all that counts. It's your office. He's your fellow agent," Zack remarked.

"Let's get the video over to forensics. If I see Harrelson soon, I'll tell him about the discovery. If I don't, I'll tell him after the results are in from the forensics team. Good?" Clare asked, seeking consensus.

"Fine with me," Zack agreed. "Everyone else?" He looked around. Everyone was nodding his head.

"I'm psyched. If we can get an approximate location, the FBI can surveil, identify the location, and send a clandestine force. If this is a lighthouse, the possibilities are narrowed to waterfront properties. Let's presume a residence somewhere in Michigan, which narrows things even further and all but eliminates the chances for any serious firearms on site. The terrorists will want to blend in with the community. The force can breach before anyone inside the house knows what hit them," Micah speculated.

"I like the way you think, but that's rather presumptuous, wouldn't you say, Micah?" Clare smiled.

"I have deep faith in the FBI, Clare. Some of my best friends—"

"I'm your only friend in the FBI."

"Well—"

"I'll get on the horn with forensics. Reed?"

"Yes?"

"Text or email me that video."

"Do you have a Dropbox account? The video is too large to text or email."

"I'll get you an account to send it directly to forensics. How does that sound?"

"Perfect."

"Cautious optimism, gentlemen—let's hold off telling the Coopers. I don't want to get their hopes up until we can identify the object. Besides, the fewer people who know about this, the better. I trust that no one in this group will leak this. I'm not sure I can trust anyone else."

"Sounds like a plan, Clare," Zack agreed. "Everyone on board?"

Clare, Micah, Reed, and Zack all nodded their heads. 'Operation Identify' was a go.

CHAPTER EIGHTEEN

R eed Spencer transmitted the video to a secure FBI data dump a few hours later. Tech nerds immediately went to work on it. Clare telephoned her favorite tech and asked her to take the point position.

The first step of the operation was to identify the object outside the window. Was it a lighthouse, as everyone suspected? Step two was to determine the object with greater specificity. If it was a lighthouse, which lighthouse was it? Step three was to identify a location that might feature a view of the object. Step four was duplicating the picture and getting a better read on the area. Step five was to surveil and determine whether a safe breach might be possible. Step six, if all else went smoothly, was to breach and rescue the hostages.

While the FBI was doing forensic work on the video, Winger Wright enjoyed the serenity of his almost beachfront Airbnb. He was in no hurry to resolve the hostage crisis. The ransom broadcast went better than expected. Contributions from like-minded white nationalists bankrolled the operation and then some. He no longer desperately needed capital and could enjoy the equivalent of a vacation at his followers' expense.

God bless America! Winger marveled at the spectacular view of the harbor and lighthouse from his zero-gravity lounge chair on the backyard deck. He enjoyed stringing the Cooper family along, peddling his anti-Semitic, racist rhetoric. Perhaps he'd record and publish another video rant. The last one raised a shitload of money, more than the movement had ever seen. He had little desire to negotiate a hostage release and delighted in his fifteen minutes of fame.

Meanwhile, Josh Cooper was being held in a windowless room, feeling guilty that his next-door neighbor was abducted because of him, but privately comforted by Chip Ellis's presence and words. Chip continued to assure Josh that his family and the police were doing all they could to secure their safe release. Josh's worst moments came when he was separated from Chip, sometimes for hours. *Where did they take him? Will they kill him? Will they bring him back?* Each time, Chip returned, surprisingly cheerful, with a positive attitude, a bright light in a very dark and dismal setting.

"Where were you?" Josh asked when Chip returned.

"They questioned me. Why do I live in Beverly Hills?"

"What's wrong with Beverly Hills?" Josh wondered.

"According to these guys? Too many Jews and Blacks," Chip explained.

"Of course, I forgot for a second who they were. What did you tell them?"

"I told them we moved from out-of-town and didn't know that the city had so many Blacks and Jews."

"Is that true?"

"Is what true?"

"That you didn't know."

"I didn't know. That's true. But I don't care, either. This is America. We all need to get along. This is a melting pot, right?"

"What's a melting pot?"

"Sorry. A melting pot is a community where people of all races, creeds, and colors live together harmoniously."

"Sounds like Beverly Hills."

"It is Beverly Hills, Josh. Guys like Wright can't stomach the concept of all races, creeds, and colors living in harmony. He believes in Christian white supremacy, where white Christians are the dominant race and religion, and everyone else is inferior or subordinate."

"You're a white Christian. Do you agree?"

"Why does that matter?"

"Do all white Christians feel this way?"

"If I'm honest, I guess you could say that all of us are somewhat prejudiced. Are there people you don't like? Certain Arab people? Palestinians, perhaps?"

"No. I don't hate anyone, especially groups of people I don't know. In school, we had a lesson about Dr. Martin Luther King."

"What about him?"

"We should judge people by the content of their character, not by the color of their skin or what religion or ethnic group they belong to."

"Do you believe that?" "Yes. That's what my mom and dad taught us. Don't you?"

"It doesn't matter what I believe. I believe we've got to get out of here."

Josh was slightly annoyed with Mr. Ellis. It was the second time he dodged the question about his own beliefs. Are the terrorists brainwashing him? Josh once watched 'The Manchurian Candidate' with his dad. Was it possible to be brainwashed in such a short period?

"Josh?" "Yes, Mr. Ellis?"

"Are you okay? You're suddenly very quiet."

"Just tired."

"Get some sleep. Hopefully, this will be over soon."

CHAPTER NINETEEN

"Hello?" Clare Gibson answered her private Bureau line.

"Clare? This is Robin Schechter. I've got some news." Schechter was Clare's favorite forensics tech at the DC lab.

"Wow! That was fast, Robin. I appreciate it. What do you have?"

"We've identified the object in the window. As you suspected, it's a lighthouse."

"Wonderful! We thought so, but we couldn't be sure. Now, we've got to narrow it down. How do we do that?"

"Well, lighthouses aren't all that distinctive. Some have unusual characteristics. We've narrowed this one to the Midwest."

"To Michigan?"

"Not yet."

"Timeline?"

"Hard to say. Anything happening on the hostage negotiation front?"

"Things are quiet. We're waiting for the next communication."

"Does Harrelson know about me?"

"Not yet?"

"May I ask why? This is his investigation, right?"

"He pulled it from me, yes."

"Pulled it from you?"

"I'm a woman. Need I say more? One good old boy gets together with another good old boy. Presto! I get bumped off the lead. It's an unfortunate reality at the Bureau."

"Can I get in trouble?"

"I don't see how. Reed Spencer sent you the video. I instructed you to report to me. How does that blow back on you? I'll take the heat. Don't worry about it."

"I've worked with Harrelson before. I much prefer you. He's quite the arrogant prick."

"To say the least. Let's crack this thing, identify the lighthouse, and arrest these racist fools before Harrelson knows what hit him. He'll take the credit. He always does. Things will work out."

"Why do guys like him get away with this crap?"

"As I said, it's a good old boy network, but, hey, look at you and me. Things are slowly changing around here."

"Like molasses."

Clare chuckled. "True, but I look at it this way. If we can rescue a thirteen-year-old Jewish kid, snatched on his bar mitzvah day, a day of celebration, and return him home safely to his mom and dad, who cares about these guys? I get a lot of satisfaction out of doing my job and doing it well."

"Amen, sister."

"Halleluiah!" The two ladies laughed. "Call me when you've narrowed it down."

"Will do." Robin terminated the call.

***

"Hello? Clare? It's Robin. I've got news."

"Hey, Robin. Good news, I hope."

"How about great news?"

"Great news is even better than good news. What's up?"

"After an exhaustive search, we've narrowed it down to two lighthouses in Michigan, Grand Haven or South Haven," Robin advised.

"That's wonderful, Robin! That makes our job a lot easier. Thanks!"

"I wasn't finished. I said great news, remember?"

"Yes. Sorry. I'm just antsy, I guess."

"You're trying to rescue an innocent thirteen-year-old hostage. You're entitled."

"I won't interrupt you again."

"I'm reasonably certain we can eliminate Grand Haven. I just sent you a text—check it out. There are multiple pictures and comparisons in addition to the original clip from the video."

"Let me check—" Clare opened her iPhone screen and scrolled for the text. Several photos were displayed on the screen. "Yes, I see them," she advised, scrolling, pausing, and studying each image.

"The first two photos are Grand Haven. Compare those to the video clip. It's hard to distinguish, subtle, but it is not a match," Robin advised.

"If you say so," Clare replied, not seeing what Robin saw.

"See the metal girding in the video clip? That's a catwalk. Only three lighthouses have one: Grand Haven, South Haven, and Manistee," Robin explained.

"We ruled out Manistee; it's white, not red. Grand Haven has two differences from South Haven. If you look closely, you'll see them. Check out photos three and four, the South Haven Lighthouse. It's over a hundred years old and guards the entrance to the Black River off Lake Michigan.

It was renovated in 2012. It's open to the public. You'll notice that it has that raised catwalk. High waves made it necessary for the lighthouse keeper to have a raised, second-level entrance. In 2011, they recorded an unprecedented twenty-three-foot wave.

"Grand Haven has two differences from South Haven. Grand is red, top to bottom, completely red. South Haven is red, too, but the beacon and cupola are painted black. See that?"

"Yes."

"Also, you will notice a guardhouse at the end of the pier in Grand Haven. In South Haven, the *lighthouse* sits at the end."

"I see that," Clare agreed.

"Let's return to the video clip. It's not easy to see, but the top of the lighthouse is black."

"Yes, I can see the difference."

"Good. If that isn't enough evidence, the view is wide enough to show that the tower is located at the very end of the pier. There are no additional structures behind it like Grand Haven. There is little doubt we are looking at the South Haven Lighthouse."

Clare paused, making sure Robin was finished. "That's wonderful, Robin. Thank you so much. You've made our jobs a lot easier."

"What's the game show where the host says, 'But wait! There's more?"

"Beats me," Clare smiled.

"But wait, there's more!" Robin exclaimed.

"You are the gift that keeps on giving. Lay it on me," Clare chuckled.

"I had my reconnaissance gurus take a close look, observe overhead maps of the area, blow up your video clip, and make a comparison. Based on the clip's view outside the window, this is a residential building, likely a rental or an Airbnb. Using our mapping and surveillance software, the home must be near Water Street, probably on Monroe Blvd, St. Joseph's Street, or Erie Street, with a back or front window facing South Beach and the Lighthouse. Does that narrow things down enough for you?"

"It does, indeed. All we need to do now is get a surveillance team out there and identify the home. Robin, you may have saved lives today."

"Happy to do my part. Anything else you need?"

"I owe you a steak dinner."

"I'm a vegetarian."

"I owe you a dinner at the venue of your choice."

"I will hold you to that. Good luck with the operation. I hope the kid's okay."

"Me too. Talk soon to set up that dinner. Thanks again. Bye."

"Bye, Clare."

Clare hung up the phone and called the FBI's Special Surveillance Group (SSG), Special Weapons and Tactics (SWAT), and Hostage Rescue Team (HRT). She coordinated a mission to identify the home where the hostages were being held and perform a breach and rescue operation.

CHAPTER TWENTY

Five days later, after SSG identified the hostages' probable South Haven location on Erie Street, one block from the Black River entrance to the lighthouse, a highly specialized HRT team with SWAT backup descended on the large Airbnb home. SSG began to focus on the home when an operative noticed that the men living there engaged in no tourist or beach activities. Its occupants subtly guarded the place, and residents drove only trucks or all-terrain vehicles.

After the initial identification, SSG sat on the place for twenty-four hours and identified artillery. There appeared to be makeshift bars on the windows. If the hostages were in South Haven, somewhere near the lighthouse, this had to be the place.

"Wake up, kid. Here's your breakfast," Barrett grumbled, nudging the boy with his foot. Josh Cooper stirred, rolled over on his back, and groaned.

"I'm not hungry. That mush you call cream of wheat is not edible. It makes me sick to my stomach. I'd rather not eat."

"Eat your breakfast, you little shit. I'm responsible if you don't keep your strength up. If you get sick or die, I'll be blamed for it. I'm not going down because a Jew kid failed to follow orders. Eat! That's an order. Or do I have to shove it down your throat?" Barrett threatened.

"I'm eating, see? I'm eating," Josh demonstrated. He shoved an empty spoon in his mouth. The boy looked emaciated.

"I'll be back in twenty to pick up the empty bowl, and it better be empty," Barrett warned. He walked out of the cell and locked the door. Barrett walked out into the dining room. Winger Wright and six other men dressed in combat fatigues were sitting at the dining room table enjoying breakfast consisting of eggs, bacon, sausage, hash browns, toast, coffee, orange juice, waffles, and pancakes. The veritable feast was carried in from a diner down the street. *If Winger wants the kid to stay strong, why doesn't he feed him? There's plenty of food.*

"The kid can't eat that disgusting mush anymore, Winger. Can I bring him some eggs? Maybe some potatoes and orange juice? Or waffles and pancakes? What do you think?"

"You going soft on the boy, Barrett? What's the health of a little Jew boy matter to you? How about you follow orders? I'll decide what the kid eats or doesn't eat," Winger snarled.

"I agree, Winger. Your hostage, your decision, but this kid looks like he's being starved. He's going to get seriously sick or worse. If he can't come to the phone and talk to his dad, they'll give up hope, and we won't get our ransom," Barrett argued.

"You hear this snotnose?" Winger surveyed the others at the table. "He thinks he's smarter than me." Everyone laughed. Barrett was embarrassed but stood his ground.

"I don't believe I'm smarter, Winger. I'm worried about the kid. He's starving, getting scrawny, and I don't think he'll be able to go on much longer."

"Give him some eggs and juice then. We don't want the kid to die, or do we? We got tons of money from the hostage campaign. We might raise more money letting this kid die than we'll get for him as a hostage. Nationalists love a Jewish funeral, especially a kid who hasn't procreated."

Everyone but Barret thought Winger was funny. Barrett was stunned by the group's inhumanity. Jew hatred is one thing. Kidnapping for profit is okay. But starving a kid to death, even a Jewish kid, crossed the line. This was still America, not Nazi Germany. Barrett grabbed a plate and piled on a healthy portion of eggs, potatoes, toast, and bacon. He poured a glass of orange juice into a Styrofoam cup and left the room.

"Did you see that plate? The kid's going soft. Do we have to worry about him?" One of the kidnappers inquired.

"He's okay. He's young, is all. He's done a good job with the boy. Anyone else want to volunteer to do what he's doing?" Wright glanced around the room. "That's what I thought, no takers. Shut the hell up!"

Barrett returned to Josh's room with the plate of food and drink. Josh lay on the floor. His uneaten food lay next to him.

"You win, kid. I scared up some decent food for you. You'll eat bacon in an emergency, right?" he asked, laughing out loud.

Josh turned over, delighted to see a large plate of eggs, bacon, toast, and potatoes. Orange juice was a treat he never expected.

"Thank you so much, sir! I appreciate it. You have no idea!" Josh effused.

"Is what it is. Hopefully, this will be over soon, and you can see your parents."

"Is that what you're hearing? Will this be over soon? I'll be freed?"

"Not sure. I figure it's about time. Eat your breakfast, stop your bellyaching, and stop asking me all these questions," Barrett snarled.

Josh began to chow down his food. The two of them heard a noise outside Josh's barred window.

"What was that?" Barrett wondered.

"I didn't hear anything," Josh lied.

"I heard a noise outside this window," Barrett declared. He went to the window and looked straight out. He turned his head to the right and left, straining to see as far as possible in each direction.

"Do you see anything?" Josh asked.

"Shut up and eat! There's nothing out there. It must have been a raccoon or a rat or something."

Ten highly trained FBI HRT soldiers assembled outside the house. The men and women wore full assault gear, carried M5s, and were gloved and masked. They hustled into position, surrounding the home's exterior, awaiting orders to breach. An HRT operative silently climbed a ladder up to the roof. He dropped a tiny camera down the chimney. Everyone was on hold, awaiting his assessment of the situation inside. The faint sound of a helicopter could be heard in the background, but not inside the house. An army of South Haven cops stood by their squad cars down Erie Street in this tree-lined lake resort neighborhood, awaiting instructions, itching for action, hoping to catch a glimpse of a terrorist kidnapper or two trying to escape HRT.

"Seven men sitting around a table, eating breakfast. I don't see the eighth kidnapper, the boy, or the neighbor," he whispered. "They are not armed. I don't see weapons. Based on previous intel, we're missing the two hostages and one kidnapper. And, of course, we know there are military-grade weapons inside."

"Who's got the floor plan?" The squad leader murmured over his comm.

"I do, boss," came the almost silent response.

"Griggs, can you pinpoint the dining room that Coleman is referring to?"

"Got it, boss."

"Where is the most logical room or rooms to detain the hostages?"

"The rooms to the south of the dining room."

"Infrared?"

"Here, sir."

"Picking up any heat signals, Rogan?"

"Two, sir, in the room directly south of the dining room with the seven men."

"What's your assessment, Coleman?"

"Seems like a good time to breach. Threat reduced from eight men to one on the south side."

"Is there a direct entry point to that south room?"

"Looks to be a small, barred window, sir. According to the blueprints, the siding is wood, blown-in insulation, studs, and drywall. Perhaps a simultaneous breach?"

"Can we get to the window without being detected?"

"Well, sir, with seven of the kidnappers in the dining room, eating, having a good time, the risk of being spotted is limited to the one dude in the south room. What's on your mind?"

"That might be the second hostage. If the two hostages are the only people in that room, I'd like to alert them to our presence and the imminency of breach."

"Stand by," another HRT operative whispered. Seconds felt like minutes.

"This is Kowalski. I'm at the window, sir. One hostage, a kid, held in the room, sir. The room has a heavily reinforced door, which is currently open. I don't see the other hostage. There's a second kid, maybe twenty, twenty-two, holding an AR-15, watching the hostage kid, who I assume is Josh Cooper. The hostage is eating breakfast. They're having a conversation, sir. If we breach the south wall, which seems feasible, we would be inside the cell with direct access to the hostage and in a ready position to take out the guard. He's just a kid with an AR-15."

"Stand by. Does anyone see the other hostage?"

"No, sir."

"What's your assessment?"

"Two possibilities, sir. Hostage two is being held at another location, or he's one of the seven men in the dining room. I don't see any restraints. We have no clear view of everyone in the room.

"Altman? What's your assessment?"

"Based on what I've heard, it seems like a good time to breach. The chances for casualties, especially to the young hostage, are highly minimized."

"Get me six mean, tough SWAT operatives. I want eight men outside the south room and eight more at the front entrance to the living and dining rooms. Prepare to breach on my command. The kid is the priority. Confirm?"

"Ten-four, sir," everyone whispered.

HRT operatives selected SWAT agents and armed them. Two teams quickly assembled at two locations, awaiting breach orders from the squad leader.

"Five, four, three, two, one. Go! Go! Go!"

Winger Wright stood at the table. The others looked at him like he was nuts.

"You hear that?" He looked up to the sky. "Is that a helicopter?"

"I don't hear anything, boss. Do you, Edgar?"

"Nothing, Carl."

"Stay put. I'll be right back," Winger advised.

As Winger Wright walked toward the east hallway, sixteen law enforcement professionals, ten skilled HRT operatives, and six SWAT team members stormed the home on two sides. The terrorists were caught flat-footed. On the south side, Josh Cooper and his captor were terrified—eggs, toast, bacon, and potatoes flew everywhere as the south wall caved in and law enforcement personnel rushed into the cell. Josh vomited on the floor. Barrett raised his AR-15. Before he could fire a shot, he was put down by an HRT marksman.

On the north side, in the dining room, stunned kidnappers reached for their weapons and were gunned down in the process. Only one kidnapper survived the assault. The man known as Edgar raised his arms and surrendered the minute the room was breached. When the assault was over, seven kidnappers lay dead. HRT secured the hostage. Josh was pale, emaciated, and probably in shock, with vomit covering the front of his body. However, to the delight of HRT operatives and South Haven police officers, the boy did not have a mark on him.

"What's your name, son?" an operative inquired.

"Joshua Cooper, sir."

"Are you hurt?"

"I don't think so."

"Let's see if we can get you cleaned up. I might have some military fatigues for you to wear. Would you like that?"

"Cool."

"You sure you're okay?"

"I'm terrified. I can't catch my breath, but I'm not hurt."

"I think you're the bravest young man I've ever met. Let's find those clothes. We'll get you squared away and back home to your parents."

Josh calmed a bit. "Thanks."

Operatives searched the house and found Chip Ellis, alive and unharmed, in a bathroom down the east hallway. He was handcuffed to a pipe under the sink.

"Are you okay, sir?"

"Considering the circumstances, I'm in pretty good shape. I'm thrilled to see you guys. Can you get these things off me?"

"Right away." an operative removed his handcuffs.

"Your name, sir?"

"Chip Ellis."

Ellis appeared to be in good physical shape. He was relieved to be rescued and gratified that he was nowhere near the dining room or the makeshift prison cell at the time of the breach. However, there was one fly in the ointment. The cops identified eight kidnappers. Only seven were accounted for. Facial recognition identified the six deceased kidnappers. All had extensive criminal records, including hate crimes. None matched the vague description of Winger Wright. Somehow, the ringleader escaped in the chaotic atmosphere of the explosive breach. In the aftermath of a successful operation, after performing multiple re-enactments and full reconstruction training sessions of the events of the morning breach, no one could figure it out.

CHAPTER TWENTY-ONE

Josh Cooper was flown home in an HRT tactical aviation helicopter, a Sikorsky UH-60 Black Hawk. As traumatized as the boy was, he called the flight the "coolest thing ever."

Clare Gibson, Micah Love, Zachary Blake, and Dan Harrelson traveled to Rich and Gail Cooper's home. They had marvelous news. Harrelson was livid with Gibson for planning and greenlighting the rescue operation behind his back. He was appeased when Clare allowed him to take all the credit.

Harrelson initially balked at including Blake and Love in the notification to the Coopers. Clare held firm—the two men were heading to Rich and Gail's home. Harrelson again backed off.

Rich Cooper answered the door. Harrelson spoke for the group.

"Mr. Cooper, I'm not certain we've met. I'm Special Agent in Charge, Daniel Harrelson."

"How do you do, sir?" He looked back and forth at the four people at his door. They were beaming. "What's up? Any news?"

"Great news, Mr. Cooper. We've located your son. Even better, we implemented an operation and rescued Josh from the kidnappers. He's fine. A bit malnourished, terrified, he's been through a horrible ordeal, but he was not hurt by the kidnappers or in the rescue operation."

Rich Cooper fell to his knees. "Oh, thank God! Gail!" he screamed. He began to sob. His wife came running to the door. She saw the four people and her husband. Rich was kneeling and crying. She assumed the worst.

"Oh, my God, no!" she cried.

Rich rose to his feet and embraced his wife. "No, honey! I'm so sorry! Josh has been rescued! Do you hear me? He's been rescued! He's fine. These are tears of joy!" he explained.

Gail trembled with shock and gratitude. "Rescued? Is he hurt in any way? Do you promise?"

"Yes, sweetheart, I promise. I'm so sorry that I scared you."

"Thank God! My prayers have been answered. Are you sure? Did you talk to him?" Gail cried, clinging to her husband.

"We have not talked to him yet, Mrs. Cooper. He's being flown home in an FBI helicopter. We can try calling the copter if you'd like," Clare offered.

"That would be wonderful," Gail sniffed.

"We'd like that very much," Rich agreed.

"Hang on." Clare pulled out her phone and called an operations center. Someone replied.

"Yes, this is special agent Clare Gibson. Yes, on the Cooper rescue. Yes. Well, thank you. It was a team effort. Yes, thanks." The operator congratulated Gibson for coordinating a successful operation. Harrelson may have taken credit, but every trained FBI agent knew it was *Gibson's* operation.

"Can you put me in touch with the Sikorsky flying Joshua Cooper home?" Clare waited. She nodded and gestured 'thumbs up.' The operator could communicate with the copter. A few seconds ticked by, and Clare spoke again.

"Yes, this is Agent Gibson. To whom am I speaking? Thank you, Agent Carlson. I appreciate it. Is Josh Cooper in any shape to talk to his parents on the telephone? They are excited to speak to him," Clare requested, nodding again. "Great! I'll put the phone on speaker."

Clare pressed a button. A loud noise was heard in the background: helicopter blades. Then, at long last, the quiet voice of a thirteen-year-old boy.

"Mom? Dad? It's Josh."

"Joshie! My baby! Are you alright? Did they hurt you?" Gail cried.

"Hi, son. I love you. How are you doing?" Rich needed to know.

"I'm exhausted and hungry, but I'm okay. These guys were disgusting, but they didn't hurt me."

"We're so glad for that, honey. When are you coming home?" Gail wondered.

"I'm not sure."

"Ask Agent Carlson," Clare intervened.

"Excuse me, sir? Do you know what time we arrive?" Josh inquired.

"We'll be landing in Troy about one o'clock. A short ride to Beverly Hills, and your boy will be home," Carlson responded.

"What's the address of the place in Troy? We'll meet you there." Gail insisted, desperate to see her son.

"My orders are to conduct a short debriefing. Might take a half-hour to an hour or so," Carlson advised.

"Josh, are you up to answering some questions when you get to Troy?" Gibson asked.

"Yes, as long as they have some food there," Josh chuckled.

"I'll bring you some Dunkin Donuts cinnamon rolls, your favorite. Would you like that?" Gail offered.

"That would be wonderful, Mom. Thanks."

"Oh, Joshie, I'm so glad you're okay, safe, and coming home!" Gail sobbed.

"Please don't call me 'Joshie' in front of these people, Mom. And stop crying. I'm fine." Everyone laughed.

"Gail? I promise. He's doing just fine. A little skinnier than usual."

"Who's this?"

"Chip."

"Chip! Thank God, Chip! I almost forgot. How are you?"

"We're both doing well. We'll be home soon."

"Thanks for watching over Josh, Chip. I feel like an idiot for saying thanks for being there, but thanks for being there," Rich remarked.

"I understand. Josh is a brave, strong kid. He didn't need me. He helped me cope more than I helped him."

"That's not true. Mr. Ellis was terrific! I don't know how I would have made it without him," Josh exclaimed.

"From the bottom of our hearts, Chip, thank you so much!"

"You're welcome, Gail. Like I said. I didn't do much. Would you guys let Tricia know that I'm okay? We'll be home soon."

"That was our next stop. Wait, let me run next door and see if she's there," Clare offered.

"I'll go," Rich suggested. He left the house and quickly returned with an anxious Tricia Ellis.

"Chip?"

"Hey, babe. How're you doing?"

"Oh, Chip! I'm fine. How are *you*? What did those scumbags do to you?"

"I'm fine, sweetheart. Josh and I are getting a neat military helicopter ride. This is the way to travel."

"I'm so glad this nightmare is over. Are you sure you're okay?"

"Yes, sweetheart. According to Agent Carlson, we'll soon be landing in Troy."

"Troy?"

"We'll fill you in, Tricia. We're going to meet the copter. Want to come?"

"You bet!" Tricia cheered.

"We're going to sign off," Carlson indicated. "Say so long and see you soon to your mom and dad, young man."

"So long, guys. See you soon."

"See you all soon," Chip echoed.

"Bye," everyone crowed.

"Thank you. From the bottom of our hearts, thank you!" Gail effused, embracing Clare Gibson. Harrelson bristled but said nothing.

"Like I said, Gail, it was a team effort," Clare advised, nodding to the boss.

"We'd like to invite the whole team to dinner one of these days."

"Just doing our jobs, ma'am," Clare insisted.

"Nonetheless, Agent Gibson, I won't take no for an answer."

"I'll see what I can arrange," Harrelson interrupted.

"Thank you, sir . . . what did you say your name was again?"

"Dan Harrelson, ma'am. Special agent in charge."

"I thought Agent Gibson was in charge."

"She handled the tactical, ma'am. I'm the agent in charge, her boss, so to speak."

"Well, thank you, too, I guess."

Clare, Micah, and Zack snickered under their breath.

Clare assembled a team of agents and vehicles, and everyone took off for the Troy airstrip. The trip took less than fifteen minutes from Beverly Hills. Fifteen more minutes passed, and a helicopter was heard in the distance. The copter landed. Carlson, Chip Ellis, and Josh Cooper alighted.

Gail was overjoyed and horrified at the sight of her son. He looked emaciated. Clare recommended a short visit to nearby William Beaumont Hospital in Royal Oak. Rich and Gail readily agreed. Chip Ellis appeared no worse for wear, which Clare noted. *Why would the terrorists treat a well-built man, the more significant threat, better than this young boy? Religious differences?* Tricia didn't notice the difference. She was pleased to welcome her husband home.

CHAPTER TWENTY-TWO

Emergency Room doctors at Beaumont Hospital in Royal Oak were concerned about Josh's condition. Much to the boy's and his parents' dismay, they decided to admit him. Doctors called in an RDN or registered dietitian nutritionist and notified Josh's pediatrician. The medical team worked up a protocol to treat what was essentially a diagnosis of acute starvation.

Starvation can have devastating effects on the body. The doctor and RDN were concerned that Josh might have difficulty healing or fighting off infections. They decided to hook the boy to a catheter, providing a cocktail of electrolyte nourishment, vitamins, minerals, and an appetite stimulant, in addition to a healthy dose of hospital food.

The boy maintained his sense of humor, commenting that the food served by the white nationalists was better than his hospital food. At his request and with permission from the nutritionist, Gail brought him a quart of his favorite ice cream, Baskin-Robbins Pralines and Cream.

Josh responded well to treatment. After a few days, doctors were confident the boy would fully recover.

***

Meanwhile, the FBI was baffled by the disappearance of the nationalist ringleader, the infamous Winger Wright. Wright was quite different from most of his ilk—a nationalist with a brain. Aside from his technical skills, Wright did a masterful job concealing his identity. The feds had only his online profile, which contained no physical description or clues about his identity.

FBI agents were convinced that Wright was a home-grown terrorist. They decided to develop a profile, guesstimating his age, working backward, hoping to locate a racist, homophobic, or anti-Semitic father or elderly relative. They also interrogated and searched for known associates of Edgar Thomas, the only surviving member of the kidnapping team.

Thomas had a long record, a complex history of minor crimes that developed into more serious offenses, including armed robbery, simple assault, assault with a deadly weapon, assault with intent to kill, and a series of hate crimes, particularly against people of color. He had no recorded history of crimes against the city's Jewish population.

Clare Gibson was chosen to lead the Thomas interrogation. Thomas was held at the Federal Correctional Institution in Milan, the closest federal prison to Detroit. He had not yet been officially charged with a crime in the kidnapping of Josh Cooper and Chip Ellis. The unit's focus was to get a lead on the identity and whereabouts of Winger Wright.

After a short initial interrogation, Thomas demanded a lawyer. He placed a telephone call, and a high profile, flamboyant, openly defiant lawyer named Ivan Lynch appeared at the prison seeking an audience with Edgar Thomas. Since the FBI could not identify any gainful employment for Mr. Thomas, agents wondered how he could secure expensive, high-profile legal talent. Was Lynch a white nationalist, too?

After a lengthy private meeting with his client, Lynch opened the prison conference room door and demanded to speak with the agent in charge. Clare Gibson entered the conference room and introduced herself.

"What can I do for you, Mr. Lynch?"

"Agent Gibson, it's more what I can do for you."

"Oh? How do you figure?"

"My client would like to negotiate."

"The Federal Bureau of Investigation does not negotiate with terrorists."

"My client is hardly a terrorist. In fact, given his circumstances, you could probably make a case that he was a victim of terrorists," Lynch argued.

"Have you reviewed your client's record? Are you a lawyer or a comedian?" Gibson snarled.

"Funny, Agent. Yes, I've seen his record. I've been his attorney for a long time. Check me out. You will see that I have represented many of his ilk. White nationalists have been very good to me. I've made a nice living off these guys."

"I'm sure your mother is very proud."

"Everyone is entitled to representation, Agent. Someone's got to do it. Why not make some money in the process?"

"Can we get to the point, please? I'll need to shower after this one. What's the negotiation you seek? What do you want, and what do you bring to the table?"

"Edgar is a low-level cog in a larger machine. The grand poohbah of white nationalist terrorism in this area is a man known only as Winger Wright."

"Go on—" Clare responded, intrigued.

"What if my client could deliver Winger Wright? Would you be interested?"

"Depends on the ask."

"Full immunity from prosecution."

"Full immunity? You've got to be kidding. We've got your client dead to rights on kidnapping and Felony Murder."

"Felony murder? How do you figure? The hostages were rescued alive. No one died at the temple."

"Seven people were killed in the South Haven raid. Kidnapping is a felony. Death during the commission of a felony is Felony Murder. Crim law 101, Counselor."

"The deaths of a bunch of terrorists in an FBI raid? Seriously? I guess I am wasting your time. That's a trumped-up charge."

"Trumped-up or not, he's going to be charged with Kidnapping and Felony Murder."

Someone knocked on a blacked-out window behind Agent Gibson.

"I'll be right back," she promised.

"We'll be here."

Clare walked out of the conference room and into an adjoining room. Dan Harrelson sat at the head of a small table. US Attorney George Brinkman sat on the opposite side. A conference phone sat in the middle of the table.

"Dan."

"Clare."

"What do you guys think?" Clare inquired, holding her breath for the answer.

"You can't dismiss immunity without at least exploring the proffer," Brinkman opined.

"Immunity is a bridge too far for a murderer, kidnapper, and domestic terrorist."

"Perhaps, but we must explore all options. The FBI wants Winger Wright," Harrelson advised.

"Do you speak only for yourself, or does this go higher?" Clare wondered.

"Higher, Agent Gibson." A voice emerged from the conference phone in the middle of the table. Clare recognized the voice. *It can't be.*

"To whom am I speaking?" Clare asked.

"This is Director Wray, Agent."

"Sir, it's an honor."

"You've done stellar work on this case, Gibson. Harrelson has kept me informed. He said good things about you."

Clare was dubious but was not about to get into a pissing contest with the director of the FBI. "Thank you, sir." She looked to Harrelson. "Thank you, Dan. I appreciate the kind words. Immunity, sir? For a domestic terrorist with a long record of hate crimes and violence? Edgar Thomas is a clear and present danger to the United States. With him in federal prison for life, we may have wiped out an entire clan of Patriotic Stormtroopers."

"I'm not certain I disagree, Agent Gibson. However, he may be a low-level grunt," Director Wray postulated.

"His record suggests otherwise, sir."

"May I call you Clare?"

"Absolutely."

"I understand, Clare, but we don't know where he fits on the pyramid. If he's low-level trash, it might be worth the trade. We must explore the option and see if the proffer supports the ask. If he can't deliver Wright, no harm, no foul."

"Understood."

"You've done your part, Clare. It's time for the US Attorney and the Justice Department to step in and handle formal negotiations. Are you on board with that, George?" The Director addressed the U.S. Attorney.

"I'm looking forward to the challenge, Director. Lynch is quite the character. We should probably offer *him* immunity. I'll bet he knows where all the bodies are buried," Brinkman retorted.

"Funny. Unfortunately, there's this little concept called attorney-client privilege. Here's another question: Do we first want to discuss this with the Cooper and Ellis families?" Clare inquired.

"Discuss and obtain their approval? I don't think so, Agent Gibson," Brinkman responded. "Let them know what we're doing? Absolutely."

"I'll defer to you, gentlemen. For the record, though, there is a lot of law enforcement and legal talent in this room, but I am opposed to negotiating a plea with this guy," Clare opined.

"Duly noted, Clare," Director Wray acknowledged. "George, you're up. Get me Winger Wright!"

"I'll do my best, sir."

CHAPTER TWENTY-THREE

"What's the offer?"

"What's the proffer?"

Negotiations for a plea deal were off to a bad start. Neither side wanted to make the first move.

"If your client offers something that directly or indirectly leads to the identification and arrest of Winger Wright, we will offer him a reduced sentence," Brinkman advised.

"That's a non-starter. If he becomes a whistle-blower in this case, his life is in danger, either in prison or out. We want full immunity, relocation, and witness protection. Otherwise, no deal," Lynch countered.

"As I indicated, any offer depends on the information and whether it leads to the arrest of Winger Wright."

"And if it does? Full immunity? Witness protection?" Lynch inquired.

"Possibly."

"Not possibly—*absolutely*, and in writing."

"He remains in custody until we get a conviction. No conviction, no immunity."

"That's not acceptable."

"Then, I'm out of here," Brinkman replied, rising to leave.

"Hold on a damn second," Edgar Thomas pleaded, speaking for the first time.

"Yes, Mr. Thomas?" Brinkman asked.

"Here's the problem," Lynch intervened. "If he gives you information that leads to the arrest of Wright, and you fail to convict, my client will most assuredly be executed in prison. Getting a conviction is *your* problem, not my client's problem. We can live with him being in custody until he testifies, but afterward, he must get immunity and witness protection."

"How about a hybrid?"

"Hybrid?"

"He must do time. In my view, given the hate crime enhancement, he must do at least five years. Assuming we capture Wright and put him on trial, your client stays in custody here, under guard, until he testifies. After his testimony, He'll do time under an alias, at a prison of our choosing, in a state or country far from Michigan. The United States Marshals Service will protect Edgar while he serves his sentence. Whether Wright is convicted or not, Edgar will go into witness protection. If Edgar behaves himself and ends his racist, homophobic, and anti-Semitic ways, he'll remain free. One slip-up, one racist text, email, or phone call; if he attends a nationalist rally or uses a nationalist bathroom, he'll do the full sentence. How does that sound if I can sell that to the AG and the Justice Department?"

"I don't think so, George. I'll need this—" Lynch began his counter.

"Hold on, just a damned minute!" Thomas interrupted. "You'll put that offer in writing?"

"As soon as we get it approved by the Justice Department."

"And I'll have full protection and a new identity in prison and after my release?"

"That's the offer."

"Will my attorney know my new identity and in which prison I do my time?"

"Yes, that's how it usually works. Prisoners need access to their attorneys," Brinkman explained.

"I'd like to talk to you without my lawyer present," Edgar declared.

"Absolutely not!" Lynch screeched. "What's the matter with you, Edgar? You can't trust these guys. You need me."

"I know I need you, sir. But I have some questions you can't hear," Edgar pleaded.

"This is highly irregular. I do not recommend this, Edgar," Lynch countered.

"I understand how you feel," he acknowledged, turning to Brinkman. "Mr. Brinkman, sir, how do I do this?"

"You would have to fire Mr. Lynch and represent yourself. You've requested counsel. The only way to proceed without counsel is to renounce your declaration, terminate Mr. Lynch, who has done a good job for you, and proceed pro se."

"Pro se?"

"Without a lawyer."

"I see. Yes, that's what I want to do."

"Edgar!" Lynch argued. He was wounded.

"That's what I want to do. Mr. Lynch, you are fired, sir," Edgar decided.

"You sure about this, Mr. Thomas? No one is forcing you to do this."

"I understand. I have my reasons, which I will explain once he's gone." Edgar advised, nodding at Lynch.

Lynch rose. "It's your funeral, Edgar. I'm out of here," he bristled.

"I would rather you stick around. I might want to rehire you after I meet with Mr. Brinkman," Edgar pleaded.

"It doesn't work that way, bud. Get another lawyer. I'm through with you. Nobody fires Ivan Lynch!" Lynch snapped. He rose and stormed out of the conference room.

"Let's get your declaration in writing, witnessed, and then we can continue our conversation," Brinkman advised.

"Thank you, sir. Looking forward to it," Edgar replied.

Thomas and Lynch prepared and executed the paperwork. After the signing ceremony, Lynch stomped out of the building, and the meeting continued.

"What's on your mind, Mr. Thomas?"

"Is Lynch gone? He's not in the other room listening or watching?" Edgar wondered.

"He's gone, sir. You have my word. Now, what can I do for you? What couldn't you discuss in front of your attorney?"

"I've never met Ivan Lynch before in my life! I don't know the guy. Someone sent him here."

"That's a fair presumption. What difference does it make? The offer still stands. Lynch did a good job for you."

"Yes, but if he knows where and who I am, it stands to reason that whoever hired him will know, too. Right?"

Brinkman now appreciated Thomas' problem. "Well, technically, no, because you have attorney-client privilege with Lynch. The guy who hires him does not. Lynch cannot ethically disclose your confidences to anyone, including the guy who hired him," Brinkman explained.

"You think Lynch is ethical and will protect me from his money source? The guy who pays him these large fees?"

"No, sir, I do not, but that is what the law requires."

"I understand that. What I know will send Winger Wright to prison for life. Winger knows that, too. So does the person who hired Lynch. I'm dead if I negotiate this deal with Lynch as my lawyer, no matter what kind of protection you offer.

"I'll be murdered in prison before I ever testify under oath."

"I see your point. So, what do you want to do?"

"I want the deal. I'll give you Wright. You give me five years under an alias, with protection and a new identity. I go into the WITSEC protection program when I'm released. I am rehabilitated, Mr. Brinkman. I will never again participate in white nationalist causes. I am willing to pay for my crimes. Where do I sign?"

"I have to get the deal approved. I don't know whether Lynch leaving and you going forward without counsel will affect the outcome, but I will explain your predicament to my superiors. By the way, off the record, I think you're doing the right thing. You're a smart man."

"A smart man wouldn't be in this mess. I'm smart enough to know that a free lawyer owes his allegiance to someone other than his client."

"Let's get this approved and in writing, and we'll continue our conversation sometime soon. In the meantime, we'll get you full-time protection."

"Thanks."

CHAPTER TWENTY-FOUR

Josh Cooper was released from the hospital and about to return home. Gail and Rich picked him up at Beaumont Hospital, where the nursing staff and the nutritionists cheered his release and departure. Considering his captivity was followed by this lengthy hospital stay, Josh was about to enjoy his first real moments of freedom since the morning he was kidnapped.

When they arrived home, Josh was treated to a hero's celebration. Many of his friends and family were present. The Ellis family from next door, Zack, Micah, Clare, and a few law enforcement types rounded out the guest list. Everyone had a great time. Zack sent in a tray from a local deli. The treatment in the hospital worked wonders. Josh looked better, felt better, and enjoyed healthy portions of everything on the tray.

When the party ended, Clare, Micah, and Zack asked if they could chat with Josh. Gail hesitated. Her son just returned home, was a traumatized youngster, and needed time to heal. But Rich and Zack argued that a conversation was necessary while things were fresh in the boy's mind. Gail reluctantly agreed, so long as it was okay with Josh. The boy readily agreed to discuss his memories of captivity.

"How about this little get-together, Josh?" Zack cheered. "You've got amazing parents."

"I sure do. I had fun and ate like a pig."

Zack admired his outlook following the disruption of his bar mitzvah. The party never happened.

"We'd like to chat about your time in captivity, Josh, if that's okay. We need to ask you some things while they are still fresh in your mind," Clare explained.

"I'd like to forget the whole thing," Josh confessed.

"Understood. We won't be too long. Most of your kidnappers aren't around anymore, so that's a good thing. Can you talk about your captors? Did they use names? Do you remember what any of them looked like?" Clare wondered.

"We wore masks the whole time. It was almost impossible to see. I'd recognize voices if I heard them again. Maybe someone's size or shape."

"How about names?"

"There was a Carl. A guy named Winger was the leader. There was Edgar and someone named . . . well . . . they talked about someone named Sinister or something like that. That's all I can remember."

"Was this Sinister person at the hideout or someplace else?" Clare asked.

"I don't think he was there. I'm trying to remember . . . he was online! That's right! He wanted to speak to this Winger guy on the phone, but they communicated online."

"And you would remember voices if you heard them again?"

"I think so."

"Did anyone sound familiar?"

"No . . . well . . . yes, but it makes no sense."

"What makes no sense, honey?" Gail wanted to know.

"Who Winger sounded like."

"Who did he sound like?" Zack interrupted.

"It's not possible. I probably made this up in my mind. I mean, he was so helpful, so supportive. It couldn't be."

"What couldn't be, Josh? Tell us, please. It may be nothing, but it may also be essential."

"The Winger guy had a gruffer, deeper voice, but he sounded like Mr. Ellis."

"Chip?" Rich was astounded.

"But Chip was kidnapped, too," Gail remarked.

"Was he?" Zack speculated. "We know he disappeared with Josh, but do we know he was kidnapped? What if he was one of the kidnappers?"

"That's not possible," Rich argued. "He's been our neighbor for years. He's a good friend. It's just not possible. Josh's mind is playing tricks on him. He heard Chip's voice every day in captivity. Naturally, Josh associates that voice with bad things. But Chip being Winger Wright? No way!"

"Dad, I understand what you are saying. I agree. I like Mr. Ellis. He saved me from going nuts in that place. But I know Mr. Ellis's voice. I remember Mr. Ellis's voice. I remember Winger's voice, too. They are different voices that sound alike. That's all I'm saying. You asked what I remembered. That's what I remembered," Josh insisted, turning back to Clare.

"Thanks, Josh. That's what I wanted from you, your memories of those days," Clare replied. "Were you able to tell what size Winger was? Was he built like Mr. Ellis?"

Josh was silent. He considered the question for a long time. "He was a big guy, but I can't say he was built like Mr. Ellis. I always had a canvas back over my head. I can't recall, sorry."

"That's okay, Josh. I only want what you remember."

"The guy who took care of me was just a kid. I saw his face. I can describe him if it helps. His name was Garrett. Did I mention him before? Did you catch him? He's a little guy, not much bigger than me. I remember. He's just a kid, eighteen, nineteen maybe, probably not much older than me. He wasn't too bad. He tried to get them to treat me better. Is he . . . still alive?"

"I'm afraid not, Josh. Sorry."

"That's okay, I guess. Being better than evil doesn't make you a good guy."

"Are you sure you're only thirteen?" Zack asked.

"Truer words were never spoken. Anything else you want to add, Josh?" Clare inquired.

"I'm tired," Josh retorted.

"That's it—up to bed or over to the couch. Mom's orders," Gail demanded.

***

"So, what do you think?" Clare asked.

"About what?" Micah replied.

"About Chip Ellis," Clare continued.

"We're the only ones who can be objective about this thing. No one saw who abducted Josh and Chip. It is certainly possible that Chip is the kidnapper," Zack decided. "It would make Rich a terrible judge of character, but it *is* possible."

"Furthermore, it fits, makes sense, or however you want to say it. Chip goes into that bathroom with Josh at the precise time the bomb detonates. Rather convenient, wouldn't you say?" Micah speculated.

"Has anyone checked his background? Where's he from? What's his family history? When did he move to Detroit? Does he have a record?" Zack wanted to cross-examine the man.

"I'm not sure, but we'll do a deep background on him now. You can count on that," Clare promised.

"If Chip Ellis is a white nationalist domestic terrorist, living in a mixed neighborhood, next door to a Jewish family, how is anyone safe in America?" Micah wondered.

"That is the question of the decade, Micah," Zack sighed.

CHAPTER TWENTY-FIVE

Edgar Thomas negotiated his immunity deal. The Sixth Amendment to the United States Constitution guarantees a criminal defendant the right to counsel. While Edgar waived his right to an attorney before negotiating the immunity and plea deal, Clare decided to have a judge appoint counsel to review the plea agreement. The lawyer would also explain Edgar's constitutional rights, assure that Edgar was of sound mind, and execute the agreement as defense counsel. Brandon Griggs was pleased to accept the appointment. He received a hefty fee for doing almost nothing.

The deal, as expected, required Edgar to plead guilty to aiding and abetting a kidnapping. He was quietly sentenced, after hours, by Federal District Court Judge Jody Kaufman. The hearing was on the record, but the transcript was sealed. Following the hearing, Edgar was transported by the U.S. Marshals Service to the Detroit office of the FBI for a formal interrogation in which nothing he said could be used against him in a court of law. Clare Gibson handled the interrogation. Dan Harrelson watched and listened in an adjoining room.

"This is a formal interrogation of Edgar Thomas, pursuant to an agreement reached by the US District Attorney's office, the FBI, Mr. Thomas, and his court-appointed counsel, Brandon Griggs. Mr. Thomas was initially charged with Felony Kidnapping and Felony Murder. He has pleaded guilty to the lesser charge of aiding and abetting kidnapping, also a felony.

"Under the terms of the negotiated agreement, Mr. Thomas has been sentenced to serve no less than five years in federal prison. Because of the sensitive nature of this plea, particularly the potential danger to Mr. Thomas, he will serve his sentence under protection at an undisclosed location. His assumed name will be known only to the United States Marshals Service. This is an ongoing investigation. At least one dangerous criminal is still at large. We must take all reasonable precautions.

"Upon his release, Mr. Thomas will go into the Witness Security Program, or WITSEC, a witness protection program, codified by 18 US Code Section 3521, administered by the Marshals Service, designed to protect threatened witnesses from great bodily harm. Mr. Griggs and Mr. Thomas are present. Mr. Thomas is under oath. Gentlemen, have I correctly stated the formal agreement?"

"You have," Griggs agreed.

"Do I have your permission to proceed, Mr. Griggs?"

"You do," Griggs assented.

"Thank you." Clare turned to Edgar. "Mr. Thomas, I direct your attention to the document before you. Do you recognize it, sir?"

"Yes, it's the plea and WITSEC agreement."

"Please refer to the last page. Is that your signature, sir?"

Edgar flipped the pages until he located his signature. "Yes," he replied.

"Has anyone coerced or threatened you into signing this agreement?"

"No, it was my idea."

"And negotiated and agreed upon by your counsel?"

Edgar was confused. He negotiated this himself. He looked at Griggs, who was nodding vigorously.

"Yes," Edgar finally stated.

"Were you part of a group of men who bombed a West Bloomfield Jewish temple?"

Edgar looked at Griggs, who nodded. "Yes."

"That group was known as the Patriotic Storm Troopers, correct?"

"Yes."

"The stated purpose of the group is the perpetuation of the white race and the extermination of people of color and people of faiths other than the Christian faith. Is that correct?"

"Yes."

"One of which is the Jewish faith?"

"Correct."

"The leader of this group is a man known as Winger Wright?"

"Yes."

"Do you know of any other name for Mr. Wright?"

"No."

"How long have you known him?"

"About five years."

"Have you witnessed or participated in other crimes perpetrated by the Patriotic Storm Troopers or Mr. Wright?"

"I must object to the question and instruct my client not to answer," Griggs interrupted.

"Why? He has immunity."

"Only for the stated crimes against the temple," Griggs concluded.

"Sorry, right you are," Clare agreed. Griggs was more intelligent and a better lawyer than she anticipated.

The questions and answers droned on. Clare took Edgar through the planning and implementation of the West Bloomfield bombing. Edgar described the kidnapping of Josh Cooper and the subsequent escape to the South Haven hideout in detail.

"Did you also kidnap a man named Chip Ellis?"

"No."

"Do you know anyone named Chip Ellis?"

"No."

"So, you are testifying, under oath, by immunity agreement, that there was only one kidnap victim?"

"Yes, the Jew boy."

"Josh Cooper?"

"Yes, ma'am."

"I'd like to show you three photographs." Clare slid the photographs across the table to Edgar. He took the photos in his hands and studied them.

"Could you please identify the individual in each photograph?"

Edgar flipped through the photos, kept one, and tossed two back to Clare. "I don't know the people in these photographs."

"What about the person in the third photo? The one you are holding in your hand?"

"That's Winger Wright."

"This photograph was retrieved after a search warrant was executed at Chip Ellis's Beverly Hills home. According to Mr. Ellis, his wife, and several other people, the person in the photograph is Chip Ellis, not Winger Wright. What do you say?"

"If that is a photo of Chip Ellis, I say that Winger Wright and Chip Ellis are the same person."

"You're certain about that?"

"No doubt about it."

***

The following day, Edgar Thomas was off to an unknown prison under an anonymous alias. Based on voice identification provided by Josh Cooper and photo identification by Edgar Thomas, Clare Gibson secured and executed an arrest warrant for Chip Ellis. Rich and Gail Cooper refused to believe their long-time neighbor was the anti-Semitic predator who kidnapped Josh. They were grateful to Chip for holding it together and caring for Josh while both were held captive.

They asked Micah Love to investigate and develop evidence that might exonerate Chip. Perhaps Micah could develop additional suspects, the very definition of reasonable doubt. They also requested that Zachary Blake represent their friend Chip. They decided Chip was innocent until proven guilty—they wanted the best of the best to represent him. If evidence demonstrated his guilt, having Zack Blake represent him would eliminate all doubt that Chip Ellis and Winger Wright were the same person.

Zachary Blake was not keen on the idea. The thought of representing a possible anti-Semite terrorist kidnapper made his skin crawl. All criminal defendants are entitled to competent counsel, but not all are entitled to the King of Justice. The evidence demonstrated that Chip Ellis was Winger Wright. While proving Ellis' guilt was George Brinkman's job, Zack was uncomfortable being forced, by friendship and loyalty, to defend a man he believed was guilty of heinous crimes against his people. Given the terrible ordeal that Rich, Gail, and Josh Cooper recently endured, he couldn't say no when Rich insisted that he take the case.

The first step was to meet with his client and try to arrange a release on his own recognizance or bail. Chip had a squeaky-clean record, so ROR was possible, and reasonable bail was likely. Zack traveled to Milan to meet with Chip at the prison. He checked in at the visitors' desk and flashed his bar card.

The officer in charge recognized Zack's name and face. He registered shock that the great Zachary Blake would take on a client as guilty and evil as Winger Wright/Chip Ellis. Zack left his belongings in a locker. After he was thoroughly searched, an officer appeared from the bowels of the prison to escort Zack to a conference room. He was told to wait while officers retrieved his client and brought him to the visitors' section.

A short while later, doors clanged, chains rattled, and a third officer led Chip Ellis into the conference room. He wore an orange prison jumpsuit.

"Chip," Zack grumbled.

"Zack," Chip murmured.

"How are they treating you?"

"As someone who just spent weeks in terrorist captivity, I guess it's not too bad," Chip chided.

"Let's talk about that, shall we?"

"Sure."

"Edgar Thomas positively identified you—"

"Who's Edgar Thomas? I do not know that name."

"Edgar is the lone survivor of Josh's kidnapping," Zack advised.

"And mine," Chip corrected. "I don't recall an Edgar."

"Edgar picked your photo from an array. He positively identified you as Winger Wright."

"Of course, he did. I'll bet he got a sweetheart deal for doing so."

"That's not our business. A positive ID from Edgar and a voice identification from the victim might be enough to convict."

"Might, might not."

"True."

"So, how do we prevent the might and get them to the might not?"

"We challenge the identification and present you as a model citizen who has never been in trouble with the law. You have no prior criminal history, do you?"

"None whatsoever."

"Why would a white supremacist move to, of all places, Beverly Hills?"

"Beats me. Why would he?"

Zack slid a piece of paper across to his new client. "Do a family tree for me. Where do your ancestors come from? How far back does the Ellis family go? Your family comes from what country? When did the first Ellis arrive in the US? What did your great-grandfather, grandfather, and father do for a living? Has any of them ever been in trouble with the law? Does anyone in your family have a history of anti-Semitic behavior? Has anyone contributed to anti-Semitic causes or activities? We need this on the Ellis side of the family and your mother's side."

"I'll have my mom work something up."

"Did anyone attend anti-Jewish rallies?"

"None that I'm aware of."

"How old are your parents?"

"My dad passed. My mom's in her seventies."

"Born in America?"

"Yes."

"And their parents?"

"Yes . . . well . . . maybe . . . I'm not sure."

"When did they start hating Jews?"

"They didn't, and I don't. Zack, you can't trick me because I'm not guilty. The eye-witness testimony of a confessed, convicted domestic terrorist and the untrained ears of a traumatized kid are hardly enough evidence to convict someone of kidnapping and murder."

"I agree. Rich and Gail talked me into taking the case. But don't assume that my taking the case means I think you're innocent. Too many factors point to your guilt."

"Such as?"

"Such as the eyewitness identification. Such as the fact that you walked out of the sanctuary at just the right time to avoid the explosion, that Josh was emaciated and traumatized, while you were well-fed and rescued in perfect health, among other things."

"Points taken. How do we counter them?"

"Let's start with well-fed and in perfect health. How do you explain that?"

"I was not well-fed, although they did feed us. Josh refused to eat what he called "crap" and "garbage." I ate every drop of food they gave me. While I was not provided adequate nourishment, I was in better shape than Josh before our captivity began. Despite my advice, Josh did nothing to keep himself from deteriorating while I worked out every day in my cell. Ask Josh. If he's honest, he'll admit what I told him to do and that he ignored my advice."

"How about the fact that you went to the bathroom at precisely the right time?"

"So did Josh, thank God."

"That cuts both ways. The prosecution will say you followed him there on purpose so you could easily abduct him and get away during the chaos and confusion of the explosion."

"But Josh also went to the bathroom. Did Josh also go to the bathroom knowing there would be an explosion? It defies common sense."

"All solid explanations."

"Good. I'm glad you think so."

"Did you practice them while you waited to see me?"

"Why are you so cynical? Until a criminal terrorist named me a criminal terrorist, I was Rich Cooper's neighbor and friend. We've lived next door to each other for over ten years. Why would I suddenly stoop to kidnapping a kid I've known and liked his whole life? Does any of this make sense to you? You don't know me. I understand that. But you do know Rich. How could he possibly be such a bad judge of character? But enough of this nonsense. Will you represent me to the best of your ability, or do I need to find another lawyer?"

"I promised Rich that I would represent you to the best of my ability."

"So, you'll do it for Rich, but not because it's the right thing to do or that I deserve the best defense possible? Does the King of Justice believe in innocent until *proven* guilty? I did not . . . I *could* not do this to Josh!"

"I promised I would defend you. I will keep my word. We'll test the evidence and see where things go. If they lead toward guilt, I will make appropriate plea recommendations. You may decide to take them or leave them. If the evidence leads toward innocence, I will apologize. Either way, you'll get my best effort. Sound good?"

"That sounds fair. How soon can you get me out of here?"

"The arraignment is tomorrow. Despite the domestic terrorism enhancement, I will try to get you ROR. Failing that, I am confident I can get this judge to set reasonable bail. Remember, you only have to post ten percent."

"I'm innocent, Zack."

"We'll see. There is one more piece of good news."

"What's that?"

"Other than Edgar, everyone who could identify you is dead."

"Yeah, I guess there's that."

"See you tomorrow."

***

The following morning, an arraignment was held in Judge Kaufman's courtroom. The Cooper family attended the hearing with Tricia Ellis. All of them, including Josh, made statements about Chip Ellis being a good friend and neighbor, someone who could not possibly be guilty of terrorism or kidnapping, a man of impeccable character.

"Your Honor? Chip Ellis has significant assets. As a free man, he is a flight risk and a threat to our key witness. We request that the defendant be retained in custody until the outcome of a trial on the merits," George Brinkman argued.

"Based on the evidence presented, I cannot, in good conscience, remand without conditions. I'm going to split the baby, as the expression goes. Bail is set at five-hundred-thousand dollars, cash or bond. The defendant shall surrender his passport. His assets are frozen—he must wear an ankle monitor. Next case."

She banged her gavel, and the hearing was over. In a few hours, Chip Ellis would be a free man. Rich and Gail Cooper were elated. Zachary Blake was on high alert, and Micah Love had work to do.

CHAPTER TWENTY-SIX

That afternoon, Chip Ellis walked out of court and prison, free on bond, with additional conditions. Zack and Micah drove to Micah's office. A meeting had been pre-scheduled between Zack, Micah, and Reed Spencer, Micah's cyber guru. The subject was proving or disproving Chip Ellis's involvement with white nationalists in general and, more specifically, the temple bombing and Josh Cooper's kidnapping.

"Reed? If Ellis is accessing the Pacific Storm Trooper website online, is there any way for you to trace that activity?" Zack asked.

"The short answer is yes unless he knows how to prevent the trace."

"And if he knows how to prevent the trace?" Micah wondered.

"That depends on his technical skill level," Reed explained. "If he's got skills, he can easily prevent the trace. Given what happened with Secure Systems, someone had next-level skills. We don't know whether that person was Chip or someone else. If it was someone else, was that person killed in the raid?"

"Good point. Let's assume the PST had a tech guru with next-level skills. Either there are remnants of the PST still operating somewhere, or Wright is now alone. If the tech guy is dead, even if we can't trace Wright's activities in the past, maybe we can trace his activities in the present or future."

"I suppose it's possible, but whether the tech guy survived or not, the infrastructure remains in place," Reed advised.

"What do you suggest?" Micah asked.

"Let me do my thing. We had no reason to investigate a link between Ellis and the PST before. Maybe someone made a mistake or two. Did the cops take Ellis's computers when they executed the search warrant on his home? They would have to permit the defense access to those computers, right?"

"Right," Zack affirmed.

"Maybe I can find a connection."

"Maybe he's innocent," Micah suggested.

"Maybe. For now, there are too many coincidences," Zack contended.

"Aside from cyber, how might we track Chip's activities?" Zack asked, turning to Micah.

"Bank accounts, bill pay, shopping, strange purchases, travel by car, train, plane, or boat, GPS in his vehicles, traffic and surveillance cameras—when he leaves home, where does he go? Maybe we can trace his movements," Micah advised.

"Yes, do it all," Zack ordered. "I'll cover fees and expenses."

"That's why I love you, man," Micah smirked.

"I love you, too. Let's get to work."

***

Zack went to court and obtained a discovery order for the evidence secured in the raid on Chip Ellis's home. He also called Chip to warn him about Reed's superior technical skills.

"The cops have terrific tech guys, Chip, but they are cops. They think like cops. They act like cops. Reed is a reformed cyber-criminal. He thinks and acts like a criminal. If you used your home computer to access the PST servers, Reed will find a connection.”

“I keep telling you, Zack. I am innocent. Reed will find no connection. I promise you that.”

“We’ll see.”

Reed Spencer was granted full access to Chip Ellis’s computers. After an exhaustive search through software and the hard drive, Reed came up empty.

“I found a big fat nothing, Zack. He’s completely clean. He plays video games online, gambles, visits fine art establishments, and does his banking online. Based on the political sites he visits, I believe he’s a Republican, but that doesn’t necessarily mean he’s a criminal. There are visits to Amazon and other shopping sites, mainly for household items and women’s clothing. I presume that’s his wife.”

“Why fine art?” Micah wondered.

“That’s what he does for a living. He’s an art broker. He brokers the sale and purchase of fine art for collectors. Makes a lot of money doing so.”

“Nothing illegal about making money,” Zack concluded. “Is it possible that the art business is a laundering operation for his terrorist activities? Can we link his art sales or purchases to the PST?”

“I couldn’t find a connection. That doesn’t mean there isn’t one, but I couldn’t find anything,” Reed replied.

“What about his bank accounts? Anything suspicious?” Micah asked.

“I didn’t do a deep dive. I still haven’t checked dark web sources for PST or offshore accounts. His primary checking, savings, and brokerage accounts show nothing unusual other than demonstrating that Ellis is well off. To the Coopers, he’s the millionaire next door.”

“Or the anti-Semite next door,” Zack warned.

***

The following day, Zack and Micah met with Clare Gibson at *Little Daddy's* near Zack's law office. While it is unusual for a criminal defense lawyer and an FBI agent to share information on a case where they represent opposite sides, the lawyer and the FBI agent had a special relationship.

"Reed went through both computers with a fine-tooth comb and came up with zilch. Either Ellis is innocent, or he is the most careful cyber-criminal in history," Zack advised.

"Did the FBI come up with anything in their search?" Micah asked.

"Nothing. Zilch, zero, nada, nothing," Clare admitted. "All we have to link Ellis to the crime is his presence and disappearance during the kidnapping, Josh's voice identification, which is iffy, and Edgar's insistence that Chip is Winger."

"Pretty flimsy, Clare. If I had to predict the outcome of Chip's trial, right now, I would predict an acquittal," Zack advised.

"That's what I'm worried about. The best of our best is tracking Chip's online footprint, using traffic and private surveillance cams to track his movements. We've also tracked his bank and brokerage accounts to follow the money. So far, nothing," Clare concluded.

"You might want to drop the charges, Clare. Let him think he's gotten away with this and put a surveillance team on him. Jeopardy has yet to attach. He's out, anyway, probably being extra cautious. If you drop the charges, maybe he'll think he's in the clear and slip up somehow," Zack suggested.

"If we do that, are you required to inform him what we've discussed? You know, as his lawyer?"

"You haven't told me what you plan to do or why, right?"

"No."

"Then I'm not required."

"What about Edgar?" Micah asked.

"What about him?"

"He'll still be protected?"

"Yes. He's in WITSEC."

"Good. His testimony may come in handy later. He must be protected. Nothing can happen to him," Zack warned.

"Agreed. If the charges are dropped, and evidence is developed that causes Ellis to be re-charged, Edgar's identification would still be part of the proofs," Clare opined.

"Okay. There's nothing more to do than wait for Brinkman to decide. You'll be talking to him, right?" Zack asked.

"Let's eat," Clare suggested, avoiding the question.

"I recommend the Tommy's Salad."

"You don't think women like Coneys?" Clare snapped.

"Of course not, Clare, I meant nothing by—" Zack replied.

"Gotcha!" Clare snapped.

"Funny, Gibson, very funny."

***

Two days later, the U.S. Attorney's office formally dropped all charges against Chip Ellis. George Brinkman received assurances that charges could be reinstated if the FBI developed additional evidence linking Ellis to the Pacific Storm Troopers or the temple bombing and kidnapping. Chip's bond was canceled. His passport was returned, assets unfrozen, and ankle monitor removed. He was now a free man. The FBI pledged to continue to investigate and surveil him, but the agency's limited government resources prevented a full-court press. Chip Ellis was innocent until *proven* guilty. The brass was hard-pressed to devote investigative and surveillance resources to an innocent man.

While the FBI's involvement with Chip was virtually over, Zack Blake and Micah Love had other ideas. They planned to continue their investigation and surveillance.

"Hopefully, he believes he's in the clear. Perhaps, one way or another, he slips up and reveals his true colors," Zack told Micah. "Whatever you need, Micah. I want no stone unturned, no corners cut. Follow the money, follow his activities, scour the dark web, find the connection, legally, illegally, by any means possible. Money is no object. I want this guy."

"I read you, boss, loud and clear. We're on it."

***

Chip's freedom was celebrated in a backyard barbeque at his home. Because they were next-door neighbors, the Coopers and other friends were invited. Most of their Jewish friends declined to attend. Many now believed Chip to be an anti-Semitic terrorist. Two of those believers were Zachary Blake and Micah Love, but both attended, hoping to catch Chip saying or doing something he would later regret.

"Thanks for coming, guys," Chip said as he approached them. "I never got a chance to thank you for helping to get me off the hook. I appreciate it."

"Innocent until proven guilty, Chip. A kid who thinks your voice may sound like the bad guy and another bad guy who picked you out of a photo array are not enough to convict a person of kidnapping and murder," Zack explained.

"Nonetheless, I appreciate you going to bat for me."

"I didn't do it for you. I did it for Rich Cooper. He believes in you."

"And you don't?"

"To be determined. I trust you'll behave yourself and accept the gift you've received."

"I've always traveled the straight and narrow."

"So, I understand you're an art broker." Micah changed the subject.

"Yes, I am."

"Is that a lucrative business?" Micah queried.

"It can be."

"For you, I mean."

"I'm aware you've investigated me, checked my assets and such. You know I do quite well." Chip admitted. He was no dummy.

"He's just making conversation. He doesn't mean anything by it. What's it like? Lots of travel?" Zack inquired.

"It can be. I've got a lot of frequent flyer mileage. The hours and the pay are often irregular. Like a contingency fee lawyer, I don't get a commission unless something sells. I've got to attend art functions, auctions, shows, lectures, and meetings, often at the last minute. It's a fun life, hectic too, and tough on a marriage."

"How so?" Zack wondered.

"Last-minute events or meetings interrupt our daily lives. Tricia makes plans and counts on me. Suddenly, I must run out of town or to someone's gallery to see a piece or participate in a sale. That can be tough, although it doesn't happen as often as it once did."

"I understand. Jennifer sure wouldn't like that. The only thing I might do that comes even close is when one of my clients is arrested, and I have to run to the prison or attend an emergency hearing."

"I guess it can be like that, but sometimes these events pull me away for days. Internet and video conferencing services help a lot. Zoom has drastically reduced my travel, especially during and after COVID."

"Do you run the business out of your home?" Zack asked, knowing the answer.

"Yes. I also have an air-conditioned warehouse . . . well, not a warehouse . . . more like a storage locker."

This was news to Zack and Micah. *A slip-up?*

"Oh? Somewhere nearby?" Micah inquired.

"EZ Storage on Southfield Road, near my house. It's air-conditioned—that's a must in my business. They've got excellent security, good rates, and top-notch service. It's perfect for me. I can store loaned pieces or pieces sold on consignment without worrying about them being damaged by the elements."

"Interesting, I wouldn't have considered that."

"The sun or intense heat can seriously damage certain pieces. Water damage is a killer. The number one issue for art dealers is theft. This place is guarded and has tremendous security. Plus, we have an alarm system."

"I need one for my office," Micah changed the subject again. "The company we use is going out of business. Do you like the company you use?"

"Yes, they're great."

"Who do you use?"

"Reliance Alarm. The guy's name is Gary Musk. I've got his number in my phone." Chip pulled out his cell phone and looked up a number. "What's your number? I'll text it to you."

Micah gave him the number. Chip pushed a few buttons. A text flashed on Micah's screen.

After Chip walked away to entertain more guests, Zack asked Micah, "What was that all about?"

"As it turns out, we now have two avenues of attack."

"Two?"

"Yep, we have the alarm company. For the right price, I'll bet Mr. Musk would be happy to share records showing each time the alarm was turned off or on. Perhaps he has online video surveillance, too."

"Track Chip's coming and going to the storage room. Good thinking, Micah. What's the other avenue?"

"He just texted me the alarm company's phone number on his private cell phone. I now have Chip's private number. I can track his 'find my phone' function, past, present, and future."

"You are brilliant, man."

"Thank you. Thank you very much," Micah imitated Elvis Presley.

"I'll bet he has computers in that storage place," Zack speculated, trying to think like an investigator.

"Very good, Mr. Blake! I'll make a private dick out of you, yet."

"If we follow the art dealer money, I'll bet dollars to donuts that some of that money did not go to purchase art."

"Very cynical, Mr. Blake."

"You don't agree?" Zack asked.

"I *do* agree."

CHAPTER TWENTY-SEVEN

R eed was excited to investigate a possible new cyber-avenue. To clone Chip's phone or computer, Reed had to be close enough to either or both. If he could access the storage facility and clone computers or find physical proof of Chip's connection to the PST and turn it over to the FBI, Zack was convinced that the evidence would be admissible.

'Fruit of the poisonous tree' is a legal concept related to obtaining evidence under false pretenses or otherwise illegally. An extension of Fourth Amendment protections, it prevents illegally obtained evidence from being declared admissible in court. Zack was an officer of the court—his involvement was a gray area. Micah and Reed were not lawyers or cops—their job was to obtain the evidence by any means possible while keeping Zack out of the loop.

Jeremy Bridges was the overnight manager at the EZ Storage location on Southfield Road. He was putting himself through college on his meager salary. It was relatively easy for Micah to persuade Jeremy to give up the number of Chip's storage unit and look the other way while Reed gained access. Micah flashed several one-hundred-dollar bills in the young college student's face. Micah and Reed had to promise, pinky-swear, that nothing would be removed from the premises. Micah spent another five big ones for a solemn promise from Jeremy that he would never tell a soul.

Reed entered the room using a key provided by Jeremy. He quickly disabled the alarm, using a private code provided by Gary Musk of Reliance Alarm—*the things people will do for money.*

As Chip described, the room was air-conditioned and filled with fine art pieces. Toward the front of the unit sat an executive desk. Two large iMac computers sat on the surface of the desk.

Piece of cake. Reed pulled out his laptop computer, punched a few buttons, inserted flash drives into each iMac, and began to download the contents onto the flash drives. While the data downloaded, Reed found a second port and covertly installed SpectorSoft CNE Investigator software on both iMacs. This software would enable Reed to monitor all future computer activity in real-time. For Reed's purposes, the beautiful part was that the installation and monitoring activity were virtually undetectable.

Reed recalled that someone in the PST had astounding next-level tech skills. That person, whoever they were, might detect and remove the threat. Reed and Micah decided to assume that the techie guy was dead, killed in the raid on the South Haven hideout. Micah wanted to proceed only with Zack's permission. Reed, the criminal mind of criminal minds, opined that if they obtained Zack's permission, Zack, as an officer of the court, would be required to disclose how the evidence was obtained. Reed didn't believe Zack would greenlight an illegal search and seizure of information. Ultimately, Micah deferred to Reed, and the two men decided to exclude Zack from anything related to their foray into Chip's storage space and alarm system, which they now called Operation EZ Access. The investigators now had present *and* future access to all data inputted into those computers.

***

Micah called Zack the following morning to report that Operation EZ Access was an unqualified success. Zack was pleased until he asked what they had and how they acquired it. Micah informed him that the information was "need-to-know," and Zack did not need to know. Zack backed off, understanding that the evidence might not pass Fourth Amendment muster.

Reed returned to the office and immediately commenced work on the information obtained from the two flash drives. Most of the material turned out to be art-related emails from dealers offering art pieces for sale or purchase. Chip kept files on dealers, other brokers, and collectors from all over the world. Reed was impressed with his knowledge of the art world and business, wondering why someone so sophisticated would be involved in white nationalism, anti-Semitism, and terrorist activity. Several hours into the investigation, Reed was finding only art business-related material. *Is he innocent?*

Suddenly, a file entitled 'Synister' popped up. The file cover included a rendition of the famous black stormtrooper mask that Darth Vader wore in the Star Wars movies. At first, Reed thought it was a video game. Upon further inspection, he discovered it was a heavily encrypted file. He could not access the documents or other stored files. The cloaking was next level. Reed concluded that someone other than Chip Ellis created and protected the file. He questioned whether the extremely cautious Chip Ellis knew it was there.

Was Synister a person, place, or event? An event from the past or one planned for the future? Perhaps, like Winger Wright, it was an alias for a terrorist. It might not be 'sinister' at all— it might be the nickname for an artist, art dealer, broker, or collector. Perhaps it was a name an artist chose to title a work of art. *If that's true, why is it encrypted?*

Reed spent the next several hours trying to hack into the file. Late into the evening, he was still trying to crack the code. His cell phone rang—it was Micah.

"Hey, Micah."

"Any luck?"

"Not yet."

"How long have you been working on it?"

Reed looked at the time on his phone screen. "About twelve hours."

"Whoa! Let's take a break."

"I'm almost there. Maybe a couple minutes, maybe an hour or two."

"Maybe never. Should we get the FBI involved?"

"And tell them what? How did we obtain this or any other file we found on the drive?"

"Make something up? I don't know!"

"If I can crack the code, I'll say I found it in the cloned files from the computers seized in the FBI raid."

"But the FBI's techies didn't find it."

"Because they aren't criminals! Leave me alone. Let me do my thing," Reed argued, bristling with frustration.

"I know you have a headache, but don't take it out on me!" Micah quoted the old commercial.

"Funny. Are we done?" Reed groused.

"Don't be a jerk."

"I'm sorry. I'm frustrated."

"I'll leave you alone. You have one hour. Pack it up and start fresh in the morning. That's an order."

"Will do, boss."

Reed terminated the call and returned to work. Encrypting or encoding information began four thousand years ago in ancient Egypt. Egyptian scribes used hieroglyphics to encode inscriptions. Reed had already sampled older, pre-computer methods like moving or shifting alphabet characters. For instance, the sender and the recipient agree to use the key '4.' 'Apple' becomes 'Ettpi' as the sender counts four letters forward in the alphabet, while the recipient counts four backward to get the coded word. Not only were these types of encryptions used by the Egyptians, but Julius Caesar also used them to send messages to his commanders. Similar codes were recently used during the First and Second World Wars.

These types of symmetric cryptography were too simple for this cipher. Reed was now trying various methods of *asymmetric* cryptography. It became apparent to Reed that different keys were used for encryption and decryption. If these files were meant to be opened by Chip Ellis, Reed was confident that he could, at some point, crack the code. After all, he believed he had far superior tech skills than the art dealer.

Still, the process was time-consuming. Reed had to test all possible keys. While computers can calculate hundreds of billions of keys per second, asymmetric cryptography was random, requiring him to experiment with more keys. All codes are crackable—the issue is time.

Reed discovered that the file was encrypted with one key but required decryption with another. Using public key technology and what is known in tech as a 'brute-force attack,' he programmed an algorithm into his computer, and the machine automatically attempted to decode the file. Per Micah's orders, he called it a night. He left the computer testing program running. When he awoke, he hoped the code would be cracked. He chose the most comfortable couch in the office, laid down, and fell asleep.

The following morning, Reed awoke, checked his phone screen, and leaped off the couch.

"Shit! I overslept!"

He raced to his computer. After randomly trying 75,428,584,265,842,110 keys, the computer cracked the code. Reed spent the next few hours applying the formula. Pieces of readable text began to slowly emerge. Most of the file documents pre-dated the temple bombing. Darth Synister, whose real name was not revealed, was involved in the planning but not the implementation of the bombing and kidnapping. The file contained detailed blueprints of the West Bloomfield temple. The terrorists flagged those points in the structure where bombs should be planted, those most vulnerable to an attack, and those where people would assemble.

It became apparent to Reed that Synister belonged to or led a second White Nationalist group acting in concert with Winger Wright and the PST in carrying out the temple bombing. A few more hours of deciphering code revealed that this second group was a fringe outfit out of Lansing called the Michigan Resistance Movement. The Movement, or MRM as the file referred to the group, was intricately involved in obtaining blueprints and explosives, conducting surveillance, and planning the event. The location and date were chosen because Winger Wright would be above suspicion as a guest at the bar mitzvah.

Reed was excited. He now had independent verification, beyond Edgar Thomas and Josh Cooper, that Winger Wright and Chip Ellis were the same person. While there were hundreds in attendance that morning, Ellis would most likely be the only attendee who possessed encrypted plans to bomb the temple and kidnap the bar mitzvah boy. Reed continued to decode the files. The process became easier as he went along. He called Micah with the exciting news.

Micah wanted to alert Zack immediately, but Reed advised against it. He wished to continue reviewing and decoding file materials. He invited Micah to join him at the office. Micah soon arrived with coffee and breakfast burritos from Taco Bell. Reed was so focused on the work he didn't realize how hungry he was.

"Thanks, I'm starving."

"Happy to oblige. Your service was above and beyond the call of duty. Did you sleep here last night?"

"Yes, the computer was working its magic, and it was too late to leave."

"You are something else. So, how do we prove that Ellis and Wright are the same person?"

"That's the easy part now that we've unlocked the cipher," Reed advised, showing Micah a copy of the decoded file.

"Ellis is Wright? No doubt?" Micah asked. "Rich Cooper will be very disappointed."

"It is what it is, as my Grampa Earl used to say."

"What's the hard part?"

"Synister and Wright are planning another attack."

"A fact made evident by encrypting these files?"

"Yes. As of now, I have no idea what they're planning, where, or when it is planned."

"When will you know?"

"I'm not sure. It could be the next minute, hour, day, week, or longer. Hopefully, the software will decipher the code while we still have time to stop the attack."

"It's time to notify Zack and Clare. What do you think?"

"I'd rather have all the information. How do I explain to the FBI that I've uncovered evidence of an attack sometime in the future? The first question the cops will ask is: "What is the source of your information?" If I give them names, dates, times, and details of the attack, they'll first move to stop the attack and ask questions later."

"I see your point. Eat breakfast, drink some coffee, clear your head, and carry on."

Three hours later, Micah and Reed had their answer.

"Check it out, Micah. It's another Jewish synagogue or temple attack.

"According to this Darth Synister character, another anti-Semitic terrorist attack is planned for B'nai Ami Temple in East Lansing.

According to his Jew-hating manifesto, this temple was chosen because of its smaller size. Fewer people—lower security levels. Because of its size, it's an unexpected target."

Neighboring Lansing was the headquarters of the MRM. While the document predicted an attack, it provided no details, dates, times, or types of attack. It read more like a memorandum of hate and an invitation to action. Written by Darth Synister and addressed to Winger Wright, it ranted against Jews and invited Wright to participate.

"Participate in what?" Micah inquired.

"It doesn't say. There are more files. We'll have to unlock each file, like pieces in a puzzle," Reed explained.

"I don't think we have enough to involve Zack or the feds. I'm sending some of my best people to Lansing to learn about the MRM organization and this Darth Synister character. I'll tail Ellis here in Detroit," Micah decided.

"You can't tail a man 24-7. You'll need help."

"I'll have Navarro and Snipes alternate shifts."

"Sounds like a plan. What do we tell Zack?"

"Tell him we're still searching the files."

"Do you think that's wise?" Reed wondered.

"We need more information. Zack must have plausible deniability about the origination of this information. Besides, you don't get much jail time for *thinking* about doing something. You get jail time for getting caught *doing* it."

"True that."

The search continued for another two days. Love operatives traveled to Lansing to commence an investigation and surveillance operation into the MRM. Micah and two other investigators began a full-time surveillance operation on Chip Ellis. One huge advantage the investigators had was that Chip thought he'd been cleared of wrongdoing. Perhaps he'd let his guard down.

At the same time, Reed continued a parallel investigation into the computer files cloned at EZ Storage. Each document contained more of the same—hate rants with no action plan. *Have these guys become all talk and no action?* Reed was dubious. They had the stones to attack a large West Bloomfield temple. An attack on B'nai Ami was a more manageable operation. He shuddered. *Here we go again.* He sighed and returned to the computer.

CHAPTER TWENTY-EIGHT

Micah Love and his surveillance crew followed Chip Ellis around town to restaurants, shopping malls, art galleries, the EZ Storage location, gas stations, and other mundane venues. For a solid week, Chip demonstrated no clandestine or hostile intent. He did nothing remotely off-kilter or close to a criminal act, not even minor traffic violations. Micah was frustrated but steadfast in his determination to prevent an attack. *When's he going to Lansing?*

Meanwhile, Love cyber-specialists continued their deep dive into the MRM. Typically, a dark web investigation would be directed by Reed Spencer, but Reed was tied up with the Chip Ellis computer files. Thus, the cyber investigation of the MRM fell to Reed's number two at the agency, Phil Greene.

The main difference between Phil and Reed was that Phil was college-educated in business, criminal justice, psychology, and computer technology. He was an effective investigator but did not think like a criminal. He was no Reed Spencer, but plenty good and extremely smart. Phil quickly unraveled the inner workings of the MRM and pieced together a management chart of chameleons. Everyone in the organization used a pseudonym. Thus, it fell to Phil to unmask as many members as possible.

Phil and his team discovered the Lansing headquarters of the MRM with ease. Unlike the Patriotic Storm Troopers, Ellis's organization, Darth Synister's hate club was more daring. Members did not hide the existence of the MRM, only its intent. To the casual observer, the organization might have been a Knights of Columbus chapter or a similar club.

According to the organizational chart, there was a five-person executive board chaired by Darth Synister. A seven-member general council operated at the direction and will of the executive committee. Micah put an investigator on each member. Photos were procured, and facial recognition identified each member. The team followed up with a detailed investigation into every member's background. The results read like a 'Who's Who' of evil, criminal hate mongers.

Every member had a record for a violent act that resulted in prison time. Each had been accused or convicted of at least one hate crime. A dark web investigation revealed that the club's principal target was Jews. However, Phil's team could not find a current action plan. Once again, they discovered a lot of talk with minimal action. The team unmasked Darth Synister—his real name was Lance Bolton. Lance was married, had two small children, and was a licensed plumber. Phil laughed to himself. *This guy is up to his eyeballs in bad shit!*

Phil wondered if Synister or Bolton accepted jobs cleaning up the plumbing messes of Jewish people. *To a white nationalist, wouldn't that be a bridge too far?* As far as Phil could tell, Lance's wife, Sally Ann Bolton, was a model citizen who had no idea she was married to a neo-Nazi.

Investigations into the other members revealed similar backgrounds. Some went to college. One was a nurse, another a paralegal for a law firm, and others were tradespeople. All members were gainfully employed, leading mundane lives, living in melting-pot communities, and blending into modern American society. *These are dangerous people*, Phil determined, *hiding in plain sight*. Their neighbors would never know what hit them.

Micah's investigators caught a break three weeks into their parallel investigation. Chip Ellis traveled to EZ Storage, opened his storage bin, sat at his desk, and woke up his computer. This was the first time since surveillance commenced and the computer monitoring device was installed that Chip spent extended time at the storage facility. It was also the first time he used his computer. Micah was juiced. He called Reed.

"Ellis is in his storage unit. He just opened one of the computers."

"On it, boss." Reed turned to a computer dedicated to monitoring and cloning computer use, websites visited, or files created by Chip Ellis's EZ Storage iMac computers. Chip pecked away at his computer for over an hour, talking on his cell phone, scheduling art meetings, making hotel reservations, and setting up appointments for his visit to East Lansing in two weeks. Reed contacted Micah.

"This must be it. The end is near."

Three nights later, during the early morning hours, a team of Love's private investigators assembled at the MRM club location in Lansing. After determining the place was void of surveillance cameras or on-site security, the investigators broke into the building and planted multiple listening devices. They cloned two computers, planted a computer bug like the one at EZ Storage, and searched the place for weapons or bomb-making material. If an explosion was planned, the material was stored elsewhere.

Bolton and Ellis became bolder and less clandestine as the days moved closer to the planned event. More communications between the two men revealed previously unknown details about East Lansing. The centerpiece of the attack was a West Bloomfield-style explosion and kidnapping. Bolton was a high school chum of Aaron Radner, a board member of B'nai Ami. A few years ago, his old friend Aaron contacted Lance about a routine plumbing job. The two men renewed acquaintances and began to get together for lunch, drinks, and an occasional Lansing Lugnuts minor league baseball game. After Aaron invited Lance and his wife to Aaron's son's bar mitzvah at B'nai Ami, a West Bloomfield-style terrorist attack plan began to take shape. The West Bloomfield attack was flawless. Why not try it again? Correct the issues that doomed the ransom—they would soon be rolling in dough.

Reed and Phil conducted a simple check of the B'nai Ami online events schedule to determine that the bar mitzvah was scheduled for Saturday, less than a week away. Winger Wright's involvement was considered payback for Darth Synister's assistance in the West Bloomfield attack. His ability to launder large amounts of money through his art broker business accounts was vital to the plot.

Love operatives continued to tail all known members of the MRM. Less than a week before the planned attack, Micah still needed to learn what explosives would be used or where they might be stored. It was time to call in the FBI. While East Lansing FBI had its own office on Eyde Parkway, Micah contacted Clare. She'd have to choose how to loop in the East Lansing folks.

A few seconds later, Clare Gibson's cell phone rang. The caller ID flashed 'Love.'

"Clare Gibson."

"Clare? It's Micah. I've got news that will turn this investigation on its head, put this whole temple bombing thing to rest, and prevent another terrorist attack at the same time."

"I'm listening."

"There's going to be a West Bloomfield-style explosion and kidnapping at a bar mitzvah in East Lansing. Winger Wright is directly involved. Are you interested?"

"That's a silly question, Micah. Here's a better one: How did you come by this information? There's been no terrorist chatter that we can decipher."

"Let's assume my means of acquiring this information were not exactly kosher. Better to call this an anonymous tip—avoid the fruit of the poisonous tree."

"Stop talking. Anonymous tip it is—here's the tipster line." Clare gave him the phone number and promised to coordinate efforts with East Lansing after the tip came in.

"So, that's it? You don't want any of the details?"

"Not if the information is about to come via an anonymous tip. I suggest that you give the tipster line operator full details. I'll take it from there. And Micah—"

"Yes?"

"Thank you. You've done a great service to your country."

"You're welcome. Anything for you."

A few minutes later, the tipster line rang.

"FBI Anti-Terrorist Tipster Line. How may I help you?"

"I have information about a possible terrorist plot on the homeland."

"Hold on, sir. Let me connect you with the agent on call."

The 'anonymous tipster' spilled his guts, providing names, dates, locations, people, nationalist groups, places, things, and how to follow the money. The agent was intrigued by the detail provided and inquired: "Where did you acquire this information, sir?"

"Call me a concerned citizen inside one or both organizations. Perhaps I'll reveal myself at some point. I am placing myself in grave danger by making this call. Can we leave it at that? I must hang up now. I suggest you take this to Special Agent Clare Gibson."

"And how do you know Agent Gibson, sir?"

"Same answer. I'm hanging up. There is very little time. I suggest you move on this . . . now!"

"Thanks for calling in this important tip, sir. Sir? Sir?" The caller had disconnected the call.

***

The following day, Chip Ellis checked into the Graduate East Lansing, a boutique hotel at Michigan State University overlooking Spartan Stadium. He unpacked his overnight bag, showered, dressed, and drove to a meeting with a collector. Afterward, he attended another meeting at a local art gallery to discuss a collector's wish list with the owner. Chip looked like an exclusive fine art broker to anyone tailing him, a man who bought and sold one-of-a-kind pieces for the rich and famous. To bolster his image on this trip, he managed to negotiate a deal for his client—she happily procured a coveted Peter Max original. An escrow deposit was immediately wired to an account monitored by Micah Love's team of investigators. Chip called his wife to deliver the good news. His activities were surreptitiously monitored every step of the way.

To anyone who didn't know Chip Ellis was an anti-Semitic domestic terrorist, nothing he did that afternoon would have caused suspicion. To Love operatives, however, his very presence in East Lansing, days before an anticipated terrorist attack on a local Jewish temple, sent all sorts of red flags.

The following morning, Chip Ellis awoke, dressed, and left the hotel to attend another meeting. This was a breakfast meeting at the *Soup Spoon Café* on E. Michigan Avenue. Chip arrived early. His client was twenty minutes late. Chip ordered coffee from a friendly server and patiently waited for his meeting counterpart to arrive. *Did something happen?*

A late model Silverado finally pulled into the parking lot. A blue-collar type exited the vehicle. He wore a blue polyester shirt, jeans, and industrial boots. He walked into the café, looked around, spotted Chip, and approached the booth. Chip was sipping his second cup of coffee. The man sat down opposite Ellis.

"Sorry I'm late," Lance Bolton apologized. "I got a last-minute call and had to change clothes. A client had an emergency. *Everything* is backed up—toilet, sink, shower. The main drain is clogged. I'm guessing it's tree roots, considering the time of year. So, how the hell are you? Ready to do some damage?"

"To be honest, Lance, I'm somewhat gun-shy. The last op went well until it didn't. The pay-off was zilch. I got lucky in court. Who knows? They could be watching me."

"Then how about not using my name? Did you spot a tail?"

"No, but we're talking FBI, the best of the best."

"They spent a pile of money trying to tie you to the West Bloomfield op and couldn't. Do you think they still have the stomach for it?"

"Who knows? I'm trying to be cautious. The good news is that my Jew lawyer and his fat Jew investigator are out of the picture. Thanks to my idiot Jew next-door neighbor, those guys are on my side. And they say Jews are sharp. Fools! So, is everything a go for Saturday?"

"That's a lot of Jews in your life!" Bolton laughed. "Talk about flirting with the enemy! Yes, we are a go for Saturday. We're putting the finishing touches on the operation as we speak. One of my guys will pick up the explosives this morning. The security system will appear functional throughout the week but will be toast when my tech guy finishes. The video will be on a continuous loop. No one will notice anything suspicious until the place goes boom. This is a small-town temple in East Lansing— security is insufficient. The explosives experts arrive from Kentucky tonight. They'll plant the stuff on the temple stage tomorrow. They've got modern equipment, high-tech rigging, and a remote detonator. These guys thought of everything. All we need to do on Saturday is press a button at the right time, grab the kid in the chaos, call in the ransom, collect our money, do not pass go."

"I'm going to be the number one suspect when the shit hits the fan. The operation is almost a carbon copy of West Bloomfield. Do you need me for anything before the kidnapping? I prefer to be shopping with my wife in Beverly Hills when the explosion happens. Plausible deniability, baby, plausible deniability."

"Shouldn't be a problem. Everything is pre-planned. Go home and make love to your cute little suburban wife. Take her out and buy something nice with your share of the ransom money."

"I never count the money I don't have. And I don't get overconfident. Watch your ass. Don't screw this up."

"Like you guys did in West Bloomfield?"

"Cheap shot. But it *is* a good lesson for you and your crew. Be careful every step of the way. Don't be afraid to call it off if something smells fishy."

"Like what?"

"I'm not sure. Something . . . anything . . . like I said earlier, I'm a little paranoid. You know what they say."

"What?"

"You're not paranoid if they're out to get you. What's good here?"

The men ate and chatted about the Lansing Lugnuts' and Detroit Tigers' misfortunes. The plumbing client offered two choice seats plus a sizeable fee for unclogging the drain and cleaning up the disgusting mess.

"And Aaron Radner will be indisposed," Lance chuckled. "Maybe you and I will go together. Would you like that?"

"Sure," Chip replied. "So long as you come to see me in Detroit. I'll take you to a Tigers game. Bring your family."

"Sounds like fun."

Anyone listening to their conversation would never guess that these two were anti-Semitic domestic terrorists about to unleash havoc on the local Jewish community.

CHAPTER TWENTY-NINE

Chip finished his business with Lance. He wished him luck, promised to see him in a couple of weeks, and exited the restaurant. He scanned the area for a tail. Satisfied he was not under surveillance, Chip returned to the hotel and checked out. He hopped on I-96 East and drove some 30 miles to Pinckney for a meeting with another art dealer and client. As fate would have it, he brokered another sale. *These joint-purpose trips are good luck. I'll have to consider doing this more often.*

He smiled to himself. To anyone who investigated him, he went to Lansing on what turned out to be a very successful business trip. He returned home well before any of the East Lansing unpleasantness occurred. Chip looked at East Lansing as redemption for the failures of West Bloomfield and South Haven. He still couldn't figure out how they located his hideout. *Where did I go wrong?* Following his successful meeting in Pinckney, he again hit I-96 East and drove back to Beverly Hills.

Meanwhile, Lance's men had everything carefully planned. The explosives were acquired and secured. The security system at the temple was disabled and placed on a sabbath service continuous loop. Anyone watching the video would think this was the present day, leading up to and including a bar mitzvah. The difference was that the earlier service was routine, and the bar mitzvah went off without a hitch. *This* service would be the *Shabbat* that East Lansing would never forget.

In the early morning hours on Friday, Kentucky-based explosives experts broke into the temple and planted powerful explosives on the *bimah*. They carefully placed them out of sight in a hatch under the *Torah* scrolls. Since the security system had been rigged on a continuous loop two weeks earlier, everything appeared quiet, with no reason for concern. All that was left to do was detonate, kidnap the kid, and commence ransom negotiations.

On Saturday morning, Lance and key board members of the MRM arrived at headquarters, six blocks from the temple. They arrived early to celebrate the glorious day that would make East Lansing history. Lance brought a bottle of bourbon. His men toasted what they hoped would be a successful mission.

After the toast, Lance left headquarters to attend the bar mitzvah of his friend's son. His number two man would have the honor of setting off the explosives. A remote switch with a spring-loaded red button sat to the man's left. Headquarters synchronized cell phones with the iMac computer in the membership office. At eleven that morning, everyone braced themselves as the man depressed the red button and waited to hear and feel the explosion six blocks away. They waited . . . Nothing happened.

Lance Bolton sat in the back of the temple near the rear exit. Ready to spring into action when he heard the explosion, he checked his Apple watch. One minute past eleven. *What the fuck?*

He excused himself to go to the bathroom, stepping over and on people trying to let him through. When he got to the temple lobby, he called MRM headquarters. His number two picked up the phone.

"Darth Synister," the man answered. "I pressed the button at precisely eleven. Did the bomb go off? We should have heard or felt the blast."

"No, you idiot. It did not go off. I planned this explosion to the last detail, and you guys screwed it up. I swear . . . if you don't do something yourself—"

At that moment, a well-dressed man in a three-piece suit approached Lance and pointed a gun directly at his head.

"Raise your hands in the air, sir. Do it . . . *now!*"

"What the hell? What's this all about?"

"Are you armed?"

"Of course not. This is a place of worship," Lance protested.

"And that matters to you?"

"Of *course*, it matters to me. Does it matter to you? What the hell is this, a robbery? I don't have much on me, but you can have it all. Just don't hurt anyone."

"No, we wouldn't want anyone in the temple to get hurt now, would we?" The man snarled, sarcastically. Lance was not the sharpest knife in the drawer; he still didn't get it. He thought he was being robbed at gunpoint. Two more men walked up, pointing their weapons.

"Three of you? For a mugging? Here!" He tendered his wallet and the money in his pocket. "Will you please leave? You're disrupting services." He started to drop his arms.

"Keep your hands in the air, Mr. Bolton. We need to search you."

"How do you know my name?" Bolton asked, while the other two men searched him.

"He's clean," one of the men advised.

"Lance Bolton? You are under arrest, sir." Bolton was officially terrified.

"For what? Attending a bar mitzvah?" He heard voices on his cell phone speaker and realized he hadn't terminated the call to headquarters.

"Freeze! You're under arrest!" All hell had broken loose at MRM headquarters. Lance dropped the phone and raised his arms.

East Lansing FBI and city police raided the MRM and arrested everyone inside. Lance faced the man with the gun.

"How? We were so careful—" Slowly, he raised his hands in surrender.

The three men led him outside to a waiting black SUV.

"I want a lawyer," he gasped, "preferably, a Jewish lawyer. I've got valuable information—"

***

Four days *before* the East Lansing operation was supposed to happen, Clare Gibson and Micah Love met at *American Coney Island* on Michigan Avenue in the heart of downtown Detroit. Established by a Greek immigrant in 1917, the restaurant sits side-by-side with *Lafayette Coney Island,* opened by the man's brother in 1924. The two restaurants are Detroit legends. Almost everyone in Detroit has a story about the restaurants and their friendly rivalry.

"Were you followed?" Clare inquired.

"No," Micah replied. "You? Does anyone at the bureau know you're here?"

"No."

"Good."

"Oh, before I forget, I bought these off book. Any further contact between me and you must be made on these phones." Clare pulled out two disposable burner phones.

"Understood. Good thinking."

"Now, what do you have?"

"I was quite detailed on the tipster line. It's all been completely sourced."

"That's what's missing. I want those source details."

"If I give them to you, you won't be able to testify."

"I don't plan to testify. I'm going to give everything to East Lansing."

"What about Harrelson? What about staying in Detroit? What about getting appropriate credit for a job well done? What about your career?" Micah demanded, nonplussed.

"My number one concern is preventing these hate crimes, bloodshed, and terror, and getting anti-Semitic, racist, asshole terrorist groups off the streets."

"Amen to that, sister, but you can do both."

"I don't want to leave anything to chance. I want to know everything. That's how we stop them. I'm all about crime prevention, not credit. You ought to know that by now."

"I do. It sucks."

"Not if we stop these attacks and get the bad guys . . . *all* the bad guys. Now, spill."

Micah spilled. The break-in, the illegal computer hacks and decoding, surveillance in Beverly Hills, Southfield, East Lansing, the MRM, the Chip Ellis connection, *everything*.

"I should retire and open a private firm. You can do much more to stop crime when you don't have to worry about the United States Constitution."

"Come work for me!" Micah exclaimed, drooling at the prospect of having a talented former FBI agent working in his office.

"I like the Constitution. However, I don't mind skirting it occasionally for the greater good. This is one of those 'greater good' moments."

"Indeed. Where do we go from here? Will you guys need backup? I suggest you get a warrant and set up a surveillance operation like ours. Make the operation completely kosher and obtain up-front evidence leading to arrests as the events unfold. I will walk you through everything. You will have a complete shadow investigation, with legally obtained evidence that will put these guys away for a long time."

"That will be appreciated. Afterward, I need you to back off."

"Yes, ma'am. What about Zack?"

"What about him?"

"I work for him. He's my client, as in the guy paying the bill. What do I tell him?"

"Nothing. He's an officer of the court. He represents Ellis. He can't know a thing. He'd have to disclose. Trust me, he doesn't want to know. Someday, he'll thank you for your discretion."

"Yes, ma'am."

"Stop saying 'Yes, ma'am,'" Clare bristled.

"Yes, ma'am."

Following her meeting with Micah, Clare contacted Dan Harrelson. She told Harrelson that the terrorist tip line received an anonymous tip from an unidentified insider that the MRM and PST were planning a joint domestic terrorist event in East Lansing. She further disclosed that she believed the operation was strikingly similar to the West Bloomfield terrorist attack and that Chip Ellis was likely involved.

The tipster revealed detailed plans with names, dates, times, and locations. She needed Harrelson to greenlight a joint operation between her Detroit task force and the East Lansing office of the FBI. Since the attack was to be in East Lansing, the East Lansing SAC could take the lead.

Harrelson was suspicious that such detailed information came from an anonymous tip, but time was of the essence, and stopping the attack was his number one priority. Besides, stopping two terrorist events against the Michigan Jewish community would enhance the currently tarnished image of the FBI, which was frequently and unfairly accused of gross ineffectiveness in combating domestic terror, especially against certain groups of minority citizens. Harrelson quickly greenlighted the mission and named Clare Gibson the coordinating agent and liaison between East Lansing and Detroit.

Following her conversation with Harrelson, Clare contacted Kurt Peck, the special agent in charge at the East Lansing office. With no time to spare, she provided a hypothetical account of Micah's operation, the need to duplicate it for Fourth Amendment purposes, and the absolute requirement that he keep everything between them.

Might Peck secure a warrant from an East Lansing federal judge to duplicate Micah's operation? The affidavit would state that the information came from an anonymous tip. Clare awaited his response. As it turned out, Peck and Gibson were like-minded believers in the *spirit* of the Fourth Amendment.

"Sometimes, you must look the other way," Peck observed.

"I couldn't agree more, Kurt. This is one of those times."

"And I know the judge to approach," he assured her. Two hours later, they had their warrant. Rather than swap the surveillance equipment, Peck decided to buy it from Love Investigations. Who would know that the equipment was in place before the purchase?

"I like this guy," Micah marveled at the ingenuity of purchasing already installed surveillance equipment. "Does he want to deputize my men?" Clare and Kurt Peck replaced all of Micah's operatives with FBI agents and East Lansing cops, but not before they received point-by-point briefings from their predecessors and on-the-spot equipment training.

The first step in the operation was to monitor a meeting between Lance Bolton and Chip Ellis. Clare was concerned that Ellis would set things in motion, leave town, and claim that he knew nothing about terror plans in East Lansing. Their waiter at *Soup Spoon Café* was an FBI agent. When the FBI found out about the meeting, they installed the agent, who took Chip Ellis to his seat and wiped off the table, simultaneously planting a listening device on the underside. The FBI was privy to and recorded the entire conversation between Chip and Lance.

The second step was to set up 24/7 surveillance on the temple, inside and outside the building. The following evening, while FBI agents looked on, a group of men in Kentucky-plated vehicles pulled up to the temple, broke in, spent about two hours inside, and left. The agents called in the bomb squad. The bomb squad carefully deactivated, disassembled, and removed the explosive devices. The entire operation was captured on video, and the Kentucky team was arrested on conspiracy to commit murder, domestic terrorism, and various weapons of mass destruction charges, as well as crossing state lines to commit a federal offense and anything else the feds thought might stick. They weren't getting out of prison anytime soon.

The third step was to set up 24/7 surveillance at MRM headquarters. Those anti-Semitic idiots proudly admitted everything, even toasting the fact that their second in command would soon be blowing up a temple, possibly injuring and killing people inside. They recorded number two proudly pressing the red button and expressing surprise when the detonator malfunctioned. FBI operatives also recorded the telephone call between Bolton and his number two following the failure to launch.

In short, the feds and the local police had enough evidence to put all co-conspirators, including Chip Ellis and Lance Bolton, away for life.

***

After what the FBI considered a highly successful mission, Dan Harrelson convened an after-action review. The review is a meeting between the brass and the agents on the ground to go over operation details. After the examination, the supervising agent prepares a report and ultimate findings of fact. The report offers praise or criticism of the agents' performance and discusses how to proceed in similar circumstances in the future.

The exercise is seen as a learning tool for the agents involved and agents who may be confronted with the same or similar circumstances. Typically, these reviews seek to answer three questions: What crime or incident were the agents investigating or trying to prevent? What was the agent's response? What would we do differently next time, or how do we improve?

In this case, however, Dan Harrelson had two additional questions: Who was the anonymous tipster? How did the agents determine the tip was reliable? Harrelson also wondered how Peck procured a warrant on such flimsy evidence.

"Let's get started, shall we?" Harrelson opened the record.

"I'm here with special agents Kurt Peck and Clare Gibson following the highly successful operation which foiled a plot to bomb B'nai Ami Temple in East Lansing and kidnap a thirteen-year-old boy. This review is being recorded. Agents Peck and Gibson, do I have your permission to record the review?"

"You do," Clare and Kurt responded in unison.

"On behalf of the Bureau, congratulations on a job well done. You saved many citizens from serious injury and possible death."

"Thank you, sir," Gibson replied.

"Yes, thanks," offered Peck, "but the day's hero is Agent Gibson. She planned the op—I was fortunate to be along for the ride."

"Weren't you the special agent in charge, Peck?" Harrelson was confused.

"It occurred in East Lansing. Per FBI protocol, that makes it an East Lansing op. As such, I was designated lead agent. But Clare received the tip, brilliantly constructed a flawless operation, and all that was left for my people was to implement her careful plan. Clare deserves all the credit."

"Very well, Peck. Agent Gibson," Harrelson turned to Clare.

"Yes, sir?"

"What can you tell us about this anonymous tip?"

"Not much, sir. It came through on the tip line. The agent on duty at the time took the call. I would have to look at the file to provide her name. She determined it to be legitimate and consequential, and our formal action plan followed the tip."

"Is it unusual to plan an op of this magnitude off an anonymous tip?"

"Sometimes, sir. The question here was, given conditions on the ground at the time the tip came in and investigations happening when we received the tip, did it seem legitimate and consequential? One that required an immediate response by our agents? I made the call to action. I take full responsibility. I felt I had no choice. Lives were at stake. The plot was formulated too close in time to a similar plot in West Bloomfield. In my judgment, we had no time to investigate the source or accuracy of the tip. We had to act on it."

"For what it's worth, sir, I agree with Agent Gibson. Clare came to me as East Lansing SAC, fully disclosed the situation, and I greenlighted the East Lansing operation. I'm pleased that I did," Peck added.

"What exactly did the tipster reveal?" Harrelson continued the questioning.

"The tipster provided details of a West Bloomfield-style terrorist plot, with names, dates, places, events, and details that were too particular to ignore. At least one of the names was a person of interest in the West Bloomfield attack. The tipster indicated that the East Lansing plot was hatched in a smaller town at a smaller temple because the terrorists concluded there would be less security."

"Please tell me about the action plan. What did you do, step-by-step?" Harrelson wanted it all on the record.

Gibson repeated the essential facts and steps in the operation. Assembling a report of the information provided by the tipster, taking it to Peck, Peck's visit to the judge to obtain the warrants, the multiple surveillance and monitoring devices planted, the crucial evidence obtained during surveillance and monitoring, the disarming of the explosives, and the arrests made as the terrorists attempted to carry out their mission. She described a flawless operation, resulting in the arrests of all involved, with no property damage and no injuries or deaths to civilians or law enforcement personnel.

"Thank you, Agent Gibson. Congratulations on a flawless execution of an almost perfect plan," Harrelson noted.

Almost perfect? What's he up to?

"Is there anything the Bureau could have or should have done differently, Agent Gibson?"

"May I speak freely, without reprisal, Agent Harrelson?"

"That's what these reviews are for, Gibson."

"I'm an experienced, highly decorated agent. I know Michigan, particularly Metropolitan Detroit. I was transferred from Detroit to Las Vegas against my will. When an SAC job opened in Detroit. I put in for the assignment and transfer. My request was deep-sixed for *political* reasons, partly because I'm a woman.

"Perhaps I come off a bit strong, I don't know, but it is always because I believe something is important to a particular aspect of an investigation—"

"Please continue. I'm listening. I'd like this on the record."

"I received a call from an investigator, Micah Love, who I know from my time in Detroit. He thought I was still in Detroit. He requested my assistance in the official investigation into the West Bloomfield attacks. However, politics reared its ugly head once more.

"Things were quiet in Vegas. DAC Hawthorne didn't need me but gave me a hard time for the hell of it. Who was he hurting—me or a case involving domestic terrorists in a town I know well? Supervising Agent Kavanaugh got involved and gave me similar treatment.

"When I got to West Bloomfield, Oakland County Sheriff Garber blustered about turf and refused to acknowledge that the FBI was far better equipped to handle the case than the sheriff's office. He loved the pissing contest. The governor of Michigan and the president had to put him in his place.

"Finally, after Kavanaugh failed to get the result he craved, he contacted his good buddy, Deputy Director Beeman, in one more attempt to usurp my authority. Beeman contacted you and put you in charge of an already active investigation. He advised that you would be flying into town to take over. I would be relegated to a subordinate role.

"With all due respect, Agent Harrelson, you can be quite the dick. Everyone at the Bureau knows it. You and I have had our differences in the past. Kavanaugh and Beeman knew this. They sent you to Detroit to rattle me, and you tried to get under my skin. Throughout this entire bureaucratic fiasco, all I did was work the case, ignore the barriers you guys put in my way, and prevent two terrorist attacks from being successful.

"What could the Bureau have done differently? Please give me the respect I deserve. Let me do the job I was born to do, a job I do quite well."

"Are you finished?"

"I am."

"The record will reflect your comments. The chain of command is an integral part of Bureau protocol. Petty grievances, personality clashes, or sexism should not interfere with our work.

"An obvious clash of personalities played an important role in delaying justice in this case. These factors could easily have led to disaster. Our agents were successful because of Agent Gibson's professionalism, determination, tenaciousness, planning, leadership, and prompt action. Supervisory agents should pay careful attention to this review and work to avoid such despicable displays in the future. Does anyone have anything more to add to the record?"

"No, sir," a stunned Gibson replied. Dirty Harry had her back. *Will wonders never cease?*

"No, sir," Peck echoed. "I would like to add that it is tough being a SAC and learning the nuances of a town. Having your judgment and expertise constantly second-guessed by people who don't know the community is counterproductive. I agree with Agent Gibson's assessment and suggest that leadership better communicate with and trust their local agents."

"Well said, Peck. Let's close the record." Harrelson signaled to the reporter to close the record and stop recording.

"I can be kind of a dick, huh?" Harrelson turned to Gibson.

"Perhaps too strong, sir. I apologize?"

"Are you asking me or telling me? If you're asking, I'd say you don't owe me a thing. There is no need to apologize. I *can* be a dick. It's part of my charm."

"Your charm, sir?"

"Yes. You wanted to solve this case, impress me, and demonstrate that you deserve respect and a transfer to Detroit, right?"

"Right."

"Dickiness *motivates*, Gibson. There's a method to my madness."

"I'll keep that in mind, sir. It worked in this case."

"That doesn't mean you were wrong. Everything you said was true. The Bureau has some work to do."

"Happy to participate in that work and grease the skids for future agents."

"I may take you up on that someday, Gibson. As for this op, well done, Agent, well done. I'll be recommending you for that Detroit SAC assignment. I'm sure you'll hear from Beeman once he pulls his head out of his ass."

Peck and Gibson laughed. "We're all attorneys, sir. I presume that comment was confidential?" Clare inquired.

"You need to ask?"

CHAPTER THIRTY

Zachary Blake sat in his home office. He and his two sons, Kenny and Jake, were discussing his representation of Chip Ellis and the recent anti-Semitic attacks in West Bloomfield. Jake was a senior at Bloomfield Hills High School. Kenny was a Junior at Michigan State University. According to a recent text from Micah, there was another similar attempt in East Lansing.

These terrorist attacks hit too close to home, geographically and religiously. While the boys weren't Jewish, they loved their adoptive father, knew the Cooper family quite well, and despised people who used religion as a pretext to commit criminal acts. After all, the two boys were once the victims of a pedophile priest. To their religious mother's dismay, they were not currently fans of organized religion.

"Another example of bad people using religion to justify their criminal behavior, Dad," Kenny argued. He was a pre-law criminal justice major at Michigan State.

"How is a bigot's bad acts the fault of organized religion, Kenny? In these two cases, what did the two temples or their members do to deserve this hate?"

"Nothing, Dad," Jake replied. "That's not Kenny's point. If people didn't have different faiths, there would be no differences and no hate, right Kenny?"

"Exactly, squirt."

"Still calling me squirt? Have you checked lately? I'm bigger than you."

"Sorry, force of habit."

"And I can kick your ass. If I wasn't a pacifist, I would," Jake warned.

"I'd like to see you try, wise guy," Kenny challenged.

"Perfect example of a non-religious squabble," Zack noted.

"I suppose there are other reasons to fight. But religious or ethnic differences are the clear number one. Look at Israel and Gaza or Ukraine and Russia," Kenny challenged. "These wars cost thousands of lives and billions of dollars."

"Men and women of good conscience and different religious and ethnic backgrounds can get along, boys. People of good will get along. People of bad will do not. It has been that way throughout history," Zack reminded him.

"Every war ever fought has some religious component. Look what your Grandpa Max went through during World War II," Jake responded.

"I agree. The Holocaust was the ultimate example of the hate we are talking about. Jew hatred seems to be a never-ending curse. The West Bloomfield and East Lansing terror plots are prime examples. However, wouldn't it be boring if we were all the same? Look at us, for example, two Christian boys with a Jewish dad. We get along fine. We love each other. We need more people of good faith to speak up and set better examples of inter-faith comradery. Drown out the voices of fear, division, and hate. Why don't you boys lead the way?"

"Right. Two boys change the world," Jake snickered.

"We've got to start somewhere," Zack encouraged. As the boys prepared to respond, the telephone rang. "To be continued," Zack sighed. "Micah's calling. It's probably about the case. I need some privacy."

The boys jumped off the couch. Jake bumped Kenny as they left the room. Kenny pushed him back, and a playful wrestling match commenced as they walked down the hall toward the kitchen. *I can't believe how big these guys have gotten—obviously not Jewish.* Zack compared his relatively diminutive size.

"Hello?" Zack answered the telephone.

"Zack? It's Micah. Let me conference in Clare."

After a few preliminary greetings, Clare gave Zack details of the thwarted East Lansing terrorist attack, Chip Ellis's apparent involvement, and the successful mission that saved the temple and its congregants. Zack's initial reaction? He was livid.

"These are the same types of characters who kidnapped and harmed my friend's kid. And Ellis is *my* client! I'm funding Micah's operation. Why wasn't I notified?" he ranted.

"There were issues, Zack. You might have compromised legal ethics to nail these guys. The fact that you were Chip's lawyer required us to keep you in the dark. When you think about the situation, you'll realize we were right," Micah explained.

Zack calmed down. "I understand. What can you tell me?"

"Acting on an anonymous tip, the FBI—" Clare began.

"Anonymous tip? I call bullshit! The whole operation was the result of an anonymous tip?" Zack cut her off.

"See? This is exactly why we couldn't loop you in. You can't help being an attorney, representing, in this case, the bad guy," Clare cautioned.

Zack calmed a second time. "Yeah, yeah, point taken . . . again. Where were we? The FBI, acting on an anonymous tip . . . I've got it. Please continue."

"The FBI, acting on an anonymous tip, set up surveillance and a wiretap on the East Lansing headquarters of the MRM," Clare explained.

"What's the MRM?" Zack asked.

"Sorry, the Michigan Resistance Movement, it's another fringe, anti-Semitic, domestic terror group, like the PST. The main difference is that this one's in East Lansing."

"These groups are crawling out of the woodwork, like roaches or termites, eating away at the cornerstones of our society. Surveillance, wiretap, please continue," Zack grumbled.

"Right, surveillance and wiretap revealed that a second temple attack was planned, this time in East Lansing. Your boy, Chip Ellis, was involved there, too."

"He's not my boy. How was he involved? What was his connection?"

"We've been following Ellis since he got released, first Micah's firm, then the FBI. Chip traveled to East Lansing on business and used the business trip as cover for his meeting with Lance Bolton. We recorded their meeting."

"Who's Lance Bolton?"

"Sorry, he's the leader of the MRM, goes by Darth Synister. He's got the explosives connections."

"Right, I remember him from the stuff we pulled off Chip's computer."

"Exactly. Anyway, at this meeting, Chip and Bolton discussed detailed plans to blow up B'nai Ami in East Lansing and kidnap the bar mitzvah boy. Sound familiar?"

"Too familiar," Zack shuddered.

"Surveillance teams followed everyone involved. On Thursday night, agents followed some MRM guys to a warehouse where they picked up the explosives. They delivered them to a bunch of explosives experts from Kentucky, who planted them on the temple stage. What's that called again?" Clare asked, trying to recall.

"The *bimah*," Zack replied.

"Right, the *bimah*. Anyway, they planted the explosives. Agents immediately arrested the MRM and Kentucky guys, and the bomb squad deactivated, disassembled, and removed the bomb."

"Wow! Cool—sounds like something out of a movie or Netflix series," Zack marveled. "What happened next?"

"We waited. Chip had left town, stopped in Pinckney, and returned to Beverly Hills."

"What's in Pinckney?" Zack wondered.

"An art dealer. He mixed business with pleasure. He was home in Beverly Hills when the East Lansing thing went down."

"What a prick! It is such a pleasure to represent guys like him. Please go on," Zack shuddered.

"On Saturday morning, all the MRM guys met at headquarters for a celebratory drink. All that was left to do was depress the remote detonator and wreak havoc on the East Lansing Jewish community. Synister's second in command, Melvin Cox, was in charge."

"Where was Darth Synister? What was his name again?"

"Lance Bolton. He went to services. He's a friend of the father of the bar mitzvah boy."

"Incredible! My Jewish brothers and sisters must find better friends or improved bullshit detectors."

"So, Cox pushes the button, and nothing happens—no go boom. Bolton, sitting as far from the bomb as possible, goes out into the hall and calls MRM headquarters. This is all recorded. While he's talking to Cox, all hell breaks loose at headquarters—FBI agents raid the place, and everyone is arrested. Bolton hears the whole thing. At that moment, he's approached by the agents who have been tailing him the whole time. Back in Beverly Hills, I had the pleasure of arresting Chip Ellis. Have you heard from him?" Clare asked.

"No."

"You will," Micah spoke for the first time.

"And all of this was initiated by Micah's private investigation?" Zack probed.

"Yes," Micah replied. "That's what you hired me for."

"And what did Micah's investigation reveal?"

"Enough—" Clare paused.

"Enough, what?"

"We're getting into an area that might cause you ethical issues."

"The anonymous tip?"

"I'm not sure what you mean," Clare waffled.

"The tip came out of Micah's shadow investigation."

"I didn't say that."

"No, you didn't. Micah?"

"I cannot confirm or deny," Micah tap-danced.

"I get it. I represent Chip. If I know where this call originated, all of this evidence might be the fruit of the poisonous tree."

"But you don't," Clare reminded him.

"Don't what?"

"Know where the call originated. Neither do I, by the way."

"Micah? Do you know?" Zack confronted him.

"Are you sure you want me to answer that, buddy? Because of this tip, we've taken down two terrorist operations and caught their leaders dead to rights," Micah cautioned. "The feds believe the tip came from an insider. It might be one of the guys who got arrested. If he comes forward and can prove he's the tipster, he'll get leniency. Right, Clare?"

"Right," Clare agreed, stone-faced.

"An anonymous tip breaks open the whole case. Got it," Zack recapped.

"That's what happened. It's what the AAR says, too," Clare advised.

"AAR?" Micah asked.

"The official FBI report. An after-action review is conducted, followed by a written report by the person who conducts the review."

"Who conducted the review?"

"Harrelson."

Harrelson! Holy shit! You *are* Wonder Woman. You turned *Harrelson*?

"He's not such a bad guy once you get to know him."

"Unbelievable," Zack exclaimed.

"Harrelson was the SAC. He brought Peck and I into a conference room to discuss the case, the arrests, any successes or failures, and what the Bureau could work on to improve in the future," Clare explained.

"Your best buddy, Harrelson? Thorn-in-your-side, Harrelson? What did you tell him? Did you make him eat shit?" Micah wanted details.

"I told him this was a flawless operation and praised every agent involved," Clare stated.

"Bullshit! Tell us the truth," Micah demanded. "How about he and his buddies railroading you out of town?"

"I did have a few things to say about politics, biases, and the chain of command."

"Bam! If I could only have been a fly on the wall for that one!" Micah exclaimed.

"What did you tell him?" Zack wondered.

"Need to know, gentlemen. Need to know."

"We *need* to know, Clare! I'm not sure about Zack, but I need to know."

"Sorry, FBI business."

"Did you let him have it with both barrels?"

"FBI business. I can tell you that Harrelson and I see each other in a new light. And I've got good news!" Clare announced.

"Arrests everywhere, a solid AAR detailing a flawless operation, and more good news? Clare, you're on a roll," Zack cheered. "What's up?"

"I'm the new SAC for Detroit."

"Wow, that is good news. Mazel tov! Well deserved!" Zack exclaimed.

"We're going to be neighbors? Can I be, like, an FBI asset? Get together for two martini lunches paid for by the Bureau and all that?" Micah salivated.

"I don't know about that, Micah, but I'm excited to be back."

"The city is lucky to have you," Zack praised. "So, what now?"

"Now, you wait to hear from Chip."

"Where's Brinkman or the East Lansing U.S. Attorney on leniency for any of these guys?" Zack inquired.

"I'm not sure. I suppose it depends on the proffer."

"I've got some ideas—" Zack thought and talked simultaneously.

"Care to share?" Clare asked.

"Anonymous tip, eh?"

"Point taken, smart-ass. I'm so glad to be home. I missed you guys."

***

"You want a Jewish person to represent you? Again? I thought you hated Jews. Are you sure?"

"Jews are the best lawyers."

"That's an anti-Semitic stereotype, but it happens to be true in this instance," Zack humbly admitted.

Zack Blake met with Chip Ellis in an attorney-client conference room at the federal prison in Milan.

"So, you'll do it? I wasn't even in Lansing at the time of the arrests. I'm innocent."

"Just like last time."

"Hey, you proved I didn't do it," Chip protested.

"Not accurate. I only proved the FBI lacked sufficient evidence to prove, beyond a reasonable doubt, that you were guilty. Big distinction. I know you did it."

"Why did you agree to represent me? Why did you get me off?"

"Because my good friend, Rich Cooper, and his son Josh asked me to represent you. Consider yourself fortunate that you know them. They're good people."

Chip remained silent. Zack continued.

"I don't get it, Chip. You have a beautiful family, a nice home, a solid business. You're even capable of *pretending* to be a good guy, which tells me there is a good guy in there somewhere. But you can't get past your prejudice, this hatred that burns within you. You've let it destroy everything good in your life."

Chip remained silent.

"Here's my one-time offer: I'll consider representing you if you do five things."

"What five things?" Chip rolled his eyes. *Fucking Jew!*

"One: Express a willingness to plead guilty. Turn State's evidence against the MRM and PST for a possible reduced sentence. Two: Reveal all remaining assets of the PST and expose all past, present, and future terrorist plots you know about. This would include the identities and crimes of fringe groups associated with the MRM and PST. Three: Sell your house and empty your bank accounts, in country and offshore. Four: With the money recovered from your personal and terrorist group assets, restore the temple to its previous condition and pay reasonable damages to the Cooper family. Five: Seek counseling and pledge to end your racist and anti-Semitic ways.

"If you pledge to complete those tasks, I will consider representing you. We will put a representation agreement together that lists these five requirements. Failing to perform any of the five tasks will terminate the relationship. Failure also voids any negotiated plea deal.

"Does your wife know you're a racist, anti-Semitic, terrorist, murderer, and kidnapper? If so, I want her to plead guilty to obstruction of justice and complete the five requirements."

"Leave my wife out of this. She's innocent. As far as she knows, I was doing art business when the East Lansing plot went down."

"I find that difficult to believe. How about this? I'll leave her out if she signs off on the asset liquidation, temple restoration, and damages award to the Cooper family. I presume she is a joint holder of your assets?"

"Most."

"Then she signs off or no deal. If she goes to prison, who takes care of the children?"

"She'll sign off."

"Do we have a deal?"

"May I think about it?"

"Sure. You have one minute." Zack pushed a button on his watch and continued to stare at it.

"A minute?"

"It's a fabulous, one-time offer. If you don't take it, I'm walking out of here. Find yourself another lawyer. There are a lot of good ones out there. You have thirty seconds."

"This is blackmail, Blake." *Damn you!*

"Sue me. Your minute's up. What's it going to be?"

"Deal." *Jew prick!*

"For a dumb terrorist bigot, you're a smart guy."

***

Zachary Blake and Chip Ellis appeared in court to put details of a plea deal on the record before Judge Kaufman. A second hearing was scheduled for the following week in East Lansing. The good news for Jews and people of color in the Detroit area was that when Chip Ellis was last arrested, there was no final resolution. Jeopardy did not attach. He could still be charged and convicted in the West Bloomfield bombing and kidnapping and was looking at the potential of life in prison.

Because of his expected allocution and restitution, the deal he and his wife made to contribute most of their fortune to the temple, and his civil suit settlement with the Cooper family, Zack negotiated a fifteen-year sentence. This was a sweetheart deal for a domestic terrorist, kidnapper, and felony murderer.

The financial aspects of the deal were concluded before the hearing. Chip and Tricia sold their Beverly Hills home, liquidated most of their assets, and turned them over to the feds. The feds, in turn, created an escrow to fund the temple restoration and restitution to the Cooper family. Chip now had to allocute in West Bloomfield and East Lansing.

As they waited in court for the clerk to call the case, Zack looked over at Ellis. His wife and children sat in the row behind him. The Cooper family sat across the aisle behind the prosecutor's table in the same row.

Zack suggested that the judge see Chip's family. There was love, compassion, and humanity buried deep in the soul of Chip Ellis. *He's a nice-looking guy with a beautiful family and a solid business. What makes such a man do the things he has done?*

When Zack thought of bigots in America, images of neo-Nazis came to mind. These were angry white men in military fatigues, marching in suburban streets, looking like soldiers mobilizing for war against people of color and non-Christian religions. But a new type of bigotry was emerging. Anti-Semites and racists in America were now ordinary people. They look like Chip Ellis or Bart Breitner. They hide in plain sight.

These newbies elected Ronald John, a self-professed bigot and president of the United States. They spew hate on social media and hide in integrated and interreligious communities. They remain silent when family members, friends, or strangers shout racial or anti-Semitic epithets. They give oxygen to these comments and space for those who make them. Tacit acceptance, this new type of bigotry, is okay with millions of our neighbors, seemingly law-abiding citizens. These 'ordinary people' create the divisions in America today. Thousands of people, willing bystanders, look the other way as violent people take to the streets.

Zack's thoughts turned to his maternal grandfather and his stories of the Holocaust. The law of large numbers turned these thousands of bystanders into millions who embraced the anti-Semitism of the Nazis. They stood by while Hitler and his cruel regime exterminated the Six Million.

There are the activists, the Klan, the Proud Boys, and their ilk. They are truly dangerous. However, for their culture to flourish, their movement also requires ordinary people willing to ignore book banning, dangerous trends, anti-woke activity, attacks on the LGBTQ community, women, non-Christian religions, and people of color. When thousands turn into multiple millions, you get Nazi Germany. These bigoted rabble-rousers cannot exist without the silent assenters.

"All rise! Federal District Court is now in session. The Honorable Jody Kaufman is presiding."

Kaufman took the bench and advised the gallery to be seated. She nodded to the clerk.

"Calling the case of *United States v. Ellis*. Please state your appearances for the record," the clerk demanded.

"George Brinkman appearing for the United States, Your Honor."

"Zachary Blake appearing for the defendant, Your Honor."

"I understand there has been a plea arrangement, gentleman. Is that correct?"

"That is correct, Your Honor. While the defendant's actions in this case are despicable, we believe the plea arrangement serves the best interest of the victims and the community at large," Brinkman postured.

"The Court has reviewed the charges and the defendant's heinous actions. While our citizens are innocent until proven guilty, a plea agreement amounts to an admission of guilt. I expect your proffer to be compelling. A plea deal for the perpetrator of *these* crimes is repugnant to the Court," the judge pontificated.

Zack smiled. He didn't care whether the judge accepted the plea or not. The financial aspects of the deal had been completed. He'd be happy to try the case and, hopefully, lose. He was surprised by the showboating, considering Judge Kaufman was a lifetime appointee.

"Mr. Brinkman? Please place the plea details on the record," the judge requested.

Brinkman regurgitated the deal. Ellis must plead guilty to conspiracy, attempted murder, and attempted kidnapping. In return for the plea and other conditions, Ellis would serve at least fifteen years in prison. In exchange for leniency, he also forfeited most of his assets to pay the Coopers' restitution and restore the temple to its former glory.

Chip would also have to provide a full allocution, admit his crimes in open court, testify against all co-defendants and other nationalist groups, and share knowledge of any additional plots against minority citizens. He would also be required to pay for counseling and education to attempt to reverse his pathological bigotry.

"Thank you, Mr. Brinkman," the judge acknowledged. She turned to Zack.

"Is that your understanding of the agreement, Mr. Blake?"

"It is, Your Honor."

"And your client intends to plead guilty?"

"Yes, he does, Your Honor."

"Does he appreciate the break he's getting?"

Ellis nodded his head. He looked at Zack, back to his family, and then to the judge.

"He does, Your Honor."

"Who will handle his allocution?"

"I will, Your Honor," Zack responded.

"Please proceed," Judge Kaufman directed.

Blake and Ellis went through the list of original charges and reduced charges. Zack included both the West Bloomfield and East Lansing incidents because the deal required him to allocute to all past and future plots and conspiracies. Chip gave detailed information about the Patriotic Storm Troopers and other groups, names, dates, plots, activities, websites, and assets—he sang like a canary and provided every detail.

"Please recite for the court your greatest accomplishments in life," Zack prompted.

"That's easy. Meeting and marrying my wife and bringing my two beautiful children into this world."

"What are your best attributes?"

"I'm a good listener. I've been a good father and husband. I've kept my family completely out of the activities and ideologies that landed me in court this morning. I'm a good provider, a talented judge of fine art, and a good teacher. Thank God I've taught my wife how to handle the business. Hopefully, she can successfully carry on while I'm . . . away."

"What are your short-term goals?"

"To see the temple restored. To make amends to the Cooper family." He looked at Rich, Gail, and Josh and nodded in appreciation. Josh nodded back. Rich and Gail looked away.

"And your long-term goals?"

"For my wife to succeed with the business. I'd like to see her thrive and rebuild. I want to serve my time in peace, complete therapy, and be a better person when I leave prison. I plan to put the past behind me and look forward to a more positive future. I hope I've learned my lesson, but actions will speak louder than any words I could utter today."

"Do you think you are being treated fairly? Is this a just punishment for your multiple offenses?"

"I believe the punishment is more than fair, sir. I've done horrible things. I have already started to make amends, as you well know."

"Your Honor. As Mr. Brinkman and I have detailed, the defendant has depleted his assets and turned them over to authorities. They've been donated to the temple's restoration and used to pay a previously negotiated civil restitution to the Cooper family. The balance has been donated to various non-profits, including the ADL, Stand Up to Jewish Hate, and Combat Anti-Semitism. I might add, Your Honor, that the Blake Law Firm has agreed to match each contribution. We are trying to turn a horrible negative into a positive."

"Thank you for that, Mr. Blake. The Court takes judicial notice of your firm's philanthropy and appreciates all you do. Please continue. Sorry for the interruption, but I wanted to get that on the record."

"Thank you, Your Honor." He turned back to Chip.

"Mr. Ellis, do you believe that leniency in sentencing will promote your respect for law and order? When you are released, do you plan to promote the law or continue your previous lawless ways?"

"What a question! It sounds self-serving to say that I have learned the error in my ways. I am under oath. I don't think it would be true. There is a great deal of hatred and anger in me, carefully honed during my childhood years and my adult associations with bigots and other haters. Bad skin is not easily shed. I pledge to try, to do my best to overcome the anger and hatred, and to become a better example. I promised my wife and kids."

"You have agreed to counseling. Do you believe that you would benefit from educational or therapeutic counseling?"

"I don't know. Is bigotry a treatable disease? Whatever I am asked to do, I will do. Whatever therapy or educational exercise they chart for me, I will participate and embrace wholeheartedly. That's all I can promise."

"Your Honor, might I state for the record that I have contacted my sons' long-time therapist, Dr. Harold Rothenberg, who advises that there is no such thing as pathological bigotry. However, if paranoia is treatable, how about racial or religious paranoia? If we can teach people to understand and eliminate bias, how about racial or religious bias? Unfortunately, there is no formal psychiatric diagnosis or DSM for pathological bigotry.

"There is a movement in the medical and psychological community to create a formal diagnosis so professionals can treat these people. According to Dr. Rothenberg, extremely hateful patients may often benefit from psychotherapy or antipsychotic medication. Of course, if a patient's hatred is linked to a clinical diagnosis, like schizophrenia, then treatment would be possible.

"In most of these cases, bigoted individuals are proud of their beliefs. There is little motivation to seek or accept treatment. In this case, however, there are two compelling reasons: One, it is a condition of this plea agreement. Two, this defendant is personally motivated to change. He is beginning to see the errors in his ways.

"I have been working with Mr. Ellis for a while now. I see a marked change in his attitude and behavior. As a Jewish person who has had some extremely negative encounters with Mr. Ellis and endured his smarmy rhetoric, I am buoyed by his change in attitude. Treatment while incarcerated should have a positive impact when he is released. In short, Mr. Ellis has done everything he promised to do to honor the plea arrangement. Time will tell, but I am extremely hopeful."

"Thank you, Mr. Blake," Judge Kaufman retorted. She turned to the defendant. "Mr. Ellis, please rise." Chip stood at attention.

"You have highly competent and wise counsel, Mr. Ellis. Consider yourself fortunate. Mr. Brinkman and Mr. Blake are distinguished members of the Michigan Bar. In conjunction with brave FBI agents and local law enforcement officers, they have worked hard to resolve this case, prevent future acts of terror, and achieve justice for all involved. I would rarely second-guess such combined ability, talent, and experience.

"However, when I first saw this plea agreement, I was dubious. Fifteen years for a terrorist? A man who conspired to kidnap a boy on the most important day of his young life? A person who plotted to destroy a sacred place of worship without concern for loss of life, limb, or property? No—fifteen years is not enough. I will not approve the deal.

"However, after listening to Mr. Blake's, Mr. Brinkman's, and the defendant's compelling presentations, I feel more positive about the arrangement. In addition to his fifteen-year sentence, the defendant has dissolved his assets and donated them to the people he harmed and to causes that fight the poisonous toxin he spread. He has agreed to receive treatment. He has provided valuable information about other anti-Semitic, racist, and homophobic domestic terrorists.

His allocution appears heartfelt—he cares about his family and realizes he has caused them significant harm. He expressed remorse for his behavior toward a remarkably supportive neighbor. I take him at his word. I respect the dedication to justice and hard work of the two lawyers involved and defer to their collective wisdom. Mr. Ellis?"

"Yes, Your Honor."

"Do not let me or these two fine attorneys down. Do you understand me? You have been given a gift, a break that few defendants receive. Use it wisely. Turn your life around."

"I will do my best, Your Honor."

"The Court accepts the plea and finds you guilty. You are hereby sentenced to fifteen years in an appropriate federal correction institution. By prior agreement, you will receive no credit for previous time served. You have already forfeited assets and made the agreed-upon restitution, which weighed heavily in the Court's decision to approve the plea bargain. I trust you will take advantage of all treatment options made available by prison authorities, not only because you are required to do so as part of this plea arrangement but because it is the right thing to do.

"To Mr. & Mrs. Cooper and Mrs. Ellis: I'm certain none of you believes this is a fair outcome. I do not judge the fairness of this plea bargain and sentence as you may see it. I judge its fairness as it relates to society at large, the safety of our community, the interests of the victims, and the interests of the defendant. It is a tough decision. Time will determine whether it is the correct decision. The defendant is remanded to the U.S. Marshals Service for transport to serve his sentence. Good luck to all. This Court is adjourned. I'll see both attorneys in my chambers."

Judge Kaufman banged her gavel and left the courtroom through a back exit to her chambers. The court officer escorted Zachary Blake and George Brinkman through the back door. Zack lightly tapped on Kaufman's open door as he and Brinkman entered.

"Your Honor?"

"Mr. Blake, Mr. Brinkman, have a seat." She pointed to two side chairs. She turned to a cabinet, opened it, and pulled out a bottle of wine. "Drink?"

"I'm driving, maybe just a little," Zack accepted.

"More than a little," Brinkman requested with a smile. "I'm walking back to the office."

"Tough case. What do you think, off the record, of course?"

"Mr. Ellis provided precious information about white nationalist terrorist networks. Hundreds of future crimes will be prevented. Thousands of criminals will be incarcerated thanks to Ellis," Brinkman advised.

"I agree, Your Honor—" Zack began.

"Call me Jodi."

"I agree, Jodi. I'm Zack. Chip appears genuinely remorseful. Perhaps he is a changed man. He's done everything he's been asked to do. Fifteen years is a long prison sentence. As a Jewish lawyer and social justice advocate who would not easily give a break to an anti-Semite, I am comfortable. And preventing future acts of terror could not happen without this plea. All things considered, you will not be sorry."

"As a Jewish federal court judge, giving an admitted anti-Semite a break troubled me, too. I almost recused myself. The allocution made me feel better. I sincerely hope you're right. He'll be sixty when he gets out?"

"Sixty-one, Your Honor . . . er . . . Jodi," Zack replied.

"Part of me hates the formality of the courtroom, that the judge is on a higher plain than a lawyer or a citizen," Kaufman declared.

"I don't know you well, but I am sure you deserved the elevation," Zack observed.

"It still makes me uncomfortable. Anything more to ease my conscience?"

"We wouldn't have negotiated or recommended the plea if we didn't think it was best for the parties or the country?" Brinkman suggested.

"Great answer. Drink up. To justice!" Kaufman raised her glass.

"Here! Here! To justice," Zack toasted.

"To closing this case. Unfortunately, there is always a next one," Brinkman raised his glass.

"Party pooper," Zack frowned. The three lawyers drank the rest of their wine.

Zack returned home from court, dragging his feet, wondering if he did the right thing. He rarely second-guessed his legal decisions, but this one was unique.

"Honey, I'm home!" he called out.

"In the kitchen!" Jennifer called back. Zack walked through the vestibule and into the kitchen.

"Hey," he greeted her.

"Hey, yourself. How was court? Did everything go as planned?"

"Yep. Chip got fifteen years. All his assets have been distributed to victims and victims causes, the whole nine yards."

"So, what's the problem? It sounds like everything you negotiated. You don't seem happy. Your client got a tremendous break."

"That's the problem. Did he deserve it?" Zack was tormented.

"What did the prosecutor say? What did the judge say? More importantly, how did the Coopers feel?"

"The judge was conflicted. The prosecutor loved the deal. Countless criminals will be prosecuted due to Chip Ellis's allocution. As for the Coopers, who knows? They've been compensated. The temple will be restored to its former glory. Everyone seems satisfied."

"So, again, what's the problem?"

"He's a fucking *terrorist*, Jennifer! *That's* the problem, Zack exploded. "Why did I agree to represent this guy?"

"Language!" She pointed to a piggy bank on the counter. "Drop a ten into Mr. Piggy." Zack did as he was told. "You represented him at Rich Cooper's request, remember?"

"Of course, I remember. But Rich thought Chip was innocent when he requested my representation," Zack sizzled.

"Watch your tone. I'm one of the good guys."

"I'm sorry, sweetheart, truly. I love you." He pulled a flower out of the flowerpot and offered it to her with an eye waggle.

"Seriously? You can do better than that."

"What do you want?"

"Hugs, kisses, and an attitude readjustment."

"Done. What's for dinner?" He gave her a hug, a kiss, and a forced smile.

"Reservations. You're taking me to *Lelli's*."

"More penance?"

"No, I'm hungry."

"But look at all this food!" There were pots everywhere. Something was roasting in the oven. The microwave was humming. "What are you making?" He took the top off a pot and stuck a spoon in. Jennifer smacked the back of his hand.

"Get out of there!" she snapped. "That's for tomorrow."

"What's tomorrow?"

"We're having company."

"Who?"

"You'll see."

"I'm tired. Besides, there's enough food here to feed an army. Why do we need to go out?"

"Penance."

"Oh, so it *is* penance. Where are the boys?"

"The boys are out. Tomorrow's a surprise."

"I don't like surprises."

"It's not for you."

"Who then?"

"I'm not telling. You can't keep a secret. You're invited, though."

"I protect client's secrets all the time."

"Not the same thing."

"What's the dress code?" he asked, searching for clues.

"Casual. Out by the pool."

"A swimming party?"

"Not necessarily. Bathing suit optional. You still look good in a bathing suit."

"Bathing suit optional? I like the way you think."

Zack walked up to her, wrapped his arms around her, and kissed her neck. He moved under her chin to the other side. He pushed her blouse over her shoulder and kissed her shoulder, then moved downward to her chest and continued to kiss.

"Get your mind out of the gutter! And cut that out!" She squirmed and pulled away. "You think I'm that easy? Not talking."

"Had to try."

"Dinner. Now."

"*Lelli's*, you said?"

"Yes."

"*Lelli's* it is. Let's go, my queen." They enjoyed a wonderful dinner overlooking the Copper Creek Golf Course and, afterward, a quiet evening at home. Zack finally began to relax.

CHAPTER THIRTY-ONE

When Zack returned home from work the following evening, there was a large tent on the front lawn, covering more than two dozen cocktail tables. Waiters and waitresses offered him hors d'oeuvres. He grabbed a cocktail frank and ran into the house.

"Jennifer? What the hell is going on out there?" Jennifer came bounding down the stairs. She wore a casual summer dress and deck shoes.

"Hi, Zack. Glad you're home. Go upstairs and change, please. Our guests will start arriving at any moment."

"Hello?" Someone called from the vestibule.

"Come on in. Zack and I have been expecting you."

Gail, Rich, and Josh Cooper walked into the kitchen.

"You said 'a quiet dinner.' What the heck is going on out there?" Gail asked.

"Well—" Jennifer snuggled next to Zack and took his arm. "Zack and I decided—"

"We did?" Jennifer shot him a look and elbowed him in the ribs.

"We did!" Zack coughed.

"We decided that Josh never had a proper bar mitzvah celebration. We got the guest list from the temple caterer and invited everyone."

Gail Cooper began to cry. She ran to Jennifer and hugged her. "This is the nicest thing anyone has ever done for us. You hear that, Josh? A bar mitzvah party with all your friends at Jennifer and Zack's pool!"

The still-traumatized boy lit up. "All my friends?"

"The entire guest list," Jennifer advised.

"Except for the Ellis family," Zack snorted.

"Zack!"

"Too soon? Wait . . . what? You didn't *invite* them, did you?"

"Of course not!"

"Well?"

"Consider the source, Jen," Rich laughed. "Seriously, though, you guys—" He teared up and hugged his wife and son.

"I've got to get changed. Let's get this party started! Go out back and check out the fabulous spread. I'll meet you out front for those fabulous hors d'oeuvres." Zack knew there was a fabulous spread. After all, this was Jennifer, the love of his life and doer of good deeds. The Cooper family joyfully jaunted out the back patio door.

"Jennifer Blake!" Zack exclaimed. "You are the most amazing woman! What a kind gesture! I love you so much!" He grabbed her and kissed her.

"You were so upset. Even though Rich asked, you didn't want to represent Chip or do him any favors. In the end, you thought Rich and Gail were angry. They didn't approach you in court. I wanted to make sure that no one had hard feelings. A friendship like yours with Rich is too precious to sacrifice for one evil anti-Semite next door."

"You are the best! Oh, look, it's the Kozlowski family. Go say hi, get them some food, send them out front, and I'll be right down." Zack raced up the stairs, changed his clothes, and raced back down.

Multiple families arrived. They greeted the Coopers and the Blakes and praised the fantastic idea of celebrating Josh's bar mitzvah at the close of the case.

Jennifer thought of everything. Josh's friends recited those annoying speeches that adults at bar mitzvahs can't stand. Everyone danced. No bar-mitzvah party can be celebrated without the traditional *Hora*, so everyone held hands and danced around the pool to *Hava Nagila*. Adults and teenagers lifted Josh on their shoulders and danced him around the pool.

At the end of a typical *Hora*, the bar mitzvah boy is returned to his family to deliver a speech. This time, Josh's friends tossed him into the pool.

Dinner was a joint effort, catered a la Jennifer, with assistance from the temple's long-time caterer. An elaborate cake was brought from the cabana for the candle-lighting ceremony.

"Incredible! How did you know?" Gail marveled.

"The caterer provided the participants and the poems you wrote. Nice job, by the way," Jennifer giggled.

"What a wonderful friend you are! I'm blown away! You must let me pay for some of this."

"Not a chance. It's my pleasure." The DJ called Josh up to the makeshift stage.

"Shush. Cake. Candles." Jennifer put her finger to her lips.

"This discussion is not over, Jen. We'll settle this later," Gail scolded. A beautiful ceremony by sunset unfolded—performed exactly as Gail Cooper planned.

"During dinner, Gail encouraged Josh to give a short speech.

"This is more than I could ever imagine. Unfortunately, I've experienced evil people who hate you for no reason. I came tonight expecting a quiet, boring dinner with four adults. Instead, I get this beautiful party at this unbelievable home with my friends, family, and all the people I love. What a terrific surprise!

"Thank you to Zack and Jennifer Blake for putting this together. My hope for the future is that love conquers hate. I hope that people who live in oppressed parts of the world can one day feel some of the love I feel tonight. I pray that the hostilities in Israel end in a lasting peace. Thank you all for coming to *both* of my bar mitzvahs. I'm guessing you're having a better time tonight than last time."

The guests roared with laughter. Josh stepped forward to his parents and embraced them. With tears in his eyes, he did the same to Zack and Jennifer.

Zack grabbed a microphone and shouted, "Joshua Cooper, everyone! How about this kid? He's going places! Give him another round of applause!" The guests cheered, and the kids shouted, "Josh, Josh, Josh." His friends hoisted him, marched him around the pool, and tossed him into the deep end one more time. Joy was contagious, and the party was on.

Toward the end of the evening, Rabbi Solomon was asked to give a toast. He stood at his table, surrounded by happy people of all ages, primarily Jewish, and other friends of the Cooper family who represented different cultures, religions, and communities.

"What a wonderful *simcha*! I am pleased to see many happy faces enjoying this party in relative peace and community harmony. Please, everyone, let's again pause and show our gratitude to Jennifer and Zachary Blake for hosting this beautiful bar mitzvah party for young Joshua Cooper, who became more than a man a few short months ago." Everyone applauded. The kids whooped and hollered. The rabbi continued after the guests settled down.

"What happened to Joshua Cooper was unique to our West Bloomfield Jewish community but not to the Jewish people. In 2017, a random poll of American citizens found that forty-nine percent of American citizens believed anti-Semitism was a critical issue in America. One month later, following a slew of vandalism and bomb threats, that number increased to seventy percent. These days, with war raging in Gaza and Israel, Jew hatred has gotten worse. Jewish kids are no longer safe on university campuses.

"We must remain vigilant. We must answer the call of *Ayeka*: Where are you? Remain strong, call out bigotry when we see or experience it. We must stand up and speak out for Josh, Israel, and Jews everywhere. The world must confront historical and modern anti-Semitism without the blinders of the past or whether it interferes with nationalism.

"We cannot and should not do it alone. A civil society must rise and stand up to anti-Semitism, racism, Islamophobia, and other forms of bigotry. It requires a global effort. We will not end prejudice and discrimination in our generation, the next, or the next. It permeates our society. Perhaps we could slow it down? Just a *bisl*?

"What is the alternative? History teaches us that this type of hate leads to terrible things, such as expulsion from Spain, the pogroms, and the Holocaust. Almost all Jewish holidays celebrate the defeat of nations who have tried to divide and destroy us but have failed. We are still here!

"Recently, there has been an uptick of hate speech against Israel. Anti-Jewish flyers fall from the sky. College students protest on behalf of terrorists. Campuses host speakers who distort the truth and lie with impunity. College presidents have difficulty condemning student chants that promote Jewish genocide. Those who try to speak the truth are silenced, ridiculed, harassed, or threatened. People call for boycotts against Israel, claiming to fight for human rights, but ignore human rights violations by Hamas or in Russia and China. Why? Because of false claims that Israel is a human rights violator. These claims are not about human rights. They are anti-Semitic rants disguised as a battle for human rights.

"In the United States, we have experienced bigotry in our government. We have seen support for neo-Nazis on the extreme right and anti-Israel sentiment on the extreme left. This is a clear and present danger to the American Jewish population and our country's support for Israel, the only true democracy in the Middle East.

"In addition to the attacks on our West Bloomfield temple and the thwarted planned attack in East Lansing, we have seen recent attacks on synagogues in Pennsylvania and California. People were fired upon during prayer. For the first time in many of our lifetimes, it feels unsafe to be Jewish. Jewish college students feel unsafe on campus. These anti-Semitic attacks, like police traffic stop shootings or school shootings, are becoming so commonplace they are no longer news. You can find the stories, usually local reports, but you must search for them.

"What can we do? First, pray for peace in the Holy Land and unite against hate. Engage other religions and invite them to join our cause. Refrain from using harsh rhetoric against others. In short, my friends, we must resist. The alternative is too terrible to consider.

"Most of you know the story of Anne Frank. Her family hid from the Nazis in Amsterdam during WWII. She wrote a diary about her experience. The diary was found by someone who hid and protected her family for over two years. I found this passage in her diary:

"Who has made us Jews different from all other people? Who has allowed us to suffer so terribly until now? It is God who has made us as we are, but it will be God, too, who will raise us up again. Who knows? It might even be our religion from which the world and all peoples learn good, and for that reason and that reason alone do we now suffer. We can never become just Netherlanders, or just English, or representative of any other country for that matter. We will always remain Jews."

"My friends. Tonight, we gather to celebrate Joshua Cooper's milestone. As Anne Frank wrote, we shall always remain Jews. We are American and Michigan Jews, Detroit, Oak Park, Huntington Woods, Royal Oak, Berkley, Southfield, Lathrup Village, Birmingham, West Bloomfield, Bloomfield Hills, Beverly Hills, Mt. Clemens, and East Lansing Jews. For thousands of years, we have been bullied and persecuted simply because we are Jewish. We shall remain defiant, strong, vocal, vigilant, and stand up for Jews everywhere. We shall do all we can to confront anti-Semitism. Perhaps, someday, we may even defeat it.

"Please raise your cups. *Baruch atah Adonai Elohainu, Melech ha'olam, shehechyanu, v'kiy'manu, v'higiyanu laz'man hazeh.* Blessed are You, the Lord our God, King of the Universe, who has kept us alive and sustained us to this glorious and joyful day.

"L'Chaim! Mazel Tov, Josh!"

THE END

About the Author

Mark M. Bello is an attorney, social justice advocate, and award-winning author of the Zachary Blake Legal Thriller series. Mark also writes for legal and political content sites and hosts the legal themed podcast, ***Justice Counts,*** on the *Spreaker* network. A Michigan native, Mark and his wife, Tobye, have four children and nine grandchildren. For more information, please visit *https://www.markmbello.com.*

Previous Books
in the Zachary
Blake Legal Thriller Series

L'DOR V'DOR –From Generation to Generation

(A Prequel Novella)

Betrayal of Faith (1)

Betrayal of Justice (2)

Betrayal in Blue (3)

Betrayal in Black (4)

Betrayal High (5)

Supreme Betrayal (6)

Betrayal at the Border (7)

You Have the Right to Remain Silent (8)

The **Zachary Blake Legal Thriller Series**

is also available in audiobook format.

Books in the Harbor Springs Cozy Legal Mystery Series

The Final Steps (1)

Books in Mark's Social Justice/Safety Series for Children

HAPPY JACK SAD JACK — A Bullying Story (1)

ONE THING OR TWO — ASHER'S DISTRACTED LESSON (2)

Other Books by Mark M. Bello

L'DOR V'DOR-From Generation to Generation, a Holocaust Era Novella

L'DOR V'DOR –From Generation to Generation II

The Blake-Lewin Family Cookbook of Traditional Jewish Recipes

Connect with Mark

Website: https://www.markmbello.com

Email: info@markmbello.com

Facebook: MarkMBelloBooks

Twitter: @MarkMBelloBooks

YouTube: Mark Bello

Goodreads: Mark M. Bello

LinkedIn:

Subscribe to our mailing list and receive your *free copy* of

L'DOR V'DOR -From Generation to Generation

and other giveaways and other surprises.

To request a speaking engagement, interview, or appearance, please email info@markmbello.com

COMING SOON FROM MARK M. BELLO!

LOVE HATE LAW

A Kramer-O'Hara Legal Romance Novel

A BRAND NEW SERIES FROM THE AWARD-WINNING AUTHOR OF THE ZACHARY BLAKE LEGAL THRILLER SERIES

ENJOY THESE BONUS CHAPTERS:

PROLOGUE

THE INSURRECTION

Rinke

Capitol Park was a canopy of color. Trees, yet to shed leaves for the winter, treated visitors to a stunning array of reds, purples, oranges, and golds. Pockets of morning dew caught beneath the pine boughs, heavy with seedling cones, fanned out their intoxicating scent on the fingers of an erratic breeze.

On this fall day in Lansing, Michigan, soon-to-be-former governor Gordon Rinke stepped to the podium. The election was over—a clear and convincing victory for the newly elected governor, Charlie Page. Deeply divided Michigan would now head in a different direction.

Not so fast, declared Rinke. In a stunning display of narcissism and political arrogance, Rinke refused to concede. "They rigged the count," he cried, making camera-grabbing protests.

He rallied his supporters, appealing to the lowest common denominator. His most significant financial contributor was Brandon North, founding member of the Michigan Watch Patrol, a far-right militia group preparing for a second American revolution or civil war. The Patrol was pro-gun and anti-government, opposed to Michigan's COVID-19 vaccination and lockdown protocol, and part of a mini-rebellion that helped sweep Gordon Rinke into office.

For weeks, Rinke encouraged followers like North to descend on the Capitol, protest the outcome, prevent certification of the vote, demand a recount, declare the election fraudulent, and induce a duly appointed legislative committee to overturn the results.

Rinke squinted in the bright sunlight, gazing at the 'magnificent turnout,' buoyed that his last-ditch ploy might work. *Is the impossible possible?* He marveled at his supporters' ignorant obedience. *If I told these guys to kidnap Page, they'd do it!*

Like a preacher, Rinke raised his arms to the sky, requesting silence. The crowd obeyed. *Remarkable!* He gazed at his supporters, some dressed in combat gear, many armed, perhaps dangerous. They could become violent, but not toward him or his people. *Who cares? These Capitol frauds certainly don't care about me!*

Police were scattered among the protestors, sticking out like sore thumbs, deeply concerned that this 'rally for justice' might turn violent. The protestors might turn their aggression toward contrary reporters or the police. Lansing and Michigan State Police were vastly outnumbered. The National Guard was on standby.

"My fellow Michiganders," Rinke began. The crowd went wild at the sound of his voice. "I come before you today for one reason only—to save Michigan. This election was not legitimate! We have a rigged system!"

The crowd roared, "bullshit, not legit." Rinke silenced the audience with a raised arm.

"Look at this crowd!" he shouted. "The media will not accurately report the size of this crowd." He gestured to camera operators to turn their cameras to the decent-sized crowd, but they refused to do his bidding. "Cowards and traitors, the lot of you," he scowled.

"The media is our state's biggest problem—fake news, everywhere!" The crowd chanted "fake news" until Rinke ordered them to stop.

"Will we stand back and see our victory stolen by our opponents?"

"Hell no!" His followers cried.

"We will rise up and declare that we're mad as hell and will not take it anymore!" Rinke borrowed the famous line from *Network*.

"This election was not even close!" His first honest remark of the day—he did not mean it as a concession to Page's margin of victory.

"We will march to the Capitol, take back our State, and restore integrity to our elections. I will lead you into the people's building. If we must fight, we will fight like hell! Break down doors and force your way in if you must. Drain the swamp and trample anyone in our way. Let's take back our Capitol!"

Rinke railed on far too long, for more than an hour. The speech finally ended, and his security team swept him away. Cheering supporters rushed toward the Capitol, chanting, "Stop the steal." State and Lansing police erected a barricade at the top of the Capitol steps and formed a defensive line on the center steps leading to the building.

As the speech droned on, a small group of Watch Patrol members gathered at the lightly guarded back entrances on the other side of the building. They quickly breached the building. Armed with assault rifles, these protestors raced through the lobby and headed toward the front entrance. When they reached their destination, they poured through the panic doors toward the line of officers. They kicked the barriers down the stairs.

Each member selected an officer, barreled into them from behind, and sent the officers tumbling down the long Capitol stairway. At the same time, Brandon North and a second group of rioters ascended the stairway and watched helpless, injured officers roll past them down the stairs. Patrol members breached the main entrance and stampeded over anyone in their path. After their tumble down the stairs, uninjured or slightly injured officers resumed upright positions and gave chase up the stairs. Legislators had quietly evacuated the Capitol *before* the breach—senators and state representatives were never in danger.

Three more hours passed before Capitol officers declared the building secure. Governor Rinke, who inspired the riot and promised to lead protestors into the Capitol, had disappeared. In the aftermath of the insurrection, this beautiful beacon of law and justice suffered millions in property and precious artifact damage. Several officers and citizens were injured—one citizen, a young legislative assistant, was trampled to death by the stampeding mob at the front entrance.

At a private, secure location a few blocks from the Capitol, the final vote certification declared Charlie Page the winner by a wide margin. The violence was for naught. Michigan had a new governor.

CHAPTER ONE

TWO MONTHS LATER

Andrea

Can someone love a career choice and hate it at the same time? Andrea Kramer was glad she went to law school and proud to graduate summa cum laude from the University of Michigan. She took school seriously—her activist parents would not have it any other way. Their activism rubbed off. While she wasn't always successful in her endeavors, it wasn't for lack of trying.

She sat in a small booth at the *Coffee Mug Café*, waiting for Mary Beth to take her order and, more importantly, pour her precious coffee. The café was known for its coffee, but Mary Beth's fantastic chocolate doughnuts brought her in that morning. Andrea was tense. Today, she celebrated the official opening of her new law office—celebrations required chocolate.

"A couple dozen of your chocolate doughnuts and a thermos filled with coffee, please?" She called out to Mary Beth, who busily slapped mugs and plates on the counter for a line of customers.

"Oh, and that's to go," she added. Law school and a short, so far uninspiring career in the law taught her to be careful with her words. She left nothing to chance. No lawyer wants to leave matters to a jury or a judge so they may draw their own conclusions. Good lawyers, like directors of award-winning movies, *directed* conclusions.

"Today, you leave the door unlocked, huh?" Mary Beth teased. "Well, it's about time. Nobody can hire you if you don't let them in . . . or maybe that's the idea?"

She tipped forward from her rubber band waist. Her practiced aim refilled Andrea's cup from two feet overhead. Like a bartender who practiced glass acrobatics, Mary Beth's steady aim resulted from a generation's worth of waiting tables. She knew her business *and* customers, the primary reason she was Andrea's favorite.

Andrea dragged herself in for a pick-me-up each morning before heading to Ann Arbor. Today, she'd stay in Saline. Dressed for painting, a scarf tied around her reddish brunette hair, not a speck of make-up was wasted. Andrea hoped to finish renovating a historic home into the Law Offices of Andrea Kramer.

The office was a unique conversion. Several years earlier, an architect converted a grain silo and barn into a modern residence. Shortly after the Dupree family moved into the home, all five family members were murdered, execution style. The murder was never solved.

A few years later, a family from out of town bought the place, then quickly abandoned it after experiencing what they called *paranormal* activity. The new owners swore, up and down, that the house had a strange smell—like something had died. The children claimed to have observed three shadowy forms in their bedroom. Presumably, these were the Dupree children.

An investor purchased the home cheaply, converted the zoning, and

listed it as a professional office. The property sat vacant for years—everyone in town knew the history.

Andrea was not superstitious. Besides, the price was right, and the conversion was intriguing. The silo had circular shelving for potential use as a working law library or file room. The barn was spacious and had a vaulted hardwood ceiling. Andrea envisioned rental offices and a beautiful conference room. The home had a kitchen, living room, three bedrooms, and a sunroom. The living room would be a waiting area, reception, and secretarial space. The bedrooms would be attorney offices, and the sunroom would be Andrea's getaway room.

Andrea loved the place but knew better than to exhibit her enthusiasm. She wrinkled her nose as Meagan Fields, an old college chum, walked her through.

"Any way to get rid of that odor?" Andrea inquired.

"I don't smell anything."

"Smells like something or someone died."

"That's the legend, but we both know it's a bunch of malarky."

"I smell something."

Meagan grunted. "Everyone who knows the history of this place 'smells something.'" She finger-signed the quotes. "If this place had no history, the rent would quadruple. We both know that."

"I don't know. It might be difficult to get staff or clients to come into the office."

Meagan shrugged. "History or no history, this is the only building in your price range. The good news is that you lock in the rate for three years."

"I saw a local documentary about the Dupree murders. People believe it's still haunted. I don't know—"

"Jesus, Andi. Please give it a rest! I'm trying to work with you here."

"Ask them to drop the rent by a few hundred, and I'll take it. Maybe I'll embrace the history. How does Kramer Law Offices at Tranquility Manor sound?"

"Wonderful." Meagan rolled her eyes. "I'll relay your offer."

"Make it five hundred."

"Five hundred what?"

"Ask for a five-hundred-dollar reduction. No rent increases for the entire lease term and an option to renew for another three years at the same rate."

"Such a lawyer—everything's a negotiation. I'll relay the message. Anything else? Do you want the guy to pay your employees? Handle your overhead?" Meagan chided.

"He could throw in utilities and paint the place," Andrea floated.

"Don't push it, Kramer. You can pay the utilities with the five-hundred-dollar discount."

"Are you saying it's a deal?"

"I'll make it work. This guy is desperate. Don't tell anyone, but I like you better than him."

"Thanks."

"This is exciting, career-wise."

"We'll see. I'm glad to be home. Looking forward to helping real people."

After she graduated from law school, Andrea spent a few years doing corporate defense work, making rich corporate types richer and helping insurance companies deny legitimate claims. She was well-paid but miserable. She hated screwing people. Without notice, she walked into the senior partner's office one day and quit.

Andrea still felt unfulfilled a year after renting an office from a small personal injury firm, doing the firm's overflow district court work, and covering scheduling conflicts. She welcomed a return to her hometown and the opportunity to help people in her community.

Meagan interrupted her thoughts.

"How's life treating you? Any interesting prospects?"

"Prospects?"

"Come on, Andi, spill. How's your love life?"

"Not everyone can be as lucky as you. Jason is quite the rising star."

"He's *too* focused on his career for my taste."

"Poor baby. Are you being ignored?" Andrea teased.

"A woman has certain desires, you know. He satisfies most of them. Look at you, the big-shot lawyer changing the subject. The question was about *your* love life, missy, not mine."

"Nothing to report, I'm afraid. Maybe after I get my office going."

"The good ones will all be taken."

"Love will come—I'm not going to force it."

"The famous last words of an old maid."

"That's a stretch—don't you think? I'm still in my twenties."

"Close to thirty."

Andrea signed the lease the next day. The landlord eyed her. "New law practice, eh? Are you sure you'll be able to make the rent?"

Andi pivoted her head to face him. "You have other takers?" She sniffed the air. "What's that smell?"

"Huh?" He grumbled and sniffed at the air. "I don't smell anything."

"Everyone else does."

"Rent is due first of the month, *every* month. Don't let me down," he warned.

"You'll get your money." She felt her temper begin to flare, and for good reason. The landlord had a nightmare on his hands and refused to admit it. In the end, he made quite a show of conciliation and left. Andrea changed the locks that same day and began sprucing the place up, making the place look like the office she envisioned.

Everything up to that point had been without risk, without penalty. She knew things would soon change. She lingered, giving the walls an extra coat, waiting for the right area rug to cover defects in the tiled floor.

Someday, these floors will be solid wood. I'll need a tax shelter and someone to share my good fortune.

After opening the office door on her first day in business, Andrea sniffed the air and smelled only fresh paint and coffee. She placed the coffee and donuts in the corner of the reception area and glanced around, proud of her work.

She walked over to what would soon be a receptionist's desk and typed a password into the computer, *DEFENSELAWYERSSUCK!*

Behind her, the front door opened. Andrea stiffened. *A client?* The moment arrived sooner than she expected.

"You the lawyer?" An older man stood in her doorway, staring at her, looking around for the receptionist or secretary who did not exist. *That will come later,* Andrea told herself.

The man wiped his hand against the thigh of his jeans, then briefly took Andrea's in the limp way a man does when confronted with the delicacy of a female hand.

"I like what you've done with the place. It's haunted, you know."

"So, I've been told. How may I help you, sir? Let's start with your name."

"I'm Arthur Longbow." He held a weathered Detroit Tigers baseball cap between roughened fingers. Every few seconds, he snuffed loudly and cleared his throat. It was a raw sound. Tears formed in his eyes.

"My daughter was at the Capitol two months ago," he whispered.

CHAPTER TWO

Michael

"What the hell?" Michael O'Hara's cell phone alarm chirped loudly enough to awaken him, ending a wonderful dream he could not quite remember. He pried his eyes open and looked around the unfamiliar room.

"Shit!" He grumbled. "Where am I?" He squirmed to the side of the bed, let his feet touch the floor, and felt a wave of dizziness and nausea as he willed his body to an upright position. That's when he saw her. A beautiful naked woman lay on top of the sheets on the opposite side of the bed.

Who the hell are you? What happened last night?

"Are you alive?" He gasped. "How could you not have heard that insidious alarm?"

He walked over to the other side and gently tapped the woman on her bare shoulder. She stirred.

Thank God! Not dead. She's got a terrific ass.

He grabbed both shoulders and shook her a bit more vigorously. She stirred, rolled onto her back, moaned, and opened her eyes.

"Morning . . . uh . . . Michael? What time is it?"

She knows my name. He studied her face and body, still trying to remember. *Who are you, beautiful? Where am I?*

He returned to his side of the bed to retrieve his cell phone. *What time is it?* He pressed a button. The screen came to life, displaying the time: nine-fifteen in the morning.

"Shit, I'm late!" He scanned the room, trying to recall *something* from the night before. His eyes settled on the bed and the naked woman. She caught him looking, stretched enthusiastically, and opened her legs. Michael sucked in a breath and paused to enjoy the view.

"Who are you? Where are we?"

"Don't you remember, darling? I'm Trudy."

Michael continued to stare at the beautiful stranger.

"We met last night at Jacoby's," she continued. "You *did* have a lot to drink."

"Jacoby's? It *is* one of my favorite places." He struggled to recall the meet.

"I was sitting at the bar, waiting for my date. You snooze, you lose, right?" she recalled.

"Huh?"

"My date was late. You were alone and transmitting vibes."

"Vibes?"

"Yeah, you know . . . vibes, like you were looking for company. You are quite a handsome man."

"Thank you. And you're a beautiful woman. I'm sure you know that." He forced a smile, still clueless.

"You moved over a few seats and introduced yourself, remember?"

"Honestly, I wish I did. How much did we have to drink?"

"Let me put it this way. You were very generous. Neither of us could drive at closing time, so you booked a room at the Greektown Hotel."

"And?"

"And what? We took an Uber to the hotel, and the rest is history. Last night was amazing!"

"I see . . . uh . . . Trudy . . . I'm beginning to remember now," he lied. "Last night was the best I've had in a long time." He glanced at his phone again.

"Listen . . . uh . . . I'm sorry to do this to you. I'm late for work. I've got to take a quick shower and run. You're welcome to stay a while if you'd like. I'll call you."

"You don't have my number."

"There's a notepad on the desk over there," he pointed. "Write it down, and I'll give you a buzz."

"You're lying. You don't remember a thing, do you?"

"I remember getting smashed," he confessed. "Not much else, I'm afraid."

"That's too bad. That *was* the best sex I've had in years. Mind-blowing!"

"I'm pleased you had a good time. I'm sure I did, too. I'd like to do this again, perhaps without the booze—"

"And the drugs."

"And the drugs." *What drugs?* "Please . . . I would love to continue this conversation. Perhaps we can meet again. Maybe get to know each other? But I am extremely late for work. Do you understand?"

"I do." The woman stretched provocatively. Michael tensed and turned. She reached out and grabbed his hand, turning him back towards her.

"I see I got your attention . . . again," she observed with a smile.

Michael pulled his hand away and looked down, embarrassed. "I've got to hit the shower. Again, stay for as long as you wish—order room service. And, please, leave your number. I'll call you."

"You're lying. You won't call, will you?"

"Why wouldn't I call? Look at you!" He continued to stare.

His phone rang, a different ringtone than the one that woke him. He answered the phone.

"Where the hell are you, Michael? Taggert is about to have a coronary." Deborah Thomas had been Michael's legal secretary since he became an associate at the Taggert firm.

"I'm just down the street." He dashed into the bathroom and turned on the shower.

"Did you just now turn on a shower?" Deb had excellent hearing.

"No," he lied. "I'm washing my hands in the sink."

"What sink? Where? You're lying, Michael. I know the difference between a shower and a sink. I'll cover for you. Just tell me where you are."

Michael hated lying to Deb. And she *always* covered for him. But these circumstances were too embarrassing. "Can we discuss it later? I'm nearby. Want me to bring you anything? Coffee? Danish?"

"Just get your ass in here. What would you do without me?"

"I refuse to even think about that possibility. I'll be there soon. Cover for me. There's dinner in it for you," he promised.

"And after dinner, my white knight?" Deb was between boyfriends. She'd been playfully flirting with the boss for years.

Michael was accustomed to the playful banter. He usually enjoyed and participated in it, but not this time. "You know my rule. No dates inside the gates."

"I quit," she kibitzed.

"You can't. I refuse to go on without you. I'll kill myself."

"Finish your shower and get the hell in here."

"You're the best."

"Yada, yada."

Michael showered and dressed in less than five minutes. Trudy still sat naked on top of the sheets. She saw Michael and parted her legs again. Michael stopped to look. Trudy seemed to revel in his body's reaction.

"Did you write down the number?" Michael turned away.

"I did, lover. Come and get it." She popped the note between her teeth.

"Please? I'm so late. I'm going to get fired." He turned back for a final look.

She frowned. He shrugged, walked to the bed, leaned over, and tried to grab the note with his teeth. She pulled him down and kissed him, which wetted and crumbled the note.

"You're a great kisser, baby," she called after him as he grabbed the note and ran out the door.

***

Michael pushed through the elevator doors at the sound of the familiar ding and swept into the law firm's lobby. The floor-length windows behind the receptionist framed a view of clouds so close a window washer could have touched them. It was the 36th floor—the named partners were Taggert, Miles & Freeman. However, Michael was the attorney currently creating firm buzz.

He was, by far, the firm's best litigator. A hot streak placed him on the partner track. As named partner, he'd earn a company Beemer, a key to the executive lounge and sports club, and a coveted country club membership. Michael could *taste* it. Once a sought-after litigator, his streak was cooled by recent trial losses and large settlements. Michael considered this a temporary aberration. What about the partners?

Michael jaunted through the hallway, entered his private office, walked to the opposite side, and opened the door separating his office from Deb's cubicle. Walking up to Deb, he leaned down from his 6'4" height and placed a key fob on the counter.

"Deb, thank you. You're a lifesaver. What do I have today?"

Deb raised her hand to halt Michael's forward movement. "Aside from your meeting with Taggert, you're clear until the six-thirty dinner.

Vicki called to say the key would be at the front desk. You turned off your phone again?"

With the fluid movement of a trained athlete, Michael returned to his office and slammed the glass door.

Michael O'Hara preferred to keep his private life private. He loved Deb but didn't share intimate details of his love life with anyone. He'd been seeing Vicki for two months and vowed to remain sober throughout the evening.

"Michael? We've been waiting." He turned to see Stu Taggert, founding partner of the firm, standing outside his door.

Michael instantly put on a smile. "Stu, sorry. I got here as soon as I could. What can I do for you? Let me grab a coffee, and I'll be right over," he chirped. *Is this the day?* The entire office had been anticipating Michael's elevation to partner. He turned to grab his coffee.

"Leave it. Bring your laptop. This is a business, not a party," Stu growled. Most mornings, Stu played nine holes at the club's premier golf course and waltzed into the office with a sunny disposition.

Michael's smile wilted in place. He carefully pulled his door shut and glanced down the hallway toward Deb. His goose was cooked if she watched with a pitiful look. *Would Stu promote another associate to partner?*

The thought twisted his gut into knots. He glanced down to inspect his shoes, then went down the hallway to where Stu had left his door partially open. Taking a deep breath, he tapped and stepped inside.

He recognized the man sitting in the conference chair. Gilbert Wallace, Michigan's Attorney General, caused Michael's gut another twist. He frantically searched his memory for any connection to the AG's office—anything he could have screwed up. Wallace read his mind.

"Relax, you're in no trouble. At least not yet," Wallace advised, with the slightest of smiles. "Sit down."

Stu motioned for Michael to take his chair. Wallace was clearly in charge of the meeting. "Excuse me," he leaned forward and extended his hand toward Michael. "Gilbert Wallace, Attorney General for the State of Michigan."

"Of course, sir. I recognized you immediately," Michael fawned, shaking the man's tanned hand. "What may I do for you?" Michael's wealthy upbringing gave him a particular aplomb in social events. He commonly encountered public figures. Business events, however, were completely different matters.

"You're familiar with recent election-denier events at the Capitol?"

"Who isn't?"

Wallace glanced at Taggert and continued. "Governor Page has ordered me to dump this case on lawyers better suited for its menial nature."

"Sir?" Michael was puzzled.

"Sorry. I guess you haven't heard about the lawsuit. Longhorn, Longfellow, Longest Yard, Long something or other—I don't remember the guy's name. That girl killed at the Capitol was this guy's only daughter, his pride and joy. You've seen one; you've seen them all. Man, I don't need to tell you."

"No, no, sir. You don't. Everyone wants to suck on the State's teat."

"Exactly. Here's the thing, Matthew."

"Michael."

"What's that?"

"Michael, sir. My name is Michael."

"Yeah, yeah, *Michael.* A lot on my mind today. So, Michael, uh, here's the thing. We live in a charged political atmosphere. There are troublemakers out there."

"I understand, sir."

"The governor won't make a big deal out of this even though he can score political points exploiting his predecessor's behavior. The media *loves* this kind of case. The governor is concerned about blowback from right-leaning and independent voters who switched their allegiance to restore normalcy and bipartisanship. God knows where this thing goes from here. The governor just assumed office. He's got enough on his plate without these annoying flies buzzing around his head."

Michael nodded and repeated, "I understand, sir."

"My office was set to handle the matter and sweep things under the rug. The young woman's family is just the old man, pretty near the grave by the looks of him. We intended to delay, deny, confuse, and refuse until the guy bought the farm." Michael encouraged Wallace to continue.

"The thing is—my office is under a lot of pressure. We can't add this to our calendar. I asked Stu to recommend someone, a young, good-looking go-getter eager to make his mark. He suggested you."

"Me, sir?"

"Yes, you, Martin. Your boss says you're a top litigator. You come from good stock. A well-connected family is good enough for me. I had some cases with your father back in the day. So, here I am, down from Lansing, to meet you in person, feel you out, and see if you might be a good fit. From my perch on high, you look mighty fine."

Michael turned from Wallace to Stuart, his sharp eyes seeking some giveaway. He *was* anxious to make his name, which was hard to do, coming from *his* family.

Michael's father, Stanley O'Hara, was a prominent lawyer, businessman, and politician. He served as Ambassador to Ireland during the Reagan years and was a huge fan of the former president and his politics.

At an early age, Michael was taught that the government could not do everything for everyone. The best thing the government could do was to clear the way for businesses and business owners to make their fortune. These businesses would, in turn, hire tax-paying workers, greasing the economic wheel for everyone. Michael worshipped his father and became a student of his business and legal philosophies.

The younger O'Hara was born and raised in the affluent suburb of Bloomfield Hills, received an exclusive private school education, and did his undergraduate work at the University of Michigan. His grades were excellent, and his postgraduate reputation was even better. He was accepted to the University's elite law school, where he graduated with honors. He was a sought-after graduate, but his father would only consider the top law firms in Detroit.

Stanley's political connections landed Michael a job at the Taggert firm. But Michael worked hard to *earn* the position. He was nobody's fool. His trial skills were superior, one reason his bosses recommended him for this assignment. Despite his recent failures in certain high-profile court appearances, Michael proved he could handle himself in a crisis. But what was at stake? *What if I fail? Am I willing to take this on? Willing to risk my partnership for this case?* He only took a moment to decide. *What choice do I have?*

"I'm honored, sir. My staff and I will immediately flyspeck every pleading and media report to date. Have someone in your office forward all relevant documents to me. I'm on this."

Stu spoke up. "The firm has already shifted your current clients elsewhere, Michael."

Michael's eyebrows rose. The decision was already made at the partner level. Michael either took Wallace up on his offer or had no cases or clients. This was the proverbial offer he couldn't refuse. The mob now dictated to the law rather than the other way around. He must win this case or kiss his partnership goodbye.

"That's very considerate of you, Stu. If there's nothing else, Mr. Attorney General, I'll get back to my office, call a staff meeting, and get things rolling."

"The sooner, the better. I'll send things over."

Michael glared at Stu. He knew this was payback for his recent courtroom failures. Taggert never praised Michael's success. In Michael's mind, he only kicked him when he was down. *Why does he always emphasize the negative? You're only as good as your last success.* Michael would embrace the assignment and demonstrate to Taggert that he was still a great litigator. Nothing would stand in his way.

Stu nodded, and Michael practically leaped from his chair and left the office, calling out orders as he strode down the hallway.

"Deb? I need anyone who's in my division here now. Put them all in the conference room and order in some deli. Cancel my dinner plans for tonight."

Michael hated to pass up a date with Vicki, but he had no choice. Taggert laid down the gauntlet. He had to prove himself *again.*

"Brock, get off your ass and find out about the firm that filed this lawsuit." He tossed the complaint on his junior associate's desk. "I want everything there is to know. What time do the firm members take a leak? Do the partners like oysters or clams? Who pisses who off? Are there women? Scandals? Illicit relationships? Who's screwing who? Got it?"

"Got it." Brock was the new boy on the block, a young associate, fresh out of the University of Detroit Law School. Michael walked in his shoes at one time. Brock would be a gopher until he paid his dues, or the higher-ups decided he earned something juicier.

With one mighty shout, Michael's voice was heard in every hallway, every office, and through every glass door.

"Anyone working in the office today, in the conference room, now!"

WATCH FOR THE RELEASE!